Ring-tailed cat   *Mallette De*

SIERRA NORTH

100 Back-Country Trips in the High Sierra

by

Karl Schwenke and Thomas Winnett

WILDERNESS PRESS • BERKELEY

First printing May 1967
Second printing July 1967
Third printing July 1969
SECOND EDITION May 1971
Second printing April 1972

Cover design by Don Denison
Front-cover photo by Karl Schwenke
Drawings by Lucille Winnett

Library of Congress card number 70-145547
ISBN:911824-14-6
Manufactured in the United States

FOREWORD

Once upon a backpack trip these authors baptized a joint endeavor in the smoke of their campfire. The endeavor we set ourselves to was to write a book containing a selection of the best back-country trips to be found in the country we knew best, the northern Sierra. We soon learned that committing a country's "feel" to labels and categories was, at best, problematical. Today, many campfires later, we confess to a good deal more humility than was present at the outset. Errors (judgmental, typographical and factual) will inevitably occur in this manuscript, and the authors humbly invite the reader's involvement by way of suggestion and/or correction.

K.S.
T.W.

FOREWORD TO 2ND EDITION

Finding one's way on the trail proves easier than finding one's way through the editorial labyrinth of a 2nd edition, but with perseverance, sweat and two blistered posteriors, we made it. This edition has entailed walking another 2,000 miles of trails and cross-country routes in preparatory research—by far the pleasantest part of the task. We then chose about 300 of these miles for actual description in this edition, while deleting only about 50 miles from the first edition.

Our intent was not a BIGGER product—the fact that this edition *is* bigger, and heavier, is an unfortunate adjunct for those who count ounces in their packs, but it is a more complete sampling. The changes and additions that we made arose from discussions with readers met on the trail, around campfires and through letters. Out of these discussions came some great trip suggestions, and a lot of new friends. For both we are grateful.

K.S.
T.W.

January 1971

ACKNOWLEDGMENTS

Many outdoorsmen and women have lent a hand in putting this book together. They have contributed their skills, their patience and, above all, their encouragement. For this the authors are grateful.

Particular thanks are due Suzanne Schwenke, David Poast, Don Denison and Lu Winnett for their great help. For the advice, information and necessary encouragement to make this sweeping revision, the authors wish to thank Tina Beal, John Burnett, Malcolm Burnstein, Verna Carlsen, Monroe De Jarnette, Thomas Dum, Donald Evers, Ron Felzer, Robert Golden, Don Harkin, Doris Headley, A. I. Kelty, Mary R. King, John McElheney, David Pesonen, Gordon Peterson, Chet Rice, Daniel Simon, Clyde Wahrhaftig and Jim Watters.

The Sierra Club has kindly permitted the reprinting of "Camping Manners for Wilderness," and "Equipment Check List" by Robert Cutter.

Table of Contents

Introduction

OUR PURPOSE

The Sierra Nevada is the longest and most extensively trailed mountain range in the United States. With its complex valley-ridge makeup, its lofty eastern escarpment, and its mild weather, it is a knapsacker's paradise unparalleled in intrinsic beauty and scenic grandeur. Much (some enthusiasts say, "most") of the finest scenery and best fishing lies in the back country, accessible only by trail. There has been, therefore, a growing trend toward wilderness trips, and with the trend has come a demand for reliable back-country trip suggestions. This book is a selective effort to meet that demand.

Galen Clark, Yosemite's beloved "Old Man of the Valley," was once asked how he "got about" the park. Clark scratched his beard, and then replied, "Slowly!" And that is the philosophy the authors have adopted in this book. Hiking descriptions, with the exception of a few "Moderate" ratings and an occasional "Strenuous" trip, are based on a leisurely pace, in order that the hiker can absorb more of the sights, smells and "feel" of the country he has come to see. Pace may not be everything, but Old Man Clark lived to a ripe old age of 96 and it behooves us to follow in his footsteps.

OUR TERMS

Sierra North encompasses the region from the barren expanses of Desolation Valley to the aspen-lined banks of Mono Creek. The authors' decision to focus on this region was an arbitrary one, based on (1) remoteness from roads, (2) scenic attractions, and (3) geographic cohesiveness.

The individual trips were selected after extensive interviews with Sierra Club trip leaders, officials of the U.S. Forest Service, and Yosemite National Park personnel. After the initial selection each trip was scouted (walked), and there followed a weeding out of those trips having poor trail maintenance, bad campsite possibilities, or routes overburdened with stock or hiker use.

Some popular routes (e.g., the John Muir Trail) were incorporated, despite their "racetrack" aspect, because in the authors' judgment they toured regions and scenic attractions unreachable by any other route. In recognition of the understandable desire to "get away from it all," there has been a compensating effort made to include the more remote and less used trails, including some cross-country routes.

Grading trips as "Leisurely," "Moderate" or "Strenuous" was done by the trip scout. Many theories and methods about how this should be done were considered but rejected because they failed to take into consideration enough pertinent factors (elevation change, heat, exposure, ground cover, terrain, availability of water, etc.). The method settled upon is a combination of the above factors together with the subjective evaluation by the scout who walked the trail. The "Trail/layover days" designation is also the recommendation of this scout, and is directly involved in the grading. (A "layover" day is one on which one does not travel to a new camp.)

The scout's subjective consideration also carries over to the evaluation of campsites and abundance of firewood. Campsites are labeled poor, fair, good or excellent. The criteria for assigning these labels were amount of use, immediate surroundings, general scenery, presence of vandalization, availability of water, kind of ground cover, and recreational potential—angling, side trips, swimming, etc.

Two other terms used in the descriptive text warrant definition. "Packer campsite" is used to indicate a semipermanent camp (usually constructed by packers for the "comfort of their clients") characterized by a nailed-plank table and/or a large, "stand-up" rock fireplace. "Improved campsite" is a U.S. Forest Service designation for places where simple toilets have been installed.

The text contains occasional references to points, peaks and other landmarks. These places will be found on the appropriate topographic maps cited in the descriptive data at the beginning of the trip.

Angling, for many, is a prime consideration when planning a trip. The recommendations in this book are the result of research into the California DF&G's fresh-water fish-stocking program, study of DF&G-sponsored surveys, "on the trail" sampling and feed evaluation, and interviews with commercial packers. When a conflict arose between "paper research" and trail sampling, the latter was given precedence, and, like the campsite designations, fishing was separated into poor, fair, good or excellent. It should be noted that these categories refer to the *quantity* of fish found in the stream or lake, and not the fishes' *inclination* to take the hook. Experienced anglers know that the size of their catch relates not only to quantity, type, and general size of the fishery, which are given, but also to factors of water temperature, feed, angling skill, and that indefinable something known as "fisherman's luck." Generally speaking, the old "early and late" adage holds: fishing *is* better early and late in the day, and early and late in the season.

Defining high-country seasons is at best a difficult chore because of altitude and latitude variations. Low early-season temperatures and mountain shadows often keep some of the higher passes closed until well into August. Early snows have been known to whiten alpine country in July and August. Some of the trips described here are low-country ones, designed specifically for the itchy hiker who, stiff from a winter's inactivity, is searching for a "warm-up" excursion. These trips are labeled "early season," and this period extends roughly from late May to early July. "Midseason" is here considered to be from early July to early September, and "late season" from then through October.

Most of the trails described here are well maintained (the exceptions are noted), and they are usually properly signed. If the trail becomes indistinct, look for blazes (peeled bark at eye level on trees) or "duck-on-the-rock" markings (cairns of two or more rocks piled one atop the other). Two other significant trail conditions have also been described in the text: (1) exposure (type and density of forest cover, meadow, brush, etc.) ; (2) underfooting (talus, broken rock, bedrock, pumice, dust, sand, duff—the last being a deep humus ground cover of rotting vegetation).

our blessing

Go,
And leave your trail
Cleaner for the feet that follow—
Pollute nothing.

Go,
Walk the forest ways.
Be as one with the wilderness,
And see your soul.

Go,
With a straight trail
And fair weather.

Backpacking Basics

Backpackers are a delightfully individualistic and unusual lot. They pride themselves on their separateness—and this is not a false pride. For in the context of today's motor-powered outdoorsmen, the backpacker is indeed utterly unique. The backpacker's horizons are his own. He is unlimited by the fetters of machinery or four-footed stock, and inclination and stamina are the only bounds to his freedom to wander.

This individuality reflects itself in equipment. One will find, on any given trail, as many outfits as he finds backpackers. There are some basic similarities, however, that may (humbly) be construed to reflect agreement on three or four pieces of basic equipment.

For the trail, one needs adequate footgear. No piece of equipment is more intimate to the hiker than his boots, so selection becomes an important, and subjective, affair. Leather boots six to eight inches high with vibram lug soles are, by consensus, the choice for the rugged Sierra trails. Tennis shoes and low-tops are just not substantial enough. Care should be taken to acquire boots with a stiff heel counter, and the boot should fit snugly at the heel and loosely around the toes.

A good-quality down sleeping bag is desirable—if not essential. Since this is by far the most expensive piece of equipment a backpacker will acquire, one hesitates to state that the success or failure of a wilderness backpack trip hinges on owning a down bag. But the amount and quality of one's sleep—particularly in the face of substantial expenditures of energy—influences one's feeling of well-being. In a sleeping bag, overlapping-tube and box-construction baffle designs are superior, and the best "all-around" bag should weigh no more than five pounds. "Mummy" and rectangular-shaped bags each have their adherents. Some cannot tolerate the close-fitting "mummy" style despite its superior thermal and weight characteristics. This is an option that the individual must exercise.

The third piece of basic equipment is a pack frame and accompanying bag. Some rigs observed on the trail rival Rube Goldberg's contraptions, but generally speaking, the frame should be constructed of lightweight, tubular aluminum. The design should not impede free movement of the hips, arms or head, and the frame's weight should not exceed three pounds. The pack bag should be roomy (for longer trips), and exterior zippered pockets are convenient. Elaborate construction is not essential, but compartments make for easy organization and keep the load from shifting. The bag should have a long "weather" flap, and the material should be waterproof.

Summers in the Sierra are fairly dry; hence many "go-lighters" forego the comfort of a tent. Sceptics who have been caught without shelter in a "rare" high-country thunderstorm carry a plastic sheet or a plastic "tube tent." These temporary shelters are strung up with light nylon cord, and extra precautions are always taken to assure an adequate air supply.

Other equipment essentials include warm clothing, raingear, ground cloth (usually plastic), air mattress (or foam pad), Sierra cup, utensils, cooking gear (lightweight aluminum), flashlight, first-aid kit (bandaids, moleskin, compresses, antiseptic, soap, aspirin, eye wash, adhesive tape, individual prescriptions), bug dope, compass, nylon line, knife, snakebite kit, waterproof matches, toilet paper, bandana, and pencil.

The following check list (courtesy of the Sierra Club) is included for the beginner who has doubts about putting in "last-minute extras":

last-minute check list
This is a check list only! Don't take everything here.

Taken by
1. **Almost** everyone   3. About half   5. Practically no one
2. Most   4. A few   ? For consideration only

TO WEAR OR CARRY

knap-sack	pack animals		ounces
1	1	Hat or cap	8
2	2	Dark glasses	3
1	1	Shirt	6-16
1	1	Trousers or shorts	6-16
1	1	Belt	3-5
1	1	Shoes or boots	32-96
1	1	Socks	2-6
2	2	Bandana or handkerchief	1
1	1	Underwear	6-24
2	2	Maps	1
3	3	Compass	3-5
1	1	Matches in waterproof case	1-3
1	1	Toilet paper	4
2	2	Watch (cheap)	2
1	1	Pocket knife (not cheap)	2
1	1	Sunburn preventive	2
2	2	Insect repellent	1
1	1	Lip ice or lipstick	1
1	3	Knapsack or packframe	16-64

1	1	Parka or jacket	16-34
2	2	Adhesive tape, moleskin, etc.	1
2	1	Raincoat, cape or poncho	3-24
1	1	Flashlight	3-9
1	1	Lunchbag (durable)	1-2
1	1	Sierra Club cup (2?)	4
1	1	Spoon	1
2	1	Swimsuit	3-24
2	2	Washing kit (for self and clothes) . . .	3
4	3	Plastic lemonade shaker	3-6
4	?	Canteen or plastic bottle	6-12
4	3	Lemonade mix, soft-drink mix . . .	3
5	5	Instant coffee, tea or bouillon	1
?	?	Water-purifying tablets	1
3	2	Fishing license	1
3	2	Camera, film	10-56

FOR DUNNAGE BAG OR KNAPSACK

?	1	Dunnage bag	24-48
2	1	Tarp or tent	16-96
1	1	Sleeping bag	36-176
3	3	Inner bag	10-24
4	4	Outer bag	16-32
2	1	Groundcloth	3-32
2	1	Air mattress or urethane pad	16-80
5	4	Pillow or pillowcase	3-12
1	1	Underwear set (lightweight)	3-8
5	4	Undershirt (wool or quilted)	12
4	3	Underdrawers (wool or quilted) . . .	12
1	1	Extra socks	5-10
4	2	Camp shoes	6-32
3	2	Extra trousers	16-32
3	3	Hiking shorts	16
2	2	Shirts (lightweight)	6-12
4	3	Shirts (wool)	16
1	1	Sweater or vest (lightweight)	8-16
4	2	Wool stocking cap or balaclava . . .	4
1	1	Bandanas	4
1	1	Powdered soap	4-8
5	3	Sewing kit (small), safety pins	1
3	2	Extra optical glasses in case	3
5	3	Extra dark glasses in case	3
1	1	Extra flashlight batteries and/or bulb . .	3-14
1	1	1/8" nylon or other cord	3-9
5	2	Plastic washbasin	3-6
4	1	Collapsible plastic bucket	4
1	1	Plastic bags (thin, assorted), rubber bands	1
?	?	Waterproof bags (strong) for camera, etc.	3
?	?	Nail brush (small)	1
?	?	Tickets, keys, money	?
5	4	Mattress-patching kit	6
?	?	Clothespins (plastic)	4
?	?	2 birthday candles or fire starters . . .	1
?	4	Gloves or mittens	3
4	2	Towel (diaper?)	2
1	1	Food	?

WILDERNESS COURTESY

Traveling in the Sierra wilderness is a privilege, not a birth-right! With the privilege comes the responsibility to keep it un-spoiled for those who follow, and it is incumbent upon every wilderness traveler to be sensitive and responsive to that obliga-tion. In recognition of that obligation, the Sierra Club, an organi-zation dedicated to the preservation of wilderness, circulates the following policy on camping and trail conduct for their group outings.

As a member of a wilderness outing party you will become familiar with the rules enumerated below. You will discover an immense satisfaction in enjoying wilderness without depreciat-ing it in any way, and in leaving no lasting sign.

Construction: Camp in the wilderness spirit. Minimize build-ing, whether for kitchen emplacements or shelter. Don't disar-range scene with hard-to-eradicate ramparts of rock as fireplaces or windbreaks. Rig tents or tarps with line tied to rocks or trees. Never cut boughs or poles, or put nails in trees. Camp should be set up where foot traffic does the least damage to fragile vegeta-tion.

Fires: Never leave a fire unattended! Build a minimum fire-place. Clear a wide circle around your fire down to mineral soil. Don't place a fire against a log or back rock. When breaking camp, drown fire completely, stir, and drown again until ashes are cold to touch. Bury ashes and charcoal. Use existing fire sites where found. If you start from scratch in places not camped be-fore, return fireplace rocks to natural positions when you leave, blackened portions hidden. Never build fires on meadows, vege-tation or duff.

Refrain from smoking while traveling; smoke only in camps and at rest stops.

Wood: Use down wood only; do not cut standing trees, living or dead, nor break off their branches. Snags are picturesque and should not be molested. Axe work on down logs and stumps mars wilderness atmosphere. Conserve wood, especially where scarce. *Keep fires small.*

Bedsites: Don't excavate. Try to find naturally level and shel-tered spot. Erase evidence of your bed when breaking camp. Double check area before you move on. Forgotten laundry is litter.

Sanitation: Latrines should be constructed when a large party plans a protracted camp. Use them when available. Latrines should be inconspicuous and placed well away from water. If no latrine, go far from camp and trail, dig deep and bury. Placing a rock over the site is not wholly satisfactory; it looks unnatural, and if small, is easily overturned by curious animals.

Swim or wash at distance, or below where camp water is drawn.

Washing: Use a small basin for laundry and sponge bathing. Prevent pollution by keeping soap or detergent out of lakes and streams. Even with care, soap is preferable to detergent for mountain use. Do your pot scrubbing and washing well back from the shoreline.

Garbage & Litter: Place candy wrappers, raisin boxes, orange peels, etc., in pocket or pack for later disposal in fire or garbage sack. Burn what will burn. *Foil does not burn!* Many packages have foil inner lining; look before you burn. Edibles may be concealed or scattered well away from camp and trail where animals can find them without digging. Carry cans, bottles, worn-out gear and foil out of the mountains. Remove ends of cans, flatten and burn cans preparatory to packing out. Garbage pits are no longer acceptable. Field-strip cigarettes.

Pack stock: Good grazing is limited, so take care to protect forage. Keep stock from concentrating on inadequate meadows; turn animals out at night whenever possible. Move picketed animals every few hours to avoid severe trampling and overgrazing of grassy areas. Saddle and groom stock away from camp to prevent accumulation of manure in camp area.

Trails: Don't cut corners. This breaks down trails and hurries erosion. Dislodged rocks may fall on others below you. Stock has right of way; stand quietly aside, preferably uphill, until animals have passed.

Off trail: Restrain impulse to blaze trees, or to build ducks (small rock cairns used as markers) where not essential. Let the next fellow find his way as you did.

Fish: Catch only as many as you need or can consume. After cleaning fish, conceal entrails ashore. Never throw entrails, head, etc., back into the water.

Noise: Be a considerate neighbor. Don't crowd others' camps or sleeping areas. Noise is out of harmony in a wilderness experience.

Maps and Profiles

Today's Sierra traveler is confronted by a bewildering array of maps, and it doesn't take much experience to learn that no single map fulfills all needs. There are base maps (U.S. Forest Service), shaded relief maps (National Park Service), artistically drawn representational maps (California Department of Fish and Game), aerial photograph maps, geologic maps, three-dimensional relief maps, soil-vegetation maps, etc. Each map has different information to impart (some more information than others), and the outdoorsman contemplating a back-country trip is wise to utilize several of these maps in his planning.

The map in the back of this book, a Wilderness Press original, is included for the reader's trip planning. Its scale is 1:253,000. Routes and campsites described in this book are shown in red, as are the boundaries of the regions that make up book chapters. Streams and lakes are shown in blue. Using this map, one can make out the general topography, watercourses and trail routes that he will encounter on a trip. Discrepancies from the topographic maps which were found while scouting the trips are incorporated into the map and the text of this book.

The profile of each trip in this book gives a quick picture of the ups and downs. All profiles are drawn with the same *ratio* of horizontal miles to feet of elevation except 47 and 87. The vertical scale in all is exaggerated.

On the trail most backpackers prefer to use a topographic ("topo") map, because it affords a good deal of accurate information about conditions of terrain and forest cover. Topo maps come in a variety of sizes and scales, but the best, because they cover the whole Sierra in one useful scale, is the U.S. Geological Survey's 15' Topographic Quadrangle series. The 15' series scale is approximately 1"=1 mile; the contour interval (elevation difference between contour lines) is 80 feet in the Sierra; and the area covered by each map is about 13x17 miles. They show most of the maintained trails (exceptions noted in the text of this book), the elevations, the relief, the watercourses, the forest cover, and the works of man. "Reading" these maps takes a little practice, but the savings in shoe leather and frayed tempers make it a worthwhile undertaking. For the convenience of the reader, the appropriate 15' topo maps for each trip are cited in the text.

A useful second map is the one published by the U.S. Forest Service. Being a base map, it lacks the contour lines, but it is

It also includes markings for water, man-made structures, and some elevations.

Anglers planning a fishing trip should acquire the "Anglers' Guides" published by Wilderness Press. These include both artistically drawn representational maps and descriptions of the fishing waters. Of this in-progress series, three guides ("Emigrant Basin," "South Boundary Yosemite Park" and "Mono Creek") apply to the regions of the northern Sierra covered by this book.

HOW TO ACQUIRE YOUR MAPS

USGS 15' Topo: U. S. Geological Survey,
                       Federal Center, Denver, Colo. 80225
                       50 cents each, less by bulk order.
                       Index map is free.

USFS base map: U. S. Forest Service,
                       630 Sansome St.,
                       San Francisco, Calif. 94111
                       An index map and the set for one
                       National Forest per order are free.

Anglers' Guides: Wilderness Press
                       2440 Bancroft Way
                       Berkeley, Calif. 94704

Desolation Wilderness

Wilderness gives a man a chance to stretch and think — a chance to renew a bond as fundamental to his well being as breathing. Federally designated Wildernesses, like the Desolation Valley region, serve this function admirably. The area is small (64,000 acres), but it contains a wide spectrum of life zones (Transition Zone through Arctic-Alpine Zone). Over 100 lakes and many miles of streams provide excellent fishing, and the feeder-system trails that focus on the main Desolation Valley/Rockbound Valley arterial are convenient entrance and egress points for short trips. The trailheads used in this section are spaced around the periphery of the Wilderness, and lend themselves to fine shuttle trips. (Three of the trailheads are located on major hiways having bus service.) U. S. 50 affords access to the trailheads at Wrights Lake (9 miles north on a good dirt road that leaves Hiway 50 five miles east of Kyburz); at Twin Bridges (on the hiway); and at Lower Echo Lake (1½ miles north of the hiway by a paved road that branches north just west of Echo Summit). State Route 89 affords access to the trailhead at Glen Alpine, which is about 6 miles south of 89 past Fallen Leaf Lake. State Route 89 also goes to Emerald Bay and Meeks Bay.

Desolation Valley proper is a high, rocky, glacially scoured basin whose cirque floor is nearly filled by very large Lake Aloha. This is a land of granite landscapes broken by spiring, wind-polished snags and gnarled lodgepole pines. One is sure to see marmots and conies along the trail, for they come with rocky, high-country slopes.

Just beyond Mosquito Pass lies Rockbound Valley. Though it is within the Desolation Wilderness, the presence of a ground cover distinguishes it from its more sterile neighbor to the south. Like Desolation Valley, Rockbound Valley was the path of an old glacier. The densely wooded valley floor belies the polished granite walls that rise on either side, and it is not until one visits one of the "hanging valleys" (feeder canyons that were sheared off by the main glacier) that one becomes aware of the size of the ice mass that covered the country. Several of these hanging valleys are in the trip descriptions that follow.

Though most of the lakes of the Desolation Wilderness are stocked with trout, some have become self-sustaining. The present fishery includes rainbow, brook, golden and brown trout. Despite heavy fishing pressure, this is real fishing country. Anglers will do well on the more secluded lakes and streams.

1   **Wrights Lake to Maud Lake**

TRIP
From Wrights Lake to Maud Lake (round trip). Topo map *Fallen Leaf Lake*. Best early season; 8 miles.

Grade	Trail/layover days	Total recommended days
Leisurely	2/0	2
Moderate	......	......
Strenuous	......	......

HILITES
This short but scenic hike makes a good "early-season muscle-lengthener." Maud Lake is set in a rocky basin at timberline, where early-season fishermen can enjoy the good angling for rainbow trout.

DESCRIPTION

1st Hiking Day **(Wrights Lake** to **Maud Lake,** 4.0 miles) : The trailhead (7000') is located at the end of a dirt road 1 mile north of Wrights Lake Campground. Beginning in a dense cover of lodgepole pine and red fir, the first ¼ mile of the route follows a level road beside a large meadow. Across the meadow, the gray granite peaks of the barren, glaciated Crystal Range rise to almost 10000'. Soon the road turns to dusty trail and we climb gently over a rocky ridge, then dip slightly to pass the Tyler Lake trail (the junction is muddy in early season). Beyond this junction we enter the expanded Desolation Wilderness. Our route then crosses the rocky ridge above the Jones Fork of Silver Creek, where there are excellent views to the northeast of the craggy heights of the Crystal Range and of the cirque enclosing Maud Lake. From this viewpoint one can make out the saddle at the head of the cirque which is Rockbound Pass. The trail then descends to ford the creek and veers northeast up a series of long granite slabs to Willow Flat. After passing the Red Peak trail, the route ascends steeply to irregularly shaped Maud Lake (7680'). Several fair campsites may be found along its western edge in the pleasant stands of lodgepole pine. Firewood is adequate, and fishing is fair for rainbow and brook (to 12").

2nd Hiking Day **(Maud Lake** to **Wrights Lake,** 4.0 miles) : Retrace steps of 1st hiking day.

Wrights Lake to Lake Schmidell

2

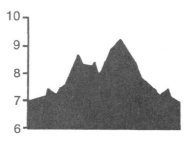

TRIP   From Wrights Lake to Lake Schmidell (semiloop trip). Topo map *Fallen Leaf Lake*. Best mid season; 16.9 miles.

Grade	Trail/layover days	Total recom- mended days
Leisurely	3/1	4
Moderate	2/1	3
Strenuous	2/0	2

HILITES   The popularity of Lake Schmidell is well deserved, being due to the relative ease of access, the usually good fishing and the highly scenic setting of this clear, green lake. This trip adds the exhilaration of returning via a high, wildflower-lined trail where views are almost constantly panoramic.

DESCRIPTION (Leisurely trip)

1st Hiking Day **(Wrights Lake** to **Maud Lake,** 4.0 miles) : See 1st hiking day, trip 1.

2nd Hiking Day **(Maud Lake** to **Lake Schmidell,** 3.5 miles) : The 960′ ascent to the summit of aptly named Rockbound Pass begins about ½ mile north of Maud Lake. As the trail switchbacks precipitously up the left face of the Maud Lake cirque, it crosses rough, loose, marmot-inhabited talus and granite slopes. The long traverse at the top of the cirque brings the traveler to Rockbound Pass (8650′), where a rest stop offers superlative views. Here one may well feel that he is on the verge of wilderness. Immediately to the northeast of the pass is tiny (5-acre) Lake Doris (8360′), with a notable stand of mountain hemlock to the south. Beyond this lake the subalpine meadows fall away into Rockbound Valley, and then rise to the eminences of Phipps Peak, Dicks Peak and Jacks Peak. The trail drops

down a rocky slope past Lake Doris (poor fishing) and strikes out across the meadows just to the north, passing the lateral to China Flat and veering northwest. In early and mid season these meadows abound in wildflowers, including penstemon, shooting star, buttercup and paintbrush. This trail segment passes through a park-like stand of lodgepole pine, silver pine and red fir before crossing a little rocky ridge to windy Lake Lois (8300'). Fishing on this lake is good (excellent in early season) for brook and rainbow (7-14"). After crossing the flow-maintenance dam on the northern edge of the lake, the trail re-enters a forest cover of lodgepole pine, red and white fir, and mountain hemlock, and tops the ridge overlooking picturesque Lake Schmidell. On this ridge it passes a trail (Rockbound Stock driveway) branching left. The steep 500' descent is made by pleasant duff switchbacks to the "Improved" campsites on the south shore and the many good campsites on the eastern edge of the lake (7900'). Firewood is plentiful, and fishing is good for brook (to 11").
3rd Hiking Day **(Lake Schmidell** to **Wrights Lake)** via Rockbound Stock driveway, 9.4 miles) : This day's hike begins by retracing the previous day's route for about ½ mile to the signed junction with the Rockbound Stock driveway, also called the Red Peak trail and Trail 16E09. This path is not immediately evident, but about 200 yards up the slope from this junction our route is marked by some ducks and blazes. The trail becomes more distinct as it climbs to the west wall of the Lake Lois cirque, switchbacks part way up the wall, and then continues upward on a fairly steep traverse. Views from the trail here are excellent of Lake Lois and the peaks beyond Rockbound Valley. The shaded, rilled slope has a great profusion of wildflowers in bloom throughout the summer, including red elderberry, sulfur flower, Douglas phlox, dense stands of red heather, spiraea, fireweed, gooseberry, elephant heads and gentian. Dwarf juniper provides ground cover over large areas.

The crest of this climb (9180'), atop the Crystal Range, is a low, broad saddle dotted with a few hemlock trees and stunted, low whitebark pines. From just west of the divide one has views of Mt. Price, Wrights Lake, Icehouse Reservoir, and the hazy, gentle west slope of the Sierra, its continuous tree cover contrasting sharply with the semi-barren slopes of Desolation Wilderness. In the rocky meadows west of the pass, the descending trail is indistinct but sufficiently ducked. Then our route passes through a lovely, grassy, high meadow from where one can look down on Top Lake and Lawrence Lake. From here the route, following a southwesterly course, crosses a small divide to a headwaters swale and descends along a sandy ridge. (Midway down the ridge, the experienced knapsacker may prefer to leave the trail and descend south-southwest from where the word "Spring" appears on the topo map, to intersect the Willow Flat trail a little way below Maud Lake.)

Leaving the ridge, our route veers west and makes a rocky-dusty 400' descent where too many bovine hooves have rather spoiled the hillside. At the foot of this descent, where snow lies all year, our ducked trail jogs north and arrives at a forested flat with a cowmen's campsite. Here it turns west to follow a series of blazes down the runoff course to a meadowy flat, where several tarns are shaded by hemlock, lodgepole and silver pine. In this flat, at a junction with the Old Barrett Camp trail, our route turns left onto the trail to Wrights Lake. This nearly level trail passes two shallow, weedy, fishless lakes and comes out onto an open chaparral slope. Here it curves northeast up a little canyon west of the Maud Lake outlet stream, and then crosses over to meet the Willow Flat trail in a stand of lodgepole at the foot of a granite-slab slope. Then our route turns right and retraces the steps of part of the 1st hiking day, trip 1.

Wrights Lake to Camper Flat   3

TRIP   From Wrights Lake to Camper Flat via Schmidell, Leland, McConnell, Horseshoe, 4-Q and Doris Lakes (semiloop trip). Topo map *Fallen Leaf Lake*. Best mid or late season; 26.4 miles.

Grade	Trail/layover days	Total recom- mended days
Leisurely	6/1	7
Moderate	5/1	6
Strenuous	3/1	4

HILITES   This route sees less use, and the hiker who wishes to get off the "beaten track" will find this loop to his liking. Some of the best fishing in the Desolation Wilderness is in the lakes that line this route.

DESCRIPTION (Leisurely trip)

1st Hiking Day **(Wrights Lake** to **Maud Lake,** 4.0 miles) : See 1st hiking day, trip 1.

2nd Hiking Day **(Maud Lake** to **Lake Schmidell,** 3.5 miles) : See 2nd hiking day, trip 2.

3rd Hiking Day **(Lake Schmidell** to **Horseshoe Lake,** 4.5 miles) : The trail to the ridge overlooking Leland Lakes is visible from Lake Schmidell. This trail section ascends steeply on a traverse of a shoulder of Red Peak. Views from the trail include Dicks Peak, Phipps Peak, Middle Mountain, and emerald green Lake Schmidell. When the trail tops the saddle above Leland Lakes, a magnificent granite amphitheater comes into view. Nestled in a pristine granite bowl beneath towering Silver Peak, Leland Lakes make an unforgettably dramatic appearance. From the saddle the trail descends 400′ over steep, glacially polished granite, and rugged, exfoliating talus slopes. This descent is a faint, "ducked" footpath that becomes increasingly hard to follow as it skirts the east side of Leland Lakes. Anglers wishing to try their luck on these deep lakes will find the fair fishing for brook (7-14″) challenging. Beyond the lakes the foot path winds through hemlock and stunted lodgepole pine as it follows the descending creek joining Leland and McConnell lakes. Just above McConnell Lake the forest cover thickens and red fir begins to appear. As the trail rounds the west side of meadowy McConnell Lake, it is close under the granite slopes of McConnell Peak. From these rocky slopes sunning marmots watch impassively as fishermen try the poor-to-fair fishing for brook and rainbow (to 8″) on McConnell Lake. The trail north of McConnell, not any better maintained than the section that preceded it, descends gently to the few campsites on the west side of Horseshoe Lake (7600′). Firewood around the lake is plentiful, and fishing is good for brook (7-13″). Anglers who wish a change of scenery—or luck—may wish to take the rocky trail that leaves our trail a few yards northeast of Horseshoe Lake, and go to granitoid Zitella and Highland lakes.

4th Hiking Day **(Horseshoe Lake** to **Camper Flat,** 4.5 miles) : The Forest Service sign at Horseshoe Lake indicating that 4-Q Lakes is only 2 miles away is in error. The correct distance is 3 miles, and this trail is extremely rough and poorly maintained. The first mile of rocky descent is correctly labeled as a hazardous stock trail and is recommended only for intermediate and experienced trail travelers. The trail drops over granite slabs, marked only by "ducks" and the garish efforts of a misguided Forest Service patrolman, to the ford of the creek that empties

Horseshoe and 4-Q lakes. Thence the trail climbs 400′ southward through an increasingly dense forest cover to 4-Q Lakes. This charming chain of lakes makes an excellent lunch stop, and fishermen will find the good-to-excellent fishing for brook (9-14″) a satisfying interlude. The remaining 1½ miles to Camper Flat (7200′) is an easy downhill jaunt that ends when it passes the trail to Rockbound Lake and Onion Reservoir and fords a tributary of the Rubicon River just below Camper Flat. There are numerous campsites in the flat, and firewood is plentiful. Fishermen will find the angling on the Rubicon good (nice holes 0.3 miles downstream) for rainbow and brown (to 9″).

5th Hiking Day **(Camper Flat** to **Lake Doris,** 4 miles) : Since this hiking day's climb (1000′ from the China Flat trail junction to Lake Doris) comes at the end of the trek, travelers are well advised to get an early start. The first 2½ miles to the foot of this climb winds pleasantly along the Rubicon River (fishing is fair for rainbow and brook 7-9″), and passes through meadows filled with wildflowers and often visited by deer. As the trail ascends toward China Flat, it passes two trail laterals to Lake Schmidell, and fords the outlet streams of Lake Lois and Lake Doris. Then, at the foot of a large, lush meadow, our route branches west toward Rockbound Pass. The remaining 1½ miles to Lake Doris is a steady ascent through a changing forest cover ending in lodgepole, red fir, and silver pine. The trail emerges from this cover to the meadows just below Lake Doris (8360′), where hikers will find several campsites among the small stands of lodgepole at the northeast end of the lake. Firewood is somewhat scarce, and fishing is poor.

6th Hiking Day **(Lake Doris** to **Wrights Lake,** 5.8 miles) : Retrace steps of 1st and part of 2nd hiking days.

Echo Lake to Lake Lucille

4

TRIP   From Lower Echo Lake to Lake Lucille, via North Lake trail or Echo Lakes boat-taxi (round trip). Topo map (15′) *Fallen Leaf Lake*. Best mid or late season; 13 miles.

Grade	Trail/layover days	Total recommended days
Leisurely	2/0	2
Moderate	—	—
Strenuous	—	—

HILITES   This is the most popular route into the Desolation Wilderness, and part of the Pacific Crest Trail and the Tahoe-Yosemite Trail. The heavy use renders the trail somewhat dusty in late season. The trail's popularity derives from the region's spectacular scenery and relatively easy access. The optional boat-taxi service operating the length of Lower and Upper Echo lakes is a unique and interesting way to begin or end a trip into Desolation Valley.

DESCRIPTION

1st Hiking Day **(Lower Echo Lake** to **Lake Lucille,** 6.5 miles) : The trailhead for this trip is at the Lower Echo Lake spillway (7414'). Those who elect to use the boat-taxi service (bypassing the first 2.9 miles of the North Lake trail) may board at the boat dock below Echo Chalet, and debark at the upper boat landing at the northern tip of Upper Echo Lake. The fairly level North Lake trail offers excellent views of the lakes and the flanking peaks : Becker Peak, Talking Mountain and Ralston Peak. Beyond the initial, rocky scrub area below Flagpole Peak, the trail enters a forest cover of lodgepole pine, where it meets the short trail lateral to the upper boat landing. This junction marks the beginning of a rocky, exposed series of switchbacks that ascend 300' to the Tamarack Lake trail junction. Anglers who are eager to wet their lines may elect to take the short (½-mile) looping trail that touches Tamarack, Ralston and Cagwin lakes. Fishing at these deep, granitoid lakes is fair for rainbow and brook (to 9"). From the Tamarack Lake trail junction, the route climbs 400' over another rocky slope to Haypress Meadows (8300'), where it levels out and passes the two trail laterals to Lake of the Woods and Horsetail Falls. Forest Service officials have removed the barbed wire that marred the meadows, and trail travelers may now enjoy the primitive beauty of this spot uncluttered by the works of man. A few yards past the west end of Haypress Meadows, our route branches north past heavily wooded Lake Margery to larger, rockier Lake Lucille (8200'). Several campsites, some with Forest Service fireplaces, may be found on the timbered west side. Fishing is good for rainbow and brook (to 9"). This beautiful lake makes an excellent base for exploratory or angling excursions to island-dotted Lake

Aloha (8100'), lying in a glacially formed basin, and for an ascent of Keiths Dome.

2nd Hiking Day **(Lake Lucille** to **Lower Echo Lake,** 6.5 miles) : Retrace steps of 1st hiking day.

Echo Lake to Heather Lake   5

TRIP   From Lower Echo Lake to Heather Lake, via North Lake trail or Echo Lakes boat-taxi (round trip). Topo map (15') *Fallen Leaf Lake.* Best mid or late season ; 18 miles.

Grade	Trail/layover days	Total recom-mended days
Leisurely	3/0	3
Moderate	2/0	2
Strenuous	2/0	2

HILITES   This route skirts almost the entire northeast shore of island-dotted Lake Aloha. Views of the spectacular Crystal Range across this glacial lake are among the most dramatic in this Wilderness. This short round trip is an eye-opener for the beginner who has never been introduced to the special feel that accompanies the alpine zone of high granitoid lakes.

DESCRIPTION (Leisurely trip)

1st Hiking Day **(Lower Echo Lake** to **Lake Lucille,** 6.5 miles) : See 1st hiking day, trip 4.

2nd Hiking Day **(Lake Lucille** to **Heather Lake,** 2.5 miles) : Taking the trail lateral rounding the northern tip of Lake Margery, this route ascends slightly to meet the Pacific Crest Trail west of Haypress Meadows. Turning right, our route passes several small melt-off tarns as it descends through lodgepole to the rocky shore of Lake Aloha. The shoreline trail from this point offers superlative views, across the blue lake waters, of Pyramid Peak (9983') and Mt. Price (9975'). The massive evidence of glacial action in this very large cirque confronts the traveler on every hand. Progress along this rocky segment of shoreline trail is slow, but the pace gives the passerby time to absorb the enormous scope of the landscape. On the north side of the trail, the exfoliating granite slopes below Cracked Crag provide numerous homesites for the buff, white-collared, yellow-bellied marmots. These furry members of the woodchuck family delight in sunning on the sun-drenched rock, and when humans get too close they scurry away with a high whistling, chirping sound. To the northwest the low, barren, rocky saddle on the skyline is Mosquito Pass, but this day's route branches east at the northeastern tip of Lake Aloha. From a few yards past this junction, one can look down the rocky descent to Heather Lake (7920') with its Forest Service "improved" campsites on the near side of the lake. Firewood is somewhat scarce, and fishing is fair-to-good for brook and rainbow (to 10").

3rd Hiking Day **(Heather Lake** to **Lower Echo Lake,** 9 miles) : Retrace steps of 1st and 2nd hiking days.

6   Echo Lake to Twin Bridges

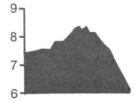

TRIP   From Lower Echo Lake to Twin Bridges, via Lake Lucille, Lake of the Woods, Horsetail Falls (shuttle trip). Topo map (15') *Fallen Leaf Lake.* Best mid or late season ; 11.4 miles.

Grade	Trail/layover days	Total recommended days
Leisurely	2/0	2
Moderate	—	—
Strenuous	—	—

HILITES   With all the scenic attractions of the south end of Desolation Valley beckoning, this route affords a different return route than trip 4 as it winds past Lake of the Woods and Horsetail Falls.

DESCRIPTION

1st Hiking Day **(Lower Echo Lake** to **Lake Lucille,** 6.5 miles) : See 1st hiking day, trip 4.

2nd Hiking Day **(Lake Lucille** to **Twin Bridges,** 4.9 miles) : Our route retraces the brief trail lateral skirting the east side of Lake Margery, crosses the Haypress Meadows/Lake Aloha trail and descends over a forested slope to Lake of the Woods. This large subalpine lake is crowded in the summer, owing largely to a Boy Scout contingent from Camp Harvey West on Upper Echo Lake. The trail "looks" across emerald waters, bounded on three sides by forest cover of lodgepole pine and red fir, to the glaciated granite of the western shore. Fishing at Lake of the Woods is fair for rainbow and brook (8-13"). Our route turns south along the east shore of the lake, and then veers west toward Ropi Lake. This section of trail is a rocky descent that levels out at barren, granitoid Ropi Lake, and crosses its outlet, Pyramid Creek, on a wooden bridge. Fishing for rainbow and brook (to 9") is poor-to-fair on Ropi, Pitt and Avalanche lakes. Following the west side of Pyramid Creek, the trail descends gently past exposed, granitoid Pitt and Avalanche lakes, which are not much more than wide spots in the creek. (The trail from Ropi Lake to Twin Bridges is not shown on the topo map.) About 200 yards west of the top of Horsetail Falls our route, marked by ducks and some white paint on rocks, begins a steep, rocky descent.

This ½-mile descent ends in a nearly level, pleasant, wooded valley where the mixed forest cover is dominated by Jeffrey pines, and the sandy trail winds among manzanita and chinquapin. Then our ducked route veers away from the creek and descends moderately, sometimes steeply, down granite slabs, levelling off again shortly before arriving at the trailhead at Twin Bridges (6100').

7   Echo Lake to Wrights Lake

TRIP   From Lower Echo Lake to Wrights Lake, via Mosquito Pass, Lake Doris, Rockbound Pass (shuttle trip). Topo map (15') *Fallen Leaf Lake*. Best mid or late season; 20.6 miles.

Grade	Trail/layover days	Total recommended days
Leisurely	5/1	6
Moderate	3/1	4
Strenuous	2/1	3

HILITES   This dramatic route samples a considerable section of the Desolation Wilderness. The landscape tells of great glacial forces at work, and at Mosquito Pass the trail traveler stands at the heads of two cirques carved by ice masses that flowed in opposite directions.

DESCRIPTION (Moderate trip)

1st Hiking Day (**Lower Echo Lake** to **Heather Lake,** 9 miles) : See 1st hiking day, trip 4, and 2nd hiking day, trip 5.

2nd Hiking Day (**Heather Lake** to **Lake Doris,** 6 miles) : From Heather Lake the trail ascends the rocky slope to Lake Aloha, where it joins the Echo Lake/Rockbound Valley trail, and then proceeds west along the northern shore of Lake Aloha. The view of Pyramid Peak to the south is a photographic favorite. Mosquito Pass (8450') is a low saddle resting between the granite heights of Mt. Price and Jacks Peak. Views from this saddle are excellent of both Desolation and Rockbound valleys, and one can easily see where two glaciers began their flows north and south from this point. This pass divides the headwaters of streams that flow into the South Fork of the American River from those that flow into the Middle Fork. Just beyond the pass, rockbound Clyde Lake nestles under the sheer granite walls of the Crystal Range, and the outlet stream from the lake marks the birth of the Rubicon River. From Mosquito Pass the rocky-dusty trail drops down into sparse hemlock and soon passes the Clyde Lake lateral. Then, as the trail gradually levels off, the forest cover becomes more dense, and lodgepole pine is added to hemlock, red fir and silver pine.

At the foot of this long, steady, wildflower-lined descent, the trail crosses the Rubicon River on boulders, and then undulates over broken volcanic rock on the west side of the river. A mile from the last ford it refords to the large, open bench called China Flat. Beyond this meadow the route passes through a "lawn" of head-high lodgepole pines, all of the same age, which succeeded the multi-height mixed forest here after it was wiped out by a large avalanche. Shortly beyond a third ford of the Rubicon River, amid this "lawn," the route reaches the junction with the Lake Doris/Rockbound Pass lateral, whence it follows part of the 5th hiking day, trip 3.

3rd Hiking Day (**Lake Doris** to **Wrights Lake,** 5.6 miles) : From Lake Doris the trail ascends the short, rocky stretch to Rockbound Pass (8650'), where the knapsacker can look back across Lake Doris to the Sierra crest. To the west this vantage point overlooks the Maud Lake cirque and the forested watershed of the Jones Fork of Silver Creek. The trail then descends steeply 970' to Maud Lake (7680') by rocky switchbacks. The slopes of this precipitous drop provide numerous opportunities for that traditional backpacker occupation — marmot-watching. These furry animals inhabit rocky hillsides and talus slopes in the higher elevations, and this particular descent may be said to be "marmot heaven." From Maud Lake our route retraces the 1st hiking day, trip 1.

Echo Lake to Wrights Lake 8

TRIP   From Lower Echo Lake to Wrights Lake, via Mosquito Pass, Camper Flat, Horseshoe Lake, Lake

Schmidell, Rockbound Pass (shuttle trip). Topo map (15') *Fallen Leaf Lake*. Best mid or late season; 32.5 miles.

Grade	Trail/layover days	Total recommended days
Leisurely	8/2	10
Moderate	6/1	7
Strenuous	4/1	5

HILITES Anglers, hikers, photographers and naturalists will like this varied route. The trip covers two distinctly different kinds of country. The first half tours the scenic grandeur of granite-bound Desolation Valley, and the second half explores the less-known and less-visited western slopes of Rockbound Valley. Because of the rugged terrain and poorly maintained trail from Camper Flat to Leland Lakes, this trip is an adventure in route picking.

DESCRIPTION (Moderate trip)

1st Hiking Day **(Lower Echo Lake** to **Heather Lake,** 9 miles) : See 1st hiking day, trip 4, and 2nd hiking day, trip 5.

2nd Hiking Day **(Heather Lake** to **Camper Flat,** 7 miles) : This day's hike begins by following the route of trip 7, 2nd hiking day, to the junction of the Rockbound Pass/Lake Doris trail. Shortly beyond this junction our trail fords the multibranched outlet of Lake Doris at the foot of a long, wet meadow. Beyond the meadow, the forest cover, which still includes some mountain hemlock, contains a few white firs; these two species are seldom found together, having different altitude preferences. After jumping across the outlet stream from Lake Lois, we pass a lateral to Lake Schmidell and continue the gentle descent beside the rapidly growing Rubicon River. A mile farther on, the trail passes the Eagle Falls/Velma Lakes trail branching right, and then another lateral to Lake Schmidell, branching left. A stone's throw north of this junction, the trail passes a short lateral leading to 2 mineral springs and arrives at sandy Camper Flat. Several good campsites may be found along the river, and firewood is adequate. Nice granite potholes (for fishing or swimming) may be found 0.3 mile downstream.

3rd Hiking Day **(Camper Flat** to **Horseshoe Lake,** 4.5 miles) : See 4th hiking day, trip 3.

4th Hiking Day **(Horseshoe Lake** to **Lake Schmidell,** 4.5 miles) : See 3rd hiking day, trip 3.

Looking south from Donohue Pass

5th Hiking Day **(Lake Schmidell** to **Maud Lake,** 3.5 miles) :
See 2nd hiking day, trip 2.

6th Hiking Day **(Maud Lake** to **Wrights Lake,** 4 miles) : See
1st hiking day, trip 1.

Emerald Bay to Velma Lakes   9

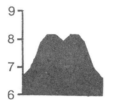

TRIP   From Emerald Bay to Middle Velma Lake (round
trip). Topo map (15′) *Fallen Leaf Lake.* Best mid
or late season ; 8.2 miles.

Grade	Trail/layover days	Total recom- mended days
Leisurely	2/0	2
Moderate	—	—
Strenuous	—	—

HILITES   Though it is a stiff 1700′ climb from the trailhead,
this trip's destination in the heart of the wooded
Velma Lakes Basin makes the effort worth while.
Good fishing for the fair-sized rainbow (and occasional brown) in these lakes is a strong plus for the
hiker, and an end in itself for the dedicated angler.

DESCRIPTION

1st Hiking Day **(Emerald Bay** to **Middle Velma Lake,** 4.1
miles) : The trailhead is at the west end of Eagle Falls Campground (6500′). The Forest Service campground is located on
the west side of Hiway 89 at the southwest end of Emerald Bay.
The trail starts on the north side of Eagle Falls Creek amid
a mature stand of yellow pine, which soon gives way to manzanita and chokebrush. After a short rocky climb beside a waterfall the route crosses the creek on a wooden bridge and levels
off somewhat as it enters a forest of mixed conifers. This route
swings south under the western cliffs of spiring Maggies Peaks

and climbs past a junction with the lateral to Eagle Lake (7040',
poor fishing). The trail section beyond the junction is a long,
brushy traverse above the lake, gaining 700' elevation. Our
trail then switchbacks steeply up into timber cover, crossing
occasional granite slabs, where views of Emerald Bay and Lake
Tahoe are very good. After passing a sandy saddle, we descend
a few feet westward and then resume a southerly, contouring
course.

At the end of a short climb the trail from Bay View·joins our
path, and the wedded route winds across undulating granite
under a sparse cover of lodgepole pine. A short ⅓ of a mile
beyond a junction with a trail (not shown on the topo map)
that leads southeast to Azure Lake is the junction with the
trail to Dicks Pass. This unsigned junction, near a small lake,
is indicated by a large cairn, and here we take the right (northward) fork. From the junction the trail makes a gentle descent
to the ford of Upper Velma Lake's outlet stream, passing
through dense hemlock and red fir. West of the ford is a Forest
Service "improved" campground and a junction with the old
Tahoe-Yosemite Trail, where this day's route turns left (south).
A level walk along the east shore of Upper Velma Lake terminates at the good campsites at the head of the lake (8000'),
where one can hear a musical cascade coming down from Fon-
tanillis Lake. The Velma Lakes are in a small, heavily wooded
basin at the apex of east and west Sierra drainages. Middle
Velma Lake flows into the Rubicon River, a major tributary
of the west slope's American River, while Upper and Lower
Velma lakes flow eastward through Eagle Falls Creek to Lake
Tahoe and out into Nevada. Fishing on all three lakes is fair-
to-good for rainbow and brook and some brown (to 12"). Firewood is adequate.

2nd Hiking Day **(Middle Velma Lake** to **Emerald Bay,** 4.1
miles) : Retrace steps of 1st hiking day.

Wrights Lake to Emerald Bay   10

TRIP   From Wrights Lake to Emerald Bay via Rockbound Pass, Lakes Schmidell, Horseshoe, and Middle Velma (shuttle trip). Topo map (15′) *Fallen
Leaf Lake*. Best mid or late season; 23 miles.

Grade	Trail/layover days	Total recom- mended days
Leisurely	5/2	7
Moderate	4/1	5
Strenuous	3/1	4

HILITES   Cross-Sierran routes are not particularly hard to
find, but this trip is outstanding in its variety of
scenery. From the invigorating heights of the barren Crystal Range to the serene calm of the Velma
Lakes Basin, this tour is for the intermediate or experienced wilderness traveler who wants to take his
time and absorb the healing balm of beautiful country.

DESCRIPTION (Leisurely trip)

1st Hiking Day **(Wrights Lake** to **Maud Lake,** 4 miles) : See 1st
hiking day, trip 1.

2nd Hiking Day **(Maud Lake** to **Lake Schmidell,** 3.5 miles) :
See 2nd hiking day, trip 2.

3rd Hiking Day **(Lake Schmidell** to **Horseshoe Lake,** 4.5
miles) : See 3rd hiking day, trip 3.

4th Hiking Day **(Horseshoe Lake** to **Middle Velma Lake,** 6.9
miles) : Proceed to Camper Flat as described for 4th hiking day,
trip 3. The trail to Middle Velma Lake branches east from the
Rubicon River trail a few yards south of Camper Flat. It fords
the Rubicon River, and climbs via a "ducked" route across a
polished granite surface. This open expanse of rock affords fine
views back across Rockbound Valley of the various "hanging
valley" lake basins flanked by Red and Silver peaks of the Crys-

tal Range. Looking northwest down Rockbound Valley, one can make out McKinstry Peak (with the bare north shoulder). The trail then enters a forest cover of red fir and hemlock, passes two trails to Stony Ridge Lake (which later join) and arrives at densely wooded Middle Velma Lake (7900'). Forest Service "improved" campsites may be found at the southeastern end of the lake. Anglers will wish to test the good fishing for rainbow and some brown (to 12") here at Middle Velma Lake and at the nearby sister lakes of the Velma group. There are good campsites at the south end of Upper Velma Lake.

5th Hiking Day **(Middle Velma Lake** to **Emerald Bay,** 4.1 miles) : See 1st hiking day, trip 9.

11   Glen Alpine to Heather Lake

TRIP   From Glen Alpine Trailhead to Heather Lake (round trip). Topo map (15') *Fallen Leaf Lake.* Best mid or late season ; 11 miles.

Grade	Trail/layover days	Total recom- mended days
Leisurely	2/0	2
Moderate	—	—
Strenuous	—	—

HILITES   This is one of the shorter routes to the Desolation Wilderness. However, the trail does not see especially heavy usage owing to the rough and rocky condition of the dirt road from Fallen Leaf Lake. This short but steep trip is made for the "weekender."

DESCRIPTION

1st Hiking Day **(Glen Alpine Trailhead** to **Heather Lake,** 5.5 miles) : The trailhead (6540') is located 1 mile south of the road forks at the south end of Fallen Leaf Lake. Advance inquiry should be made. Write to : U. S. Forest Service, Lake Tahoe Visitor Center, South Lake Tahoe, California, to determine whether this road section is open to automobile traffic. The trail soon leaves the forest cover about Glen Alpine Creek and then climbs steadily past the short lateral to Grass Lake. This ascent parallels Glen Alpine Creek, and from the rocky switchbacks the traveler has good views of the spectacular granite formation to the west known as Cracked Crag. Soon after re-entering forest cover, the trail levels out and fords Glen Alpine Creek. In a setting of several lovely melt-off tarns, the trail passes the junctions of two trails leading to Dicks Pass, and crosses a rocky ridge to granitoid Susie Lake (7840′, fishing for rainbow and brook to 9″ is poor-to-fair). Towering Jacks Peak dominates the western skyline as the trail circles the south end of Susie Lake and climbs to Heather Lake (7920′). Forest Service "Improved" campsites are on the north side of the lake, and firewood is somewhat scarce. Fishing on Heather Lake is fair-to-good for brook and rainbow (to 10″).

2nd Hiking Day (**Heather Lake** to **Glen Alpine Trailhead,** 5.5 miles) : Retrace steps of 1st hiking day.

Meeks Creek to Rubicon Lake   12

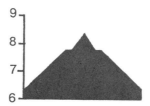

TRIP From Meeks Creek Roadend to Rubicon Lake (round trip). Topo maps (15′) *Tahoe, Fallen Leaf Lake.* Best early to mid season ; 12.4 miles.

Grade	Trail/layover days	Total recommended days
Leisurely	2/1	3
Moderate	2/0	2
Strenuous	—	—

HILITES This weekend trip, which visits six lakes in six miles, is for anglers and swimmers alike. Hemlock-bordered, emerald-green Rubicon Lake has the loveliest setting of the six, and the least foot traffic. This

trip makes a fine introduction to the wilderness west
of Lake Tahoe.

DESCRIPTION

1st Hiking Day **(Meeks Creek Roadend** to **Rubicon Lake,** 6.2
miles) : This hike follows the first portion of the Tahoe-Yosemite
Trail, a route that ends 180 miles away at Tuolumne Meadows
in Yosemite. The trailhead is at the end of a dirt road that
leaves Hiway 89 across from the Meeks Bay Theater. From
the trailhead (6300') the trip begins on a gently ascending sandy
trail in a forest of white fir, incense cedar, Jeffrey pine and
lodgepole pine. After a short ¼ mile the trail enters the Desolation Wilderness, where motorized travel is prohibited. As the
ascent becomes moderate up a gray granite slope, we pass a
spring where currant bushes and corn lilies thrive, and flowers
of purple lupine and red paintbrush decorate the slope above
the spring. Beyond the spring the trail levels, becomes sandy
again, and starts to approach Meeks Creek, whose happy splashing sounds foretell the sight of its tumbling waters.

Crossing a seep in this sandy section, we see that its moisture
sustains paintbrush, monkeyflower, groundsel, thimbleberry,
delphinium, columbine and tiger lily — their blossoms a spectrum of bright hues. The trail then crosses three meadows set
close together, and after a short ascent we come to the old Tahoe-Yosemite Trail, marked *Abandoned*. A few yards farther is
a boulder ford of Meeks Creek; in early season it may be
advisable to go fifty yards upstream to cross on a log. From the
ford the trail makes a loop to the east, ascending steadily to
gain the height of a cascade we can glimpse through the mixed
forest cover that has come to include mountain hemlock. Beyond the cascade is Lake Genevieve, a shallow, green, warmish,
pine-rimmed lake with some fair campsites that get heavy use.

A short, gentle ascent of ¼ mile brings us to Crag Lake and
some more fair campsites, which are also heavily used. From
this lake the trail ascends moderately on rocky underfooting
to a boulder ford of Meeks Creek, where a sign points the way
to Hidden Lake, a few yards west. Beyond this sign the trail
veers away from the creek and ascends through a dense pine
and fir forest, passing above meadow-bordered, lily-dotted
Shadow Lake. This short, steady ascent beside rapids and cata-
racts brings the traveler to Stony Ridge Lake, largest of the
series of lakes, where fair-to-good campsites may be found
near the outlet and along the west shore. Anglers may wish
to pause here to sample the fair fishing for rainbow, brown and
lake trout (to 14").

At the head of Stony Ridge Lake we bear right, and begin a moderate ascent that overlooks the green, marshy meadow above the lake. This 500′ ascent passes through dynamite-blasted granite, and then switchbacks up the cool, north-facing head of Meeks Creek Canyon to a little saddle. From this saddle it is an easy descent to the shores of hemlock-rimmed Rubicon Lake (8340′). There are several good campsites on the east shore, and fishing is good for eastern brook (to 11″). Firewood is ample.

2nd Hiking Day **(Rubicon Lake** to **Meeks Creek Roadend,** 6.2 miles) : Retrace steps of 1st hiking day.

Meeks Creek to Velma Lakes   **13**

TRIP   From Meeks Creek Roadend to Emerald Bay via Velma Lakes Basin (shuttle trip). Topo maps (15′) *Tahoe, Fallen Leaf Lake.* Best mid season; 14.9 miles.

Grade	Trail/layover days	Total recommended days
Leisurely	3/1	4
Moderate	3/0	3
Strenuous	2/0	2

HILITES   This shuttle trip over Phipps Pass offers perhaps the finest views along any trail through the Desolation Wilderness. It visits 10 lakes and three stream valleys, and offers the angler a choice of varied angling for four trout species.

DESCRIPTION (Leisurely trip)

1st Hiking Day **(Meeks Creek Roadend** to **Rubicon Lake,** 6.2 miles) : See 1st hiking day, trip 12.

2nd Hiking Day **(Rubicon Lake** to **Velma Lakes,** 4.6 miles) : From Rubicon Lake the trail climbs past a looping lateral trail to Grouse Lakes. Continuing to the top of a little rise, we look down into the gray-green valley of Eagle Falls Creek and across it to the snow-streaked north slope of Mt. Tallac and its western ridge. From here the trail ascends moderately on rocky under-footing, with constantly good views that include the Grouse Lakes, Cascade Lake and parts of Lake Tahoe. The trail here is rather exposed, with a broken forest cover of hemlock, lodge-pole and silver pine. Then a nearly level traverse leads to a steep section, where we find some Forest-Service-constructed water bars that are more of a hazard than the natural terrain.

Beyond the water bars the trail departs from what is shown on the topo map. Instead of descending to the saddle labeled "Phipps Pass" on the map, our route climbs above the saddle, levels off, and gradually curves far around the south shoulder of Phipps Peak. At the highest point on this shoulder (8850') reddish-brown Dicks Peak comes into view, and a short dis-tance farther on we look down on all three Velma Lakes at once. From this open vantage point the experienced knapsacker may choose to descend cross-country straight to Middle Velma Lake, for the trail route to there, described below, is indirect.

The trail then swings around to the west, and brings the traveler to excellent views of the cirque-scalloped northern part of the Crystal Range. Finally, at a hairpin turn, the trail heads back toward Velma Lakes. A few yards northwest of the turn is a fine viewpoint overlooking much of Rockbound Valley, including Rockbound Lake. Here we begin a steady, sandy descent of more than a mile, including two long switch-back legs. After walking through a moderate-to-dense forest cover of red fir, interspersed with some silver pine, lodgepole and hemlock, we arrive at the junction of the Miller Lakes trail. The next short mile of the route is complicated by a number of trail junctions not shown on the map, but following a course almost due south will take one to a ford of the outlet stream from Middle Velma Lake. Beyond this ford we turn southeast and climb to the southwest end of the lake.

Skirting a cove here, the trail rises above the lake into a dense red-fir forest and then passes a junction with the trail to Dicks Pass. Two hundred yards farther on is another trail junc-tion, with signs pointing to Emerald Bay. Near the junction is a Forest Service "improved" campground (7960'), where wood is adequate. More primitive campsites with better views and adequate wood lie at the upper end of Upper Velma Lake. Fishing on the Velma Lakes is fair-to-good for rainbow, brook and brown (to 12"), and occasional larger fish may be caught.
3rd Hiking Day **(Velma Lakes** to **Emerald Bay,** 4.1 miles) : Retrace steps of 1st hiking day, trip 9.

Land of Fire and Ice

Called the "land of fire and ice" by one awestruck pioneer emigrant, this large slice of the northern Sierra encompasses the area stretching south from Hiway 50 to the North Boundary of Yosemite National Park. The pioneers who first trod this wilderness saw and recognized the black basaltic crests of this region for their fiery origins, and in stories of arduous crossings over snow and ice-capped summits, they expressed a profound appreciation for the evolutionary contrasts. Today's geologists tell us that lava once covered that area from Sonora Pass west to Knights Ferry to a depth of 1500 feet. Millions of years passed before the juggernaut forces of time, glacial ice and water cut through this thick layer, and today more than half of this region consists of re-exposed white-and-gray granite, the hallmark rock of the Sierra. The traveler passing through the backcountry cannot help but notice the sharp delineation between the older batholithic granites and the volcanic overlays.

These sharp contrasts are most apparent in the deeper river cuts, and it is here that the observer will witness the most vivid example of the next step in the evolutionary cycle. Here, in the mineral-rich alluvial river bottoms, life in the form of dense forest, brush and grass continues the process of mountain-leveling. The experienced mountaineer will notice immediately that timberline is usually lower than in Yosemite, Devils Postpile or the Fish Creek/Mono Creek country — a fact owing to the latitudinal differences.

Historically, this region offers much to intrigue the visitor — particularly if this visitor is on foot (either on two or four). Many of the trips described here trace old emigrant trails, and it is easy for backpackers, afoot like the emigrants, to identify with these pioneers. Preceding the emigrants were the footloose pathfinders. Explorers like Fremont, Walker and Smith first looked upon these mountains, and Fremont and Walker made crossings that cut across some of the routes described here. Before the white man, however, the Indian established hunting trails that made a network over the foothills on both sides of the Sierra crest. The Maidu and the Miwok occupied and hunted the west side of the crest, and the Washoe and Piute coexisted on the east. It is of interest to the mountaineer to know that most of these Indian trails are located on top of the ridges, and not, as is the white man's custom, along the muddy, snowy canyon bottoms.

After the Indians and the explorers came the emigrants. The Bartleson-Bidwell party of 1841 was the first overland emigrant group to cross the Sierra, and its route, tentatively identified, showed the way — later changed in places — for those who followed. This route still bears blazes placed on trees by westward-bound emigrants. There is, for example, a blazed tree near Emigrant Lake (in Emigrant Basin) which still shows the epitaph of a traveler who died there in October 1853. Still another emigrant route followed Fremont's old route up the West Carson River to Caples (formerly Twin) Lake, and thence descended the west slope past yet another "Emigrant Lake."

These routes were the predecessors of roads — first toll roads, and finally public highways. Today, with the devastating intrusion of roads into these wild spots, Californians have come to a (curiously) reluctant recognition of the necessity of preserving wilderness integrity. To this end they have established, through federal auspices, Wilderness Areas that are supposed to preserve a wild area in its intrinsic primitive state. The Mokelumne Wilderness has been included in this category, and there are plans to enlarge the Emigrant Basin Primitive Area, renaming it Emigrant Wilderness. There is also a plan for a Carson-Iceberg Wilderness that will encompass the area between Ebbetts Pass Hiway and Sonora Pass Hiway. Both planned wildernesses have, at this writing, notable administrative exclusions. In the Emigrant Wilderness it has been proposed to exclude the mining claims and their access road, which cuts across the Sierra crest at Emigrant Pass. And in the planning stages of the Carson-Iceberg Wilderness it is proposed that the present Clark Fork road be left to intrude like a dagger into the heart of the Wilderness Area. Administrative decisions of this caliber offer slim hope that future decisions will be made to extend the protective mantle of a Wilderness Area designation to other deserving areas such as that scenic east-side region in the West Walker River drainage. Here the present policy remains one of wilderness attrition by "recreation roads" (a gross contradiction) and unless prompt action is taken, it too will become another dusty traffic jam suitable only for trail bikes and tent cities.

The back-country hiker who knows the beauty of unspoiled wilderness comes to know the threat implicit in the unrestrained use of machines. With an objectivity born of an appreciation of fundamentals, and an individual wholeness that results from relying on his own resources, he recognizes the automobile as a cultural blight that is responsible for the destruction of thousands of acres of Sierra wilderness. Only recently have Forest

Service officials begun to realize the burgeoning threat of trail bikes and snowmobiles, and this dawning awareness has prompted an administrative proclamation that has closed many of the trails on the Eldorado National Forest to jeeps and trail bikes. Hopefully, similar restrictions will be placed upon the equally disastrous presence of snowmobiles in the back country.

The Emigrant Basin area has long been a fisherman's mecca, and for good reason. Hundreds of lakes and miles of streams offer excellent angling for brook, rainbow, brown and golden trout. Some of the better fishing in the area may be found at Wire Lakes, Cow Meadow Lake, the North Fork of Cherry Creek, and the upper reaches of Falls Creek (Jack Main Canyon). California fishing licenses are required.

This area is served by numerous trailheads. From north to south they are:

Echo Summit: One half mile south of Echo Summit at the end of a summer-home-tract road.

Carson Pass: One mile west of Carson Pass on Hiway 88.

Carson Pass: A few yards east of the pass on the old road.

Lake Alpine: At the end of a summer home tract road midway along the north shore of Lake Alpine, on Hiway 4.

Iceberg Meadow: At the end of a 9-mile blacktop hiway that leaves Hiway 108 20 miles east of the Pinecrest "Y"

Sonora Pass: One mile west of Sonora Pass on Hiway 108. (One can drive some distance up the dirt road that runs north from the hiway here.)

Kennedy Meadow: One mile up a paved road from Hiway 108, 29 miles east of the Pinecrest "Y".

Gianelli Cabin: At the end of a dirt road (4N34) reached via dirt road 4N26, which leaves Hiway 108 one mile east of Cold Springs. (Until 4N34 is completed, Gianelli Cabin may be reached via a 7-mile dirt road — very rough — that branches north from the oiled loop road at Dodge Ridge ski resort.)

Crabtree Camp Trailhead: An unsigned junction on Road 4N45Y, which branches south from Road 4N34 (see above) about 2½ miles east of Aspen Meadow. Crabtree Camp is about ¼ mile east of this road-trail junction.

Bell Meadow: Reached by taking dirt road 4N26 (see above) to Aspen Meadow and then taking the road forking right for 3 miles to Bell Meadow.

O'Shaughnessy Dam: At the end of the paved road turning north from Hiway 120 at San Jose City Camp, or the one turning north at the junction two miles west of the Big Oak Flat entrance to Yosemite. (Both routes merge at Mather and continue on to the dam.)

14 **Carson Pass to Showers Lake**

TRIP   From Carson Pass to Showers Lake (round trip).
Topo map *Silver Lake*. Best mid season; 8.6 miles.

Grade	Trail/layover days	Total recommended days
Leisurely	2/1	3
Moderate	2/0	2
Strenuous	—	—

HILITES   Showers Lake is one of the best camping places between Hiway 50 and Hiway 88, with numerous campsites and good angling for brook trout. En route, the trail through the upper Truckee Valley offers panoramic views of immense volcanic formations and promises potential close-up glimpses of many birds and mammals.

DESCRIPTION

1st Hiking Day **(Carson Pass** to **Showers Lake,** 4.3 miles):
From a small parking area (8350') 1 mile west of Carson Pass our dusty route climbs steadily northward on an old jeep road. (Although it is now closed to motor vehicles by a sign, a cable, a fence and some immense boulders, one often sees the tracks of 2-wheeled vehicles circumventing these obstacles.) The slope is moderately forested with red fir, lodgepole pine and clumps of aspen. Leaving the tree cover behind, we climb steeply up a slope covered by sagebrush and mule ears. In the warm sun of this open slope the sage odor adds spice to the thin, clear air. After ascending 400 feet in ½ mile, the trail reaches a saddle on the divide between Truckee River drainage and American River drainage. From this saddle views southward of Round Top Peak and its snow-draped satellites are excellent. In the north, we see Mt. Tallac, Dicks Peak and Jacks Peak, all west of Tahoe. Here we begin a descent down the long, green, tree-dotted valley of the upper Truckee. Nearby on the east, Red Lake Peak is topped by slablike volcanic outcroppings resembling a stegosaur's back plates. Little runoff streams that spring from porous volcanic rocks trickle their water onto flower gardens of iris, yarrow milfoil, Mariposa lily, sulfur flower, lupine and paintbrush. Descending moderately to steadily from the

summit, we cross three runoff streams (dry in late season), then a westward-flowing tributary, and finally the infant Truckee River — all via easy fords.

Just past another easy ford are the buildings of a cow camp, and near them the Round Lake trail (not shown on the topo map) branches right. The meadows here are full of little gray Belding squirrels, commonly called picket-pins, and often a Swainson hawk soars overhead, hoping to surprise one of them. Continuing the level walk from the Round Lake junction, we pass an unsigned trail to Meiss Lake, visible as a meadow-fringed blue sheet toward the northeast. Then one last time we ford the river, on boulders, and a few feet beyond the ford an old jeep road forks right toward Meiss Lake, as our route bears left. (From this point on the route is not shown on the topo map.) We pass a trail to Schneider Camp (not shown on the topo map and unsigned but marked by a blazed "S" on a lodgepole), and ascend out of Dixon Canyon on a gentle grade. From the crest of this little ascent, the trail dips past a shallow, weedy pond and continues on the old two-track jeep road. After crossing two runoff streams, we begin a steady-to-steep ascent of $\frac{1}{4}$ mile, first up a wash filled with smoothed, round rocks, and then on a rocky-dusty trail, under moderate-to-dense forest cover of red fir, hemlock, silver pine and lodge-pole pine. Sixty yards after the jeep tracks emerge from this forest onto a meadowy slope lush with lupine and mule ears, a trail veers slightly left and uphill from the tracks, and we take the trail. (The old jeep road also goes to Showers Lake.) This trail section traverses a bountifully flowered, meadowy slope to a forested saddle overlooking Showers Lake, from where it descends to the fair-to-good campsites on the west and east sides of the lake (8650'). Wood is adequate, and fishing is good for eastern brook (to 12"). From a base camp here, one may easily walk cross country to Four Lakes, where fishing and swimming are often good in mid-to-late season.

2nd Hiking Day **(Showers Lake** to **Carson Pass,** 4.3 miles) : Retrace steps of 1st hiking day.

15   Carson Pass to Echo Summit

TRIP   From Carson Pass to Echo Summit (shuttle trip). Topo maps (15′) *Silver Lake, Fallen Leaf Lake.* Best mid season; 10.8 miles.

Grade	Trail/layover days	Total recom-mended days
Leisurely	2/1	3
Moderate	2/0	2
Strenuous	—	—

HILITES   This trip offers one of the easiest ways in the whole northern Sierra to get away from the crowd, and it is an excellent choice for a two-party shuttle. With a minimum of effort, the hiker can traverse some high, scenic, little-used country, where the wildlife is as plentiful as the people are scarce.

DESCRIPTION

1st Hiking Day **(Carson Pass** to **Showers Lake,** 4.3 miles) : See 1st hiking day, trip 14.

2nd Hiking Day **(Showers Lake** to **Echo Summit,** 6.5 miles) : Heading northwest from the southwest shore of Showers Lake, we soon find the trail, and then ascend gently for several hundred yards through mixed conifers. Coming out onto open slopes, we ford a year-round stream fed by the snow cornice that drapes the ridge of Little Round Top above. Where we cross this stream, its banks are lined with thousands of blossoms of the showy yellow flower *Arnica chamissionis.* In fact, this whole open bowl is laced with runoff streams and lavishly planted with colorful bushes and flowers: blue elderberry, green gentian, swamp whiteheads, mountain bluebell, aster, wallflower, pen-stemon, spiraea, cinquefoil, corn lily and columbine. As we walk around this bowl on the boundary between volcanic rocks above and granite below, we have good views of Stevens Peak and Red Lake Peak, both built up of layers of richly colored vol-canic flows.

Finally, the trail ascends out of the bowl and enters a sparse cover of lodgepole and silver pine. At the crest of this ascent,

the pine gives way to hemlock as we pass a cattle drift fence
(close the gate) and level off through open high country. Reaching a willowy meadow, one may lose the trail momentarily, but
it is easy to find if one continues straight across the meadow. A
short distance beyond is a junction with a signed trail to Schneider Cow Camp, which leads west. One third of a mile beyond
this junction our route crosses, at right angles, an unsigned but
well-grooved trail which is used by local stockmen, and then
continues its almost level, winding course northward under a
sparse-to-moderate mixed forest cover.

We then pass a collapsed stock fence and make a short, steep
descent down a hemlock-covered hillside to a meadowy slope
where marsh marigolds, their white and yellow petals set off by
their rich green leaves, bloom in the wetness of melting snows
until late in the season. Our sandy footpath soon passes a trail
(not shown on the topo map) that winds down Sayles Canyon,
and then we continue north to a summit from where views of
the Crystal Range, including Pyramid Peak, are good. From
here it is a gentle descent under hemlock, silver and lodgepole
pine to Bryan Meadow. Here one may camp except in late season, when the stream is dry. A collapsed log cabin in the meadow
sprawls near the confluence of routes leading to Showers Lake,
Hiway 50 and Benwood Meadow. Heading for Benwood Meadow, we ascend a gently rising sandy trail through meadowy,
open stands of lodgepole pine, with some sagebrush. The alert
hiker here may spot a red-shafted flicker on one of its characteristic undulating flights between trees. At the top of this sandy
climb the trail levels off and becomes indistinct, but the route
is well marked by blazes. A short, steep descent then brings us
to a willow-filled bowl where an unnamed stream rises. We cross
the young stream and on the far slope veer right, on a trail that
soon switchbacks down a red-fir-covered slope. At the foot of
the slope is another willowy meadow, and shortly beyond that
another steep downslope, also shaded by red fir, where following the route may require attention to the frequent ducks. The
trail then levels out in a large meadow that was once a lake,
skirting the west side of it.

The trail from this meadow to Benwood Meadow is sometimes
indistinct, but there are sufficient blazes and ducks. At Benwood
Meadow the flora is quite noteworthy: along the wet meadow
margin the flower-spotter is kept busy by the plenitude of aster,
corn lily, snow plant, alpine lily, monkeyflower, penstemon,
False Solomon's seal, squawroot, pennyroyal, groundsel, columbine, larkspur and mountain bluebell, to say nothing of the ferns,
grasses and sedges.

Past Benwood Meadow, our nearly level trail dips to cross the outlet of a lily-filled pond, and then ascends gently up a rather exposed slope, where a few mixed conifers partially shade a ground cover of huckleberry oak, pinemat manzanita and Sierra chinquapin. Finally, the rocky-dusty trail ends at a blacktop road (7520') that serves a small tract of summer homes half a mile south of Echo Summit.

16   Carson Pass to 4th of July Lake

TRIP From Carson Pass to Fourth of July Lake (round trip). Topo maps (15') *Silver Lake, Markleeville*. Best mid season; 10.4 miles.

Grade	Trail/layover days	Total recom-mended days
Leisurely	2/1	3
Moderate	2/0	2
Strenuous	—	—

HILITES This trip tours the exhilarating high country around Carson Pass. The constantly good views of majestic, richly colored volcanic heights and long, tree-clad valleys make it a good trip choice for lensmen, and for history buffs there is a chance to "meet" Kit Carson.

DESCRIPTION

1st Hiking Day **(Carson Pass** to **Fourth of July Lake,** 5.2 miles) : From the trailhead (8550') a few yards east of Carson Pass on the old hiway, a short, rocky climb of ½ mile gains 300' elevation to a plateau where Frog Lake lies. Somewhere on this plateau John C. Fremont made the first winter crossing of the Sierra crest, in February 1844, with Kit Carson as his scout. From an encampment in Faith Valley a few miles to the east, Fremont climbed Red Lake Peak, the first peak north of Carson Pass, and from the summit he saw the great mountain lake we now call Tahoe. Fremont's diary entry is the first recorded mention of Lake Tahoe, and the climb of Red Lake Peak was the first recorded ascent of a Sierra peak that we can identify. At Frog Lake, the domelike red prominence we see to the south is a volcanic hill called Elephants Back. Large red-tailed hawks are often seen soaring on the air currents that rise up the sides of this dome. Farther ahead up the trail is Round Top (10380'), which has large snow fields on its north side all year long. At Frog Lake the trail leaves silver and lodgepole pine behind, and levels off through a high plateau of whitebark pine and mountain hemlock. The stands of high-altitude-loving whitebark provide nesting places for the host of Clark's nutcrackers which swoop back and forth over the passing hiker.

A mile-and-a-half level stroll along a hillside then brings us to deep, blue Winnemucca Lake, where numerous fair-to-good campsites line the northwest shore. At the outlet of this lake, the trail forks, the right fork going down to a roadend at Woods Lake. The left fork fords and then leads up over a gentle saddle to Round Top Lake. Near this saddle, one has views of a small arc of Lake Tahoe. In midseason the trail over the saddle has fine specimens of the rare red-purple flower called rockfringe. Descending from the crest to the outlet of Round Top Lake (good campsites), our trail passes another lateral leading down to Woods Lake, and then circles around the northwest shoulder of Round Top. The excellent views along this curving stretch of trail, from east to north to west, include Markleeville Peak, Hawkins Peak, the Crystal Range, and the green-clad slopes of upper Caples Creek.

From the shoulder of Round Top the trail descends to a saddle on the border of the Mokelumne Wilderness — a region of 50,450 acres where only foot travel is permitted. The border is a major watershed, separating the watershed of the American River from the Mokelumne River basin. From the divide our trail switchbacks steeply down a mile on dusty, decomposed granite to Fourth of July Lake (8100'), where there are good-to-excellent campsites on the east and south shores, and beside the inlet. Fishing is good for eastern brook (to 10"), and the supply of camp firewood is adequate.

2nd Hiking Day **(Fourth of July Lake** to **Carson Pass,** 5.2 miles) : Retrace steps of 1st hiking day.

17 Carson Pass to Summit City Canyon

TRIP From Carson Pass to Summit City Canyon (round trip). Topo maps (15') *Silver Lake, Markleeville.* Best early-to-mid season; 21.4 miles.

Grade	Trail/layover days	Total recom- mended days
Leisurely	4/1	5
Moderate	3/0	3
Strenuous	2/0	2

HILITES This trip takes the solitude-lover to trail's end in the Mokelumne Wilderness. Its route winds beside a secluded year-round stream at the bottom of a deep, glaciated canyon.

DESCRIPTION (Leisurely trip)

1st Hiking Day **(Carson Pass to Fourth of July Lake,** 5.2 miles): See 1st hiking day, trip 16.

2nd Hiking Day **(Fourth of July Lake to Summit City Canyon,** 5.5 miles): At the outlet of Fourth of July Lake, our trail begins a gentle-to-moderate traversing descent into steep-walled Summit City Canyon. The timber cover of silver pine, red fir and lodgepole pine soon disappears, and our sandy trail (contrary to the topo-map trail) bears eastward among granite outcroppings toward the unnamed pyramidal peak (point 9381' on the topo map) lying on the Sierra crest at the head of Summit City Canyon. Where the trail begins to level off, it enters a cover of sparse red fir and lodgepole, which rise above a flora of sagebrush, snowbrush, creamberry and spiraea.

On the canyon bottom we meet the Summit City Canyon trail, and turn right onto it. The streamside trail descends gently under a dense cover of lodgepole, passing a packer campsite and fording two jump-across tributaries of Summit City Creek. After the last ford the sandy footpath descends steadily, and the forest cover becomes moderate to sparse — a few yellow pines along with lodgepole and red fir. Then, where the trail enters open slopes, the hiker has excellent views of the granite walls towering 2000 feet and more above him; green fingers of brush poke upward between granite outcroppings, and the black color of lichen on the granite cliffs reminds one of the same aspect on the walls of Yosemite Valley.

Leaving these open slopes, the trail re-enters a moderate forest cover, where some white fir is now seen, along with red fir, lodgepole and yellow pine, and occasional aspen. Shortly beyond the Horse Canyon trail junction the trail crosses the Horse Canyon stream, and passes several fair-to-good campsites. Horse Canyon was part of the route of one emigrant trail, and eye bolts can still be found in some trees up the canyon, where they were used to rope the wagons up or down. There are numerous campsites along Summit City Creek along the next mile and a half of trail. About ½ mile beyond Horse Canyon we pass Telephone Gulch (no water in midsummer) and then a timbered meadow with a sign *Grouse Creek* pointing east. There is no obvious trail up to Grouse Lake, but a cross-country scramble to this lake will enable the angler to cast for trout to 14". A few hundred yards beyond this sign is a good campsite. It is located beside Summit City Creek, at the point where the trail shown on the topographic map ends (6640'). Fishing here is good for rainbow (to 12") and firewood is ample. The hiker with an urge to explore can find little-traveled country down the canyon from here, as well as up either canyon wall.

3rd Hiking Day (**Summit City Canyon** to **Fourth of July Lake,** 5.5 miles) : Retrace steps of 2nd hiking day.

4th Hiking Day (**Fourth of July Lake** to **Carson Pass,** 5.2 miles) : Retrace steps of 1st hiking day.

18 Carson Pass to Lake Alpine

TRIP   From Carson Pass to Lake Alpine via Summit City Canyon (shuttle trip, part cross country). Topo maps (15′) *Silver Lake, Big Meadow, Dardanelles Cone*. Best early-to-mid season; 22.2 miles.

Grade	Trail/layover days	Total recom- mended days
Leisurely	5/2	7
Moderate	4/1	5
Strenuous	3/0	3

HILITES   This trip tours some of the least-visited country in the northern Sierra, on the banks of the Mokelumne River. Virgin forests here shade the cool green river, and large brown trout often rise to the fly.

DESCRIPTION (Moderate trip)

1st Hiking Day **(Carson Pass** to **Fourth of July Lake,** 5.2 miles) : See 1st hiking day, trip 16.

2nd Hiking Day **(Fourth of July Lake** to **Summit City Canyon,** 5.5 miles) : See 2nd hiking day, trip 17.

3rd Hiking Day **(Summit City Canyon** to **Camp Irene,** 4.1 miles, part cross country) : A trail was surveyed from the campsite where this hiking day begins down to the Mokelumne River. But then a new Forest Service policy was announced calling for an end to trail-building in the wildernesses of the Eldorado National Forest (the Desolation and Mokelumne wildernesses).

Downstream from the campsites at the end of the trail, our route crosses Summit City Creek and climbs the east bank, then descends southward above the creek, often out of sound of the cascading waters. This moderate-to-steady descent leads down to the elevation of incense cedar and black oak, and then sugar pine — trees that are characteristic of the Transition life zone. The route returns to streamside at a good campsite near a sandy beach beside a large pool. From here to the Mokelumne Canyon floor the hiker should stay above the stream and east of it, but not more than 100 yards or so away from it. In the last ½ mile before the river, Summit City Creek forks into two branches, which separately flow into the Mokelumne River (good campsites nearby). Our route follows the more easterly branch to the river bank, turns right (southwest) and fords the two branches to a little clearing a few yards west of the confluence of the western branch and the river. At a sign in this clearing proclaiming the Cedar Camp trail, maintained trail begins again. This trail climbs slightly away from the river under a cover of sparse-to-moderate incense cedar, Jeffrey pine, ponderosa pine and black oak. As the trail becomes rocky and exposed, we see a few sugar pines and white firs.

The almost level trail winds through moderate-to-dense mixed forest, fording two jump-across streams and passing beneath some magnificent first-growth sugar pines that have strewn the forest floor with their great cones. One-eighth mile beyond the second stream is an unsigned trail junction. The topo-map trail up to Long Lake from this junction no longer exists, and the map trail beside the river from here to Camp Irene is washed out.

At this junction our route continues straight ahead, southwest, making a short climb to an open hillside with a sparse cover of mixed conifers. Just beyond the second of two little crests is a junction, where we turn down toward the river (on Trail 17E31). From the junction, the trail to Camp Irene winds down an exposed slope on rocky underfooting to the good campsites on the Mokelumne River (5200'). Fly fishermen will be understandably eager to begin casting for brown trout (to 18"), and swimmers will find swimming holes fine for a medium-warm dip. A trail of use continues down the west side of the river to Cedar Camp, offering the chance to visit wild stretches of the river.

4th Hiking Day **(Camp Irene** to **Lake Alpine,** 7.4 miles) : This day the hiker makes a small payment for the solitude along the Mokelumne River: a 3600' climb up the south canyon wall. After crossing the river to the east side on a large log, the trail ascends gently, parallel to but out of sight of the Underwood Valley stream for about ¾ mile. Then it ascends steeply beside the stream, leaving black oak, cedar and sugar pine below. Where the stream turns eastward, we continue a steady ascent southward. At breather stops on this long, hot ascent, one may appreciate the greater oxygen content of the air at these relatively low altitudes. Veering southeast up Lake Valley, we pass a fair campsite and then resume the stiff climb. Near the top of this day's ascent the trail passes beneath dark, cliffed, volcanic outcroppings from which chocolate-brown boulders have broken off and rolled down across the trail route.

Views improve constantly on this climb, and after the route leaves the Mokelumne Wilderness at a saddle east of Mt. Reba and passes onto a dirt road, we see ahead pyramidal Stanislaus Peak, and Leavitt Peak to the right of it. For a round-the-compass panorama, one may detour a few yards north onto the 8800' prominence that has been used as a fire lookout. From here we can see Round Top to the north and a long series of peaks around to the east. Mokelumne Peak looms strong in the northwest, and the volcanic peaks overlooking Silver and Caples lakes complete the circle.

Returning to the dirt road, we follow it southeast for ½ mile through fields of mule ears, whose leaves rattle in the afternoon wind. Just after stepping across a runoff stream, we leave the road and walk east to the lowest saddle on the divide, where we encounter another dirt road. From that point our trail drops steeply eastward into Bee Gulch (not labeled on the topo map). This trail is at times hard to follow, but Lake Alpine provides a good landmark to reckon on. Beyond the steep descent, at an unsigned junction, we veer slightly to the right and descend moderately under dense lodgepole and red fir. After almost a mile of sparse forest, the trail turns left at another junction, and soon it comes onto a road (7360') that serves the summer home tract on the north shore of Lake Alpine.

Sonora Pass to Clark Fork   **19**

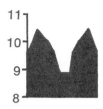

TRIP   From Sonora Pass Trailhead to Clark Fork Meadow
(round trip, part cross country). Topo map (15')
Sonora Pass. Best mid season; 7 miles.

Grade	Trail/layover days	Total recom- mended days
Leisurely	2/0	2
Moderate	—	—
Strenuous	—	—

HILITES   Clark Fork Meadow is secluded by the steep sides
of the deep bowl which protects it, and here—only
two airline miles from a state highway—one can get
away from it all even on a short weekend. On the
way, the views from the pass are among the most
sweeping in the entire Sierra.

DESCRIPTION

1st Hiking Day (**Sonora Pass Trailhead** to **Clark Fork Meadow,**
3.5 miles) : The trailhead is located about ½ mile up a dirt road
(shown as trail on the topo map) which leads north from Hiway
108 about 1 mile west of Sonora Pass. From a parking area
(9760') we walk up the jeep road toward timberline, through
sparse lodgepole and whitebark pine understoried by considerable sagebrush. The pinkish soil here slowly and steadily
gives off its stored winter water, and these slopes are dotted with
a pleasant variety of high-elevation wildflowers throughout the
season. Beyond a small runoff stream that flows all summer, the
road becomes trail, and after a short level section we veer eastward and ascend steadily. A breather stop here allows us to look
south and see the great peaks of the Emigrant Basin and northern Yosemite. Below us is the threadlike highway curving up to
Sonora Pass, and beyond the pass we see unnamed peak 11245.
West of this imposing if nameless height, the long chocolate-
brown west ridge of Leavitt Peak shows its snowy north slope,
and even a few tiny glaciers.

The crest of this little climb (10440') is called St. Marys Pass. Here we obtain a view far to the north—on clear days, as far as the peaks west of Lake Tahoe. Looking north and south, we realize we are standing right on the boundary between the rugged High Sierra of Yosemite and beyond, and the lower, less rugged northern Sierra. Immediately below us to the north, the bowl that contains Clark Fork Meadow is so deep that we cannot see the bottom of it.

From the pass we turn southwest and follow a sporadically ducked route near the top of a granite ridge for about one mile, dipping slightly to cross several runoff streams not shown on the topo map. In mid season these seemingly bare slopes boast a profusion of blue flax, lavender phlox and yellow woolly sunflower. Once past the billowy granite outcroppings that line most of the route for the first mile from St. Marys Pass, we veer north and start down the valley of a little stream not shown on the topo map. We follow the ridge that lies east of the upper basin of this stream until, at about timberline, we drop down next to the stream and parallel it into the thick hemlock forest, where we may find occasional ducks. This route passes close under the west face of the cliffs that are ½ mile southeast of the meadow.

At the bottom of the steep descent we ford the infant Clark Fork on a log, turn west, and almost immediately ford a tributary on boulders. Half a mile of level walking under a moderate forest cover of silver, lodgepole and whitebark pine and some hemlock brings us to the good campsite at the northwest edge of the meadow (8875'). Firewood is ample, and fishing in the Clark Fork is good for eastern brook (to 9").

2nd Hiking Day **(Clark Fork Meadow** to **Sonora Pass Trailhead,** 3.5 miles) : Retrace steps of 1st hiking day.

Sonora Pass to Iceberg Meadow   **20**

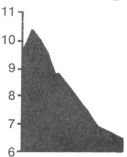

TRIP From Sonora Pass Trailhead to Iceberg Meadow (shuttle trip, part cross country). Topo map (15') *Sonora Pass*. Best mid season; 10.5 miles.

Grade	Trail/layover days	Total recommended days
Leisurely	2/1	3
Moderate	2/0	2
Strenuous	—	—

HILITES Few trips are downhill most of the way, but this one ascends only 800' and then descends 4000'. The descent follows the canyon of the Clark Fork of the Stanislaus River from its wellsprings above timberline through meadows and down granite gorges to a thickly forested, gently flowing section of the river.

DESCRIPTION

1st Hiking Day (**Sonora Pass Trailhead** to **Clark Fork Meadow,** 3.5 miles) : See 1st hiking day, trip 19.

2nd Hiking Day (**Clark Fork Meadow** to **Iceberg Meadow,** 7 miles) : From the campsites, we walk to the foot of the meadow and cross the Clark Fork on boulders. On the west side, a few yards downstream, we encounter ducks, and this ducked route soon becomes a trail—although none is shown on the topo map. The trail passes a stock-drift fence (close the gate) and makes a short, steep descent under a moderate forest cover of hemlock, silver pine and lodgepole. At the foot of the descent we enter redfir forest and this superb conifer is frequent for the rest of the hiking day. A short mile from Clark Fork Meadow is a boulder ford to the east side of the stream, and several fair-to-good campsites lie just beyond it. After the ford, the sandy trail veers away from the stream and descends gently to moderately, fording a small runoff stream every half mile or so.

After paralleling and then fording a larger tributary, the trail enters a sloping meadow considerably marred by the hooves of grazing cattle. The route across this slope is indistinct, but we find the trail again in granite sand under red firs near the Clark Fork. After crossing another tree-shaded meadow with fair campsites, we begin a steep, switchbacking descent on a rocky, dusty trail down to an almost level valley, where the Clark Fork swings west. At the foot of the descent, the trail crosses Boulder Creek and meets a trail not shown on the topo map which leads off up the creek. From this junction the route descends along a shaded sand/duff trail, close to the alder-lined Clark Fork now big enough to call a river. Numerous good campsites line this shaded canyon, with its dense forest cover of white fir, incense cedar, alder and ponderosa pine. Nearing Iceberg Meadow the trail makes a short, steady-to-steep descent and then parallels the river on pleasant sandy underfooting to the roadend (6460′).

21   Kennedy Meadow to Sheep Camp

TRIP From Kennedy Meadow to Sheep Camp (round trip). Topo maps (15′) *Sonora Pass, Tower Peak.* Best early-to-mid season; 16 miles.

Grade	Trail/layover days	Total recom-mended days
Leisurely	2/0	2
Moderate	—	—
Strenuous	—	—

HILITES A part of this route follows the historic Emigrant Trail used by the pioneers in crossing the Sierra from the area around Bridgeport to Columbia and

points west. Relief Peak was a major landmark for
these early travelers, and the terminus of this trip,
Sheep Camp, lies in this unusual formation's shadow.
The scenery along the way is an absorbing study in
glacial and volcanic terrain.

DESCRIPTION

1st Hiking Day **(Kennedy Meadow** to **Sheep Camp,** 8 miles) :
The trailhead (6400′) is located alongside the Middle Fork of
the Stanislaus River at Kennedy Meadows Resort and Pack Sta-
ion. Amid a dense forest cover of Jeffrey pine, incense cedar
and white fir, the trail crosses a small ridge to Kennedy Meadow
itself and skirts the east side of the meadow, offering panoramic
views of the lush grasslands. Beyond the meadow, the trail
crosses the river via a bridge and immediately veers west onto
a new trail section not shown on the topo map. This trail section
ascends gently past the foot of a small granite dome and then
switchbacks up a steeper grade between this dome and its larger
neighbor. Under a sparse-to-moderate forest cover of mixed conifers, the route ascends steadily up a little canyon to a saddle,
where it turns eastward to descend to Summit Creek. After
paralleling the creek for a few steps, the trail crosses it on a
bridge and meets the abandoned trail a few yards south of the
Kennedy Lake trail junction, near the PG&E dam-maintenance
station.

This route then skirts the east side of Relief Reservoir. The
trail section paralleling the shore offers excellent views to the
west before it descends to the timbered shallow at the Grouse
Creek ford. Fishing on Relief Reservoir is poor owing to severe
water-level fluctuation. From the south end of Relief Reservoir
the trail ascends steadily over a series of rocky switchbacks, and
then veers southeast as it passes the Upper Relief Lake trail.
The forest cover at this point is a mixture of fir and aspen scattered in small stands amid fields of granite and moraine till. This
steady ascent is relieved when the trail drops into the little pocket
encompassing Saucer Meadow. Travelers who pass through here
in early-to-mid season will find the heavy wildflower growth a
colorful study. The gravesite, indicated on the topo and USFS
maps, was that of a passing emigrant. Traces of this site have
been vandalized but the cairned monument can still be seen. The
section of trail beyond this point was part of a major trans-
Sierra route, used during the middle of the 19th Century—the
Emigrant trail. With the many-hued volcanic rock of Relief
Peak on the left, and white, glaciated granite on the right, the
trail climbs along Summit Creek past several optional campsites

to a small meadowed area known as Sheep Camp (8800'). Good campsites are available along the creek, and firewood is abundant. Fishing along the creek is poor; however, anglers who have an extra day may elect to take the cross-country route (west) to Lewis, Sardella and Iceland lakes for good fishing for brook and golden (7-11").

2nd Hiking Day **(Sheep Camp** to **Kennedy Meadow,** 8 miles) : Retrace steps of 1st hiking day.

22 Kennedy Meadow to Emigrant Meadow

TRIP   From Kennedy Meadow to Emigrant Meadow Lake via Brown Bear Pass (round trip). Topo maps (15') *Sonora Pass, Tower Peak.* Best mid or late season; 28 miles.

Grade	Trail/layover days	Total recommended days
Leisurely	4/0	4
Moderate	3/0	3
Strenuous	2/0	2

HILITES   A good portion of this trail follows the historic Emigrant trail, and travelers today have an excellent opportunity to identify with these hardy pioneers. Scenically, this route splits the terrain into two distinctly different parts : To the north the basaltic and pumice slopes vividly disclose the vulcan overlay that gives the country its colorful reds and blacks. To the south mirrorlike stretches of glacially polished granite add contrast and interest.

DESCRIPTION (Leisurely trip)

1st Hiking Day **(Kennedy Meadow** to **Sheep Camp,** 8 miles) : See 1st hiking day, trip 21.

2nd Hiking Day **(Sheep Camp** to **Emigrant Meadow Lake,** 6 miles) : Winding above Summit Creek, the trail soon leaves timber cover, and crosses a pumice slope above Lunch Meadow. This meadow is subalpine, dotted with sparse stands of lodgepole and mountain hemlock. At the east end of Lunch Meadow our route passes the trail lateral to Emigrant Lake. North of the trail red and black volcanic columns thrust up from the otherwise smooth, red, pumice slopes, and punctuate the skyline with their tortured shapes. Directly to the east the traveler can discern the bifidated saddle that is Brown Bear Pass. The trail to the pass is a gradual but steady ascent offering colorfully contrasting views of Granite Dome and Relief Peak to the west. It is easy to see why the emigrants who used this same route relied upon the distinctive outline of Relief Peak as a landmark. At the summit of Brown Bear Pass (9700'), the grassy expanses of historic Emigrant Meadow present themselves, and the serenity of this pioneer waystop is enhanced by the placid blue waters of Emigrant Meadow Lake.

As the trail descends from Brown Bear Pass on a long traverse, the visitor cannot help being impressed by the gigantic scale of this grassy, granite-walled basin. It seems a fitting stage for the enactment of the "great move westward," and it doesn't take a great deal of imagination to hear boisterous shouts, the creaking of wagons, the barking of dogs, and the tired, hungry lowing of trail-weary stock. This great meadow saw the frenzied summertime travel of thousands of pioneers headed for the town of Columbia on the western slope, but of their passing all that remains is an echo in the wind. Fair campsites may be found around the western perimeter of Emigrant Meadow Lake (9400'), but firewood is relatively scarce. Fishing for rainbow (8-13") is good, with a midseason slowdown.

3rd Hiking Day **(Emigrant Meadow Lake** to **Sheep Camp,** 6 miles) : Retrace steps of 2nd hiking day.

4th Hiking Day **(Sheep Camp** to **Kennedy Meadow,** 8 miles) : Retrace steps of 1st hiking day.

23   **Kennedy Meadow to Emigrant Lake**

TRIP   From Kennedy Meadow to Emigrant Lake (round trip). Topo maps (15') *Sonora Pass, Tower Peak.* Best mid-to-late season ; 28 miles.

Grade	Trail/layover days	Total recommended days
Leisurely	4/1	5
Moderate	3/1	4
Strenuous	3/0	3

HILITES   A long-time favorite of anglers, Emigrant Lake is often used as a base camp for short fishing trips to the surrounding lakes. This route to Emigrant Lake allows the traveler to take in the geological variety of the country. Alpine meadows surrounding isolated melt-off tarns compete for attention with vast slopes of red pumice and fields of polished granite.

DESCRIPTION (Leisurely trip)

1st Hiking Day **(Kennedy Meadow to Sheep Camp,** 8 miles) : See 1st hiking day, trip 21.

2nd Hiking Day **(Sheep Camp to Emigrant Lake,** 6 miles) : The trail leaves Sheep Camp by gradual, winding ascent over an exposed pumice slope to a point above the foot of Lunch Meadow, and then descends by a long traverse to the ford near the head of the meadow. Serpentining Summit Creek bisects this subalpine meadow, and its willow-lined banks provide a haven for bird life. At the east end of the meadow, this route branches right (south), fords Summit Creek, and ascends through a sparse mountain hemlock cover to a long, low saddle. Views along this segment of trail present a wide range of colors. The superimposed vulcanism of Relief Peak and the ridge to the east are a potpourri of pastel shades of reds, blacks, yellows and ochres. Black Hawk Mountain to the west is granite in varying shades of dun, gray, and buff brown. The saddle through which our trail winds is a series of granite fields that are delightfully broken by tiny, wildflower-filled meadows. Often these meadows are further enhanced by one or two small melt-off tarns. The saddle ends at the long, shallow watershed of a stream lateral feeding the North Fork of Cherry Creek, where there are excellent views across the Cherry Creek watershed south to Michie and Haystack peaks. The trail descends on the west side of this tributary to the large meadow marking the inlet to large (230-acre) Emigrant Lake (8800'). There are several good-to-excellent campsites at the inlet, on the north side, and at the outlet. Firewood is ample at most sites. This lake is glacial in character with sparse forest cover, and fishing for rainbow (8-18") is good (excellent in early and late season).

3rd Hiking Day (**Emigrant Lake** to **Sheep Camp,** 6 miles) : Retrace steps of 2nd hiking day.

4th Hiking Day (**Sheep Camp** to **Kennedy Meadow,** 8 miles) : Retrace steps of 1st hiking day.

Kennedy Meadow to Emigrant Lake   24

TRIP From Kennedy Meadow to Emigrant Lake via Middle Emigrant and Emigrant Meadow lakes (semi-loop trip). Topo maps (15') *Sonora Pass, Tower Peak.* Best mid or late season ; 32.4 miles.

Grade	Trail/layover days	Total recom- mended days
Leisurely	5/2	7
Moderate	4/2	6
Strenuous	3/2	5

HILITES　Like the previous trip this route tours a part of the historic Emigrant trail and visits large Emigrant Lake. By linking Emigrant Lake with Emigrant Meadow Lake, this route makes a good fisherman's loop as well as adding scenic variety.

DESCRIPTION (Leisurely trip)

1st Hiking Day **(Kennedy Meadow** to **Sheep Camp,** 8 miles) : See 1st hiking day, trip 21.

2nd Hiking Day **(Sheep Camp** to **Emigrant Lake,** 6 miles) : See 2nd hiking day, trip 23.

3rd Hiking Day **(Emigrant Lake** to **Emigrant Meadow Lake,** 4.4 miles) : Beginning at the Buck Lakes trail/Maxwell Lake trail junction at the inlet to Emigrant Lake, this route crosses the log bridge over the North Fork of Cherry Creek and ascends the moderately forested (lodgepole and hemlock) slope to Blackbird Lake (9000', poor fishing) and the junction of the trail to Middle Emigrant Lake. (Anglers who have the time, inclination, and extra head of steam may elect at this point to enjoy the excellent fishing for brook at little-visited Shallow Lake (9000'). The fisherman's trail—4 miles round trip—branches west from this trail ½ mile south of Blackbird Lake.) From Blackbird Lake this route is unmaintained as it winds northeast and ascends on the south side of the meandering North Fork of Cherry Creek. After fording the creek, the trail climbs over a rocky plateau to the soggy meadows just south of Middle Emigrant Lake. This is a glacial, granitoid lake with meadowed fringes and little forest cover. Anglers will find the fishing fair-to-good for rainbow (7-10"). The trail skirts the west side of the lake, fords the inlet stream, and crosses a low, rocky ridge to the large meadows surrounding Emigrant Meadow Lake (9400'). Fair campsites may be found on the western side of the lake. Firewood is relatively scarce. Fishing for rainbow (8-13") is good—with a mid-season slowdown.

4th Hiking Day **(Emigrant Meadow Lake** to **Sheep Camp via Brown Bear Pass,** 6 miles) : See 2nd hiking day, trip 22.

5th Hiking Day **(Sheep Camp** to **Kennedy Meadow,** 8 miles) : Retrace steps of 1st hiking day, trip 21.

Kennedy Meadow to Cow Meadow Lake 25

TRIP   From Kennedy Meadow to Cow Meadow Lake via
Sheep Camp, Emigrant Lake, Buck Lake (loop
trip). Topo maps (15') *Sonora Pass, Tower Peak.*
Best mid or late season; 47 miles.

Grade	Trail/layover days	Total recommended days
Leisurely	7/2	9
Moderate	5/2	7
Strenuous	4/2	6

HILITES   This is a fine choice for a mid-season fishing trip, as
it circles the lake-dotted Cherry Creek watershed.
A day's walking from one or another base camp will
permit the fisherman to sample from almost 100
lakes. The route also tours some of the finest scenery in the Emigrant Basin Primitive Area, which
should provide adequate incentive for the nonfisherman as well.

DESCRIPTION (Leisurely trip)

1st Hiking Day **(Kennedy Meadow** to **Sheep Camp,** 8 miles):
See 1st hiking day, trip 21.

2nd Hiking Day **(Sheep Camp** to **Emigrant Lake,** 6 miles): See
2nd hiking day, trip 23.

3rd Hiking Day **(Emigrant Lake** to **Cow Meadow Lake,** 6
miles): From the trail junction at the inlet to Emigrant Lake,
our route traverses the long, timbered north side of the lake, and
passes the junction with the poorly maintained trail to Cow
Meadow Lake via the North Fork of Cherry Creek. It then
crosses a low, forest-covered saddle and descends to ford Buck
Meadow Creek. After crossing the long meadow at the north
end of Upper Buck Lake, the trail circles the west side of Upper
Buck Lake (passing the trail to Deer Lake), crosses the isthmus
separating the two lakes, and follows the eastern shoreline of
Lower Buck Lake. Upper Buck Lake is a good-sized (50-acre)

glacial lake with numerous good campsites around the shore. Fishing for rainbow (to 13") is good. Lower Buck Lake is somewhat deeper and rockier, though about the same size, and fishing is usually about the same as at the upper lake. At the south end of Lower Buck Lake, the trail passes the Wood Lake lateral, and amid a nice forest cover of lodgepole descends steeply (500') to the Kibbie Ridge trail junction and lovely Cow Meadow Lake (7840'). There are excellent campsites along the northern edge of the lake, with an abundant supply of firewood. This 55-acre lake is connected by lagoons with overhanging banks. A DF&G dam at the south end keeps the water level fairly constant, and fishing for rainbow and some brook is excellent (8-18"). Angling on the stream above the lake is good.

4th Hiking Day **(Cow Meadow Lake** to **Maxwell Lake,** 7.5 miles)**:** From the east side of Cow Meadow Lake the trail ascends 560' via a very poorly maintained trail to the bench containing rocky, deep, granitoid Lertora Lake (8400'). This 25-acre lake offers only fair angling for brook and rainbow (7-13"). At the west end of Lertora Lake this route passes a short lateral to the west end of Huckleberry Lake, then veers eastward along the south side of Lertora, and descends over a very rough trail to the northeast end of large (200-acre) Huckleberry Lake (8000'). This subalpine, granitoid lake provides good fishing for brook and rainbow (8-18"), and the East Fork of Cherry Creek above the lake often provides excellent angling. From the meadows at the northeast end of Huckleberry, the trail fords the East Fork of Cherry Creek and ascends the canyon. Views of the unusual granite island known as Sachse Monument dominate the northern skyline as the trail passes a currently active tungsten mine. At this point the trail joins the mining road, and then passes the Twin Lakes trail lateral. The road crosses to the north side of the East Fork of Cherry Creek, and at the south end of Horse Meadow our trail branches northwest up a timbered slope to Maxwell Lake (8700'). Maxwell Lake (46 acres), an emerald-green gem with a tufty meadow fringe, affords excellent angling for brook (8-14"). The polished granite of Sachse Monument towers over the south side of this charming lake, and the choice campsites on the north side of the lake have an uninterrupted view of both the lake and the monument. Firewood is abundant.

5th Hiking Day **(Maxwell Lake** to **Emigrant Meadow Lake,** 5.5 miles)**:** The trail climbs by a series of switchbacks through a dense forest cover of lodgepole, silver pine, and mountain hemlock and then winds through a long, rock-lined meadow to Blackbird Lake and the junction with the trail to Emigrant Meadow Lake. At this junction our route branches right (north) past several small tarns that are usually dried up by late season. The trail soon becomes faint since this lateral is unmaintained, and one must keep a sharp eye out for "ducks" and blazes. This footpath ascends along the south side of the wandering North Fork of Cherry Creek for about 1½ miles, and then fords the creek. From the ford onward, the trail is rutted into meadowy turf, but has become overgrown due to lack of maintenance. The trail becomes a little steeper just south of Middle Emigrant Lake, and then levels out at the wet meadows at the foot of the lake. Anglers who wish to try their luck on this fair-sized, granitoid lake will find the fishing fair-to-good for rainbow (7-10″). The trail rounds the west side of the lake, fords the inlet stream, and crosses a low, rocky ridge to the Emigrant Meadow Lake basin (9400′). This huge meadow was the traditional stopping place for emigrant trains on the first leg of their Sierra crossing. This hiking day terminates at the open and exposed camping sites (fair) on the west side of the lake. Firewood is relatively scarce, but fishing in Emigrant Meadow Lake is good for rainbow (8-13″).

6th Hiking Day (**Emigrant Meadow Lake** to **Sheep Camp,** 6 miles) : See 2nd hiking day, trip 22.

7th Hiking Day (**Sheep Camp** to **Kennedy Meadow,** 8 miles) : See 1st hiking day, trip 21.

Kennedy Meadow to Hetch Hetchy   **26**

TRIP   From Kennedy Meadow to O'Shaughnessy Dam (Hetch Hetchy Reservoir) via Brown Bear Pass and Jack Main Canyon (shuttle trip). Topo maps

(15') *Sonora Pass, Tower Peak, Pinecrest, Lake Eleanor.* Best mid or late season; 45.4 miles.

Grade	Trail/layover days	Total recommended days
Leisurely	7/2	9
Moderate	5/1	6
Strenuous	4/0	4

HILITES This is a trip of contrasts. The route divides the volcanic and glacial terrain north of Bond Pass. It is, as one writer aptly described it, "a land born of fire and ice." As beautiful as the terrain is northwest of Bond Pass, the primitive, unspoiled beauty of Jack Main Canyon has to be the high point. Glacial, subalpine meadows like those around Emigrant Meadow Lake impress the visitor, but it remains for the lower grasslands of Grace Meadow with its meandering Falls Creek to claim the heart. This is an excellent trip for the intermediate as well as the seasoned wilderness traveler.

DESCRIPTION (Leisurely trip)

1st Hiking Day **(Kennedy Meadow** to **Sheep Camp,** 8 miles): See 1st hiking day, trip 21.

2nd Hiking Day **(Sheep Camp** to **Emigrant Meadow Lake,** 6 miles): See 2nd hiking day, trip 22.

3rd Hiking Day **(Emigrant Meadow Lake** to **Dorothy Lake,** 5 miles): From Emigrant Meadow the route climbs over a rocky ridge to Grizzly Meadow (9700') and two unnamed lakes. Fishing here is fair-to-good for rainbow (to 10"). This area is subject to the Forest Service's Multiple-Use land program; hence the traveler may encounter summer-grazing steers. Further evidences of this program mar the serenity of this Wilderness just beyond the lakes, where this trail encounters a mining road. Our route follows this road as it descends to the Summit Meadow trail junction, a distance of about 2 miles. From here our route follows another mining road across the northern fringe of the meadow, and then ascends by a series of switchbacks to the gentle saddle called Bond Pass (9700'). Amidst a clump of red fir marking the summit, the trail leaves the dirt road and crosses into Yosemite National Park. There are excellent views, eastward from the summit, of Saurian Crest and Tower Peak.

The descent on the east side of the pass winds through dense lodgepole and fir to the junction of the ½ mile trail lateral to Dorothy Lake (9440'). This lateral is a gentle ascent that brings

the traveler to the scattered campsites on the west shore. Firewood is ample around most of the sites, and anglers should ready
their tackle for the good-to-excellent fishing for brook and rainbow (8-15"). Dorothy Lake, with its pleasant meadow fringes
and bunched stands of lodgepole, makes an excellent option for
a base camp from which to explore the surrounding lakes and
terrain. Of particular interest is the "rock glacier" beneath nearby Forsyth Peak. A discovery side trip to the lake just south
of Dorothy Lake provides excellent views of this geologic wonder. Like their ice counterparts, "rock glaciers" are moving
masses.

4th Hiking Day **(Dorothy Lake** to **Grace Meadow,** 3.2 miles) :
Jack Main Canyon begins at Dorothy Lake, and from the start
it is a great hiker's route. A whole spectrum of wildlife may be
found along this trail, and the abundance of the wildlife is testimony to the effectiveness of the National Park System. In the
meadowed fringes of Dorothy Lake, the piping of the Belding
ground squirrel ushers the traveler past the marmot-inhabited
opposite slopes. If one is on the trail early enough, deer still out
grazing will keep him entranced with their graceful movements.
Ample signs of the black bear that roam this section of the park
will be found along the trail — particularly during gooseberry
season. Scenically, this short stretch of trail is an idyllic series
of tiny meadows alongside murmuring Falls Creek. To the east,
somber Forsyth Peak and abruptly divided Keves Peak (juxta-
posed black gabbro and white granite) cap the canyon walls.
The trail gradually descends through a dense forest cover to
the northern end of long, rolling Grace Meadow (8720'). In
contrast to the wide-open, windy stretch of Emigrant Meadow,
Grace Meadow possesses a soft, intimate "feel" that makes it
a favorite base camp. Excellent campsites with abundant firewood line the creek, and anglers should be ready for excellent
brook and rainbow (to 13") along Falls Creek.

5th Hiking Day **(Grace Meadow** to **Meadow Junction of Jack
Main Canyon/Benson Lake trails,** 8 miles) : From the lower
end of Grace Meadow the route stepladders down through smaller meadows on a well-maintained trail paralleling aptly named
Falls Creek. Directly to the south there are excellent views of
the massive granitic upthrust named Chittenden Peak, and as
the trail descends alongside this landmark the terrain becomes
rougher. Our route passes the Tilden Lake lateral and continues
to descend through rocky terrain that shows increasing signs
of glacial action. Chittenden Peak, at a higher elevation and
greater exposure, shows signs of progressive erosion on its exfoliating dome. Lower down in the canyon, by contrast, the

smooth, polished surfaces of the rock look as though they had just emerged from their glacial sleep.

Two miles south of the Tilden Lake lateral the trail passes sheltered Wilmer Lake (called "Wilma Lake" on the topo map). Set off to the side of the trail, this blue mountain jewel is fringed with meadows and lodgepole and mountain hemlock. There are good campsites and good fishing for rainbow and brook (8-13"). In late season swimming is excellent in the potholes along Falls Creek and in some of the shallower lakes. From Wilmer Lake the trail crosses a small rocky ridge and descends through a narrow canyon. Here the surroundings change dramatically. Quaking aspen groves are more frequent, and the previously dashing Falls Creek has become a series of tranquil, lakelike, turgid lagoons. The trail now winds through dense fern and willow until it arrives at the meadowed junction with the Benson Lake/Tiltill Valley trail (7680'). Just before this junction, the trail passes an unnamed, charming, picturebook lake, perfectly flanked by a towering granite cliff across the lake from the trail. There are several campsites on the long meadow with an abundant supply of firewood. Fishing on the lake and in Falls Creek is fair for brook and rainbow (to 9").

6th Hiking Day **(Meadow Junction of Jack Main Canyon/ Benson Lake trails** to **Beehive,** 8 miles) : From the meadow the trail goes past granite-domed Andrews Peak, and passes several small, unnamed lakes before ascending the steep, rocky "Golden Stairs" to Moraine Ridge, At the foot of this rocky ascent, the trail veers away from Falls Creek, and travelers get an excellent view down to the meadowed flats surrounding Lake Vernon. The ascent to the crown of Moraine Ridge is marked by a magnificent stand of red fir and lodgepole. The panorama from the top of the ridge includes Tiltill Mountain and Andrews Peak to the east, Bailey Ridge and Mahan Peak further north, and Forsyth Peak, Saurian Crest, Tower Peak, Pettit Peak and Mt. Conness on the eastern skyline. The trail across the crest of Moraine Ridge becomes very sandy as it descends past the trail junction to Lake Vernon and on to Beehive (6500'). Beehive is a charming meadow campsite set in a classic red-fir forest. At one end of the meadow is a fenced-off, coldwater spring. Even in the driest years, this meadow is a splash of wildflower color.

7th Hiking Day **(Beehive** to **O'Shaughnessy Dam,** 7.2 miles) : At Beehive this route passes the trail lateral to Laurel Lake, and continues south on a duff trail that winds through dense stands of fir that alternate with small, wildflower-filled meadows. As this route descends gradually past a second lateral to Laurel Lake, it becomes rockier, and finally drops via steep, rocky switchbacks. The forest cover changes with the advent of incense cedar and black oak. One final grove of mature sugar pine, red fir, and incense cedar marks the end of the trail as it joins with the Forest Service road from Lake Eleanor to O'Shaughnessy Dam. This arterial winds by long, dusty switchbacks over a steep slope covered with black oak and lilac. From this 4-mile stretch of road views are excellent of the Grand Canyon of the Tuolumne, Kolana Rock and Le Conte Point. Shortly before arriving at the dam (3796') the hiker passes through a long tunnel blasted out of a solid granite wall on the north side of the dam.

Gianelli Cabin to Y Meadow Dam Lake **27**

TRIP   From Gianelli Cabin to Y Meadow Dam Lake (round trip). Topo map (15') *Pinecrest*. Best mid or late season; 10 miles.

Grade	Trail/layover days	Total recommended days
Leisurely	2/0	2
Moderate	—	—
Strenuous	—	—

HILITES   Except for the short distance from Gianelli Cabin to Burst Rock, this trip is within beautiful Emigrant Basin Wild Area, and the route parallels a segment of the historic Emigrant trail. Enroute to Y Meadow Dam Lake, anglers can try their luck on two small but fairly productive lakes, and early-trip views, from Burst Rock, are panoramic.

DESCRIPTION

1st Hiking Day **(Gianelli Cabin to Y Meadow Dam Lake,** 5 miles) : At Gianelli Cabin (8560') — now only the log cabin's base remains — the trail begins in a meadow and ascends a steep slope covered with red fir, silver pine and lodgepole. In the past this segment has been used as a jeep trail; hence it is somewhat eroded. The trail tops the ridge at Burst Rock (9161'), a landmark for the old Emigrant trail, and crosses the Emigrant Basin Wild Area boundary (no motorized vehicles allowed). This vantage point offers excellent views to the north of Liberty Hill, Elephant Rock, the Dardanelles, Castle Rock, and the Three Chimneys. As the trail bears eastward along the ridge, the traveler has excellent views of the Stanislaus River watershed to the north and the Tuolumne River watershed to the south.

The trail descends gradually to the low saddle overlooking granitoid Powell Lake. This small 9-acre lake offers fair fishing for brook in early and late season, and the fine views to the northeast makes this an attractive spot for a lunch break. The trail then crosses a small ridge, descends through a forest of lodgepole, fir, and mountain hemlock, and arrives at the open stretches of meadowy Lake Valley. A faint fisherman's trail (0.7 miles) to Chewing Gum Lake turns south through the meadow. Anglers with a yen will want to try the fair-to-good fishing for brook on this small (5-acre) lake before continuing. From Lake Valley it is but a mile across another broad ridge to the turnoff to Y Meadow Dam Lake. Here our route turns south for one undulating mile to the fair campsites at the north end of Y Meadow Dam Lake (8600'). Firewood is plentiful, but the water level fluctuates so much that the lake cannot support fish life. However, anglers accustomed to cross-country walking may elect to try the waters of Granite Lake (0.7 miles south) for the good fishing for brook (8-13"). There are some poor-to-fair campsites at Granite Lake.

2nd Hiking Day **(Y Meadow Dam Lake** to **Gianelli Cabin,** 5 miles) : Retrace steps of 1st hiking day.

28   Gianelli Cabin to Wire Lakes

TRIP   From Gianelli Cabin to Wire Lakes (round trip). Topo map (15') *Pinecrest*. Best mid or late season; 24.8 miles.

Grade	Trail/layover days	Total recommended days
Leisurely	4/1	5
Moderate	4/0	4
Strenuous	2/1	3

HILITES   This round trip penetrates the heart of the Emigrant Basin Wild Area as it wends through a delightful series of meadows and over high, open ridges. Wire Lakes, the destination for this trip, is a stepladder set of three memorable high-mountain lakes that afford excellent angling and several fine choices for secluded camping.

DESCRIPTION (Leisurely trip)

1st Hiking Day **(Gianelli Cabin** to **Y Meadow Dam Lake,** 5 miles) : See 1st hiking day, trip 27.

2nd Hiking Day **(Y Meadow Dam Lake** to **Upper Wire Lake,** 7.4 miles) : Retrace your steps from Y Meadow Dam Lake to the trail junction of the Gianelli Cabin/Whitesides Meadow trail. Our route turns right (northeast) through very large Whitesides Meadow. Travelers should be prepared for the probability of seeing summer-grazing cattle on these broad expanses (Forest Service Multiple-Use land program) but these bovine occupants should not detract too much from the appreciation of this subalpine grassland. Midway across the meadow our route passes the Eagle Pass trail lateral, and then ascends the steep, moderately timbered slope at the southeast end. The forest cover at this point is largely lodgepole, mixed occasionally with silver pine and mountain hemlock. As the ascent levels off, this route passes two trails to Upper Relief Valley and Kennedy Meadow, and then dips down to ford the West Fork of Cherry Creek (sometimes dry in late season) at Salt Lick Meadow (8500'). From here the trail crosses a small ridge and descends past several picturesque tarns to Spring Meadow. Tiny lakes dot the green expanse of the meadow, and early-to-mid season trailpounders will find the grassland areas spiced with lupine, paintbrush and buttercup. Fishermen will find the fishing for brook fair-to-good along the tributary (Spring Creek) flowing through Post Corral Canyon, and good-to-excellent for brook from the banks of little Starvation Lake. The latter lake lies somewhat hidden just to the left (east) of the trail as it ascends the densely forested slope at the east end of Spring Meadow. A few yards farther south, a marked duff fisherman's trail (unmarked on the topo map) winds the remaining 0.6 miles along a ridge to the excellent campsites on the northwest side of Upper

Wire Lake (8800'). Equally good campsites may also be found at Banana Lake (Middle Wire Lake), 0.3 miles southwest by an unmaintained fisherman's trail. Fishing on the Wire Lakes is good-to-excellent (with a mid-season slowdown) for brook (8-14"). Campers will find one of the several secluded campsites on these high, montane, granitoid lakes an idyllic setting for a base camp. Firewood is plentiful.

3rd Hiking Day **(Upper Wire Lake** to **Y Meadow Dam Lake,** 7.4 miles) : Retrace steps of 2nd hiking day.

4th Hiking Day **(Y Meadow Dam Lake** to **Gianelli Cabin,** 5 miles) : Retrace steps of 1st hiking day.

29   Crabtree Camp to Bear Lake

TRIP   From Crabtree Camp to Bear Lake (round trip). Topo map (15') *Pinecrest*. Best early-to-mid season; 8 miles.

Grade	Trail/layover days	Total recom- mended days
Leisurely	2/0	2
Moderate	—	—
Strenuous	—	—

HILITES   Bear Lake usually is a good bet for an early season trip, when fishing for the rainbow trout that inhabit the lake waters is best.

DESCRIPTION

1st Hiking Day **(Crabtree Camp** to **Bear Lake,** 4 miles) : The trail situation at the beginning of this trip is complicated by logging operations. When they are completed, probably in 1971, the Forest Service plans to put up sufficient signs. Until then, advance inquiry of the Forest Service may be best. One may even choose to drive to Bell Meadow and take the trail (not shown on the topo map) which leads up the valley of Bell Creek to Crabtree Camp. From the present logging road the trail descends over a slope covered with lodgepole and red fir to the flats north of Crabtree Camp. After crossing Bell Creek the trail climbs to the timbered slopes above Pine Valley, where it passes the short lateral to the valley and then winds through a fir and lodgepole forest cover to Camp Lake (7600'). This heavily timbered and heavily used lake contains a fair population of annually planted brook trout. At the east end of Camp Lake the trail passes several picturesque tarns and then, at the Bear Lake trail junction, branches left (north) 1 mile to granitoid Bear Lake (7750'). Campsites on the western periphery of this high, montane lake have been somewhat vandalized (paint on rocks), but they are the best to be had. Firewood is ample, and swimming in late season is invigoratingly good. Fishing on this 30-acre lake is fair for rainbow (7-10").

2nd Hiking Day (**Bear Lake** to **Crabtree Camp,** 4 miles) : Retrace steps of 1st hiking day.

Crabtree Camp to Deer Lake   **30**

TRIP From Crabtree Camp to Deer Lake (round trip). Topo map (15') *Pinecrest.* Best mid or late season ; 24.8 miles.

Grade	Trail/layover days	Total recommended days
Leisurely	6/2	8
Moderate	5/2	7
Strenuous	4/2	6

HILITES Fine fishing and the pristine beauty of the Emigrant Basin Wilderness highlight this round trip. A variety of wildlife is present along the route as it touches three life zones, and the higher ridges offer impressive views of the glaciated terrain.

DESCRIPTION (Leisurely trip)

1st Hiking Day (**Crabtree Camp** to **Bear Lake,** 4 miles) : See 1st hiking day, trip 29.

2nd Hiking Day (**Bear Lake** to **Piute Lake,** 5.4 miles) : This hiking day begins as we retrace our steps over the undulating

1-mile trail, to the junction with the Crabtree Camp/Deer Lake trail, where our route turns left (east). From the junction, the trail descends to the ford of Lily Creek and then ascends steeply around a densely forested slope. After a moderately difficult climb, the trail gradually descends past an unnamed lily-padded lake with a meadowed fringe, and then drops steeply down a rocky slope by switchbacks to Piute Meadow. The crown of this ridge marks the western boundary of the Emigrant Basin Primitive Area (no motorized vehicles allowed). The trail-maintenance station at Piute Meadows, intermittently manned by the Forest Service (emergency aid), is a few yards north of the trail as it fords Piute Creek. At the east end of the meadow our route passes the short lateral to Groundhog Meadow and ascends a saddle on the ridge to the east. This trail segment is rocky and poorly maintained, but the summit of the ridge above Piute Lake affords excellent views of glaciated Louse Canyon and the Buck Meadow Creek watershed. The trail then descends to the meadowed fringes of Piute Lake (7920') and the good campsites on the north side. Firewood is abundant, and fishing for rainbow (8-12″) on the shallow, small (2-acre) lake is fair-to-good.

3rd Hiking Day **(Piute Lake** to **Deer Lake,** 3 miles) : From Piute Lake the trail fords the West Fork of Cherry Creek and ascends a rocky section to tiny Gem Lake (poor fishing). This lake is a favorite of photographers, for its southern edge drops off dramatically into Buck Meadow Creek Canyon. Only somewhat less steep than the previous climb, the trail to Jewelry Lake is a rocky ascent. Our route skirts the north side of the meadow fringes surrounding Jewelry Lake, and anglers will want to try their luck for the fair-to-good fishing for rainbow (to 10″) in the lake and the lagoons about the inlet. From the east end of Jewelry Lake, it is 1 mile by rocky, gently ascending trail to the excellent campsites on the north side of Deer Lake (8560'). This long, large (50-acre) lake is granitoid, with meadow fringes on the northern side. The forested campsites look out over the lake's island- and rock-dotted surface. Fishing for nice-sized rainbow (8-16″) is good-to-excellent on both the lake and the inlet stream. Firewood is ample.

4th Hiking Day **(Deer Lake** to **Piute Lake,** 3 miles) : Retrace steps of 3rd hiking day.

5th Hiking Day **(Piute Lake** to **Bear Lake,** 5.4 miles) : Retrace steps of 2nd hiking day.

6th Hiking Day **(Bear Lake** to **Crabtree Camp,** 4 miles) : Retrace steps of 1st hiking day.

Gianelli Cabin to Crabtree Camp   **31**

TRIP   From Gianelli Cabin to Crabtree Camp via Wire
and Deer Lakes (shuttle trip). Topo map (15')
Pinecrest. Best mid or late season; 27.9 miles.

Grade	Trail/layover days	Total recom-mended days
Leisurely	5/2	7
Moderate	4/2	6
Strenuous	3/2	5

HILITES   This route has proved popular with angler, naturalist, photographer and hiker alike. High, coldwater lakes and streams vie with deep fir forests and
alpine meadows for the attention of the visitor. The
shortness of the shuttle for this trip makes it a near-
loop.

DESCRIPTION (Leisurely trip)

1st Hiking Day (**Gianelli Cabin** to **Y Meadow Dam Lake,** 5
miles): See 1st hiking day, trip 27.

2nd Hiking Day (**Y Meadow Dam Lake** to **Upper Wire Lake,** 7.4
miles): See 2nd hiking day, trip 28.

3rd Hiking Day (**Upper Wire Lake** to **Piute Lake,** 5.5 miles):
From Upper Wire Lake the traveler has the option of circling
to Deer Lake by the longer trail route or descending through
the Wire Lakes basin and going cross country to the west end
of Deer Lake. The trail route, after retracing the short fisherman's lateral, rejoins the Spring Meadow/Deer Lake main trail
and then turns south. The remaining distance to Deer Lake is a
steady descent over a forested streamcourse that passes several
small, unnamed lakes. At Deer Lake this route passes the Buck
Lake trail and turns right (west) toward Jewelry Lake. The
cross-country route from Upper Wire Lake to this point first
follows a faint fisherman's trail to Banana Lake (Middle Wire
Lake), where the trail vanishes. The easiest descent from this

point is to take the clear route through the meadowed area east of Banana Lake and then descend via the usually dry streamcourse to the Jewelry Lake/Deer Lake trail. The trail from Deer Lake to Jewelry Lake is a 1-mile rocky descent that brings the traveler to the pleasant meadow fringes surrounding Jewelry Lake. This lake has placid lagoons forming its inlet that provide fair-to-good fishing for rainbow (to 10″). Crossing the inlet stream, the route descends by rocky trail to tiny Piute Lake (7920′) and the good campsites on the north side. From this lake-edge campsite one has a dramatic view across the lake to the precipitous dropoff into Buck Meadow Creek Canyon. Fishing for rainbow (8-12″) is fair-to-good.

4th Hiking Day **(Piute Lake** to **Bear Lake,** 6 miles) : See 2nd hiking day, trip 30.

5th Hiking Day **(Bear Lake** to **Crabtree Camp,** 4 miles) : See 1st hiking day, trip 29.

32 Gianelli Cabin to Kennedy Meadow

TRIP From Gianelli Cabin to Kennedy Meadow via Deer and Emigrant Lakes (shuttle trip). Topo maps (15′) *Pinecrest, Tower Peak, Sonora Pass.* Best mid or late season ; 35 miles.

Grade	Trail/layover days	Total recommended days
Leisurely	5/2	7
Moderate	4/2	6
Strenuous	3/2	5

HILITES This trip journeys through a cross section of the Emigrant Wilderness. The route touches some of the justly popular base-camping lakes, and from these points the traveler has access to the unusual and exciting surrounding country. Taken at the Leisurely pace, this route affords one of the best possible week-long excursions in this country.

DESCRIPTION (Leisurely trip)

1st Hiking Day **(Gianelli Cabin** to **Y Meadow Dam Lake,** 5 miles) : See 1st hiking day, trip 27.

2nd Hiking Day **(Y Meadow Dam Lake** to **Upper Wire Lake,** 8.5 miles) : See 2nd hiking day, trip 28.

3rd Hiking Day **(Upper Wire Lake** to **Emigrant Lake** via Deer and Buck lakes, 7.5 miles) : The traveler going to Deer Lake has a choice of going by the trail or cross country. The trail route entails retracing the short fisherman's trail to its junction with the main trail from Spring Meadow. There our route turns right (south), and descends gently past several unnamed tarns to Deer Lake. The cross-country route descends by faint trail through the Wire Lakes basin to Banana Lake (Middle Wire Lake), and then veers east a short distance through a meadowed basin (no trail). At the end of this meadow a long, usually dry streamcourse descending to the south gives access to the west end of Deer Lake (8560'). This is a large, granitoid, meadow-fringed lake offering good-to-excellent fishing for nice-sized rainbow (to 16"), and anglers who have had an early start will want to try these waters.

The trail to Buck Lakes continues east over a low rocky ridge, and then descends to join the Emigrant Lake/Cow Meadow Lake trail on the west shore of Buck Lakes. At this junction our route turns left (north) along the west side of Upper Buck Lake, and follows Buck Meadow Creek as it crosses the long meadow at the lake's north end. Our route then veers east, fords Buck Meadow Creek, and crosses the steep, low ridge separating the Emigrant Lake and Buck Lakes basins. At Emigrant Lake (8800') the trail follows the long north shore to the several good-to-excellent campsites at the inlet. Emigrant Lake is the largest lake (230 acres) in the Wilderness, and is a long-time favorite of fishermen because of the good-to-excellent rainbow fishing (8-18") in its deep waters. Those who prefer stream fishing will find the lagoons near the inlet exciting sport, but the fish are smaller. Firewood is ample.

4th Hiking Day **(Emigrant Lake** to **Sheep Camp,** 6 miles) : See 2nd hiking day, trip 23.

5th Hiking Day **(Sheep Camp** to **Kennedy Meadow,** 8 miles) : See 1st hiking day, trip 21.

33   **Kennedy Meadow to Gianelli Cabin**

TRIP   From Kennedy Meadow to Gianelli Cabin via Brown Bear Pass, and Emigrant Meadow, Maxwell, Buck, Wire, and Y Meadow Dam lakes (shuttle trip). Topo maps (15′) *Sonora Pass, Tower Peak, Pinecrest.* Best mid or late season; 44.5 miles.

Grade	Trail/layover days	Total recommended days
Leisurely	7/3	10
Moderate	5/2	7
Strenuous	4/2	6

HILITES   After visiting the northern side of the Emigrant Basin Wilderness, this route turns south and traverses the beautiful, lake-dotted country of the Cherry Creek watershed. At Emigrant Meadow the trail joins the old Emigrant Trail, and history buffs will have the opportunity of seeing this historic crossing as the pioneers did. Counting the lakes within easy walking range of a base camp, this route takes one to over 100 named and unnamed lakes.

DESCRIPTION (Leisurely trip)

1st Hiking Day **(Kennedy Meadow to Sheep Camp,** 8 miles):
See 1st hiking day, trip 21.

2nd Hiking Day **(Sheep Camp to Emigrant Meadow Lake,** 6 miles): See 2nd hiking day, trip 22.

3rd Hiking Day **(Emigrant Meadow Lake to Maxwell Lake,** 5.5 miles): See 5th hiking day, trip 25.

4th Hiking Day **(Maxwell Lake to Cow Meadow Lake,** 7.5 miles): See 4th hiking day, trip 25.

5th Hiking Day **(Cow Meadow Lake to Deer Lake,** 3.5 miles):
Leaving Cow Meadow Lake, the trail passes the junction with the Kibbie Ridge trail going south and the unmaintained short

lateral to Emigrant Lake going north. Just past this junction the trail ascends steeply (500') amidst a dense, predominantly lodgepole forest cover to the junction with the Wood Lake lateral and the southwest end of Lower Buck Lake. Lower Buck Lake (42 acres) is a rocky, deep, glacial lake that is separated from Upper Buck Lake by a narrow isthmus. Fishing on both lakes for rainbow (to 13") is good. Our route crosses the isthmus and turns north, where it strikes the Deer Lake trail. Here our route turns left (west) and crosses the low, rocky ridge to the excellent campsites on the north side of Deer Lake (8500'). This long lake is roughly the same size as Upper Buck Lake, and has the same kind of subalpine meadow fringing on the north side. The fine campsites, situated in small stands of lodgepole, look out across the lake's island-dotted surface. The firewood supply is ample, and fishing for rainbow (to 16") is good-to-excellent.

6th Hiking Day **(Deer Lake** to **Y Meadow Dam Lake,** 9 miles) : The mileage for this hiking day is calculated on the basis of bypassing Wire Lakes. However, those who elect to visit this charming lake chain (good fishing) should examine the alternative route offered in the description of the 3rd hiking day, trip 31. From Deer Lake our trail route proceeds north on a gentle ascent to a series of unnamed tarns. These tarns mark the usual turnoff for the wooded cross-country route to Long Lake (1 mile east). A short distance beyond, our route passes the fisherman's trail going left (west) to Wire Lakes, and then descends via a densely forested slope to the east end of Spring Meadow. Good-to-excellent fishing for brook can be found at the end of the ¼ mile faint fisherman's trail bearing east from the middle of this descent that leads to little Starvation Lake, and the fishing is fair-to-good for brook on Spring Creek above the meadows. Spring Meadow is a vast, lakelet-dotted grassland that is lush with buttercups, lupine and paintbrush. One frequently sees cattle grazing here and on Whitesides Meadow because of the National Forest Multiple-Use land program.

From Spring Meadow the trail crosses a small ridge and then descends gradually through a sparsely wooded section to Salt Lick Meadow, where it crosses the tiny West Fork of Cherry Creek (sometimes dry in late season). Beyond Salt Lick Meadow the trail ascends, passing the first of two trails leading north to Upper Relief Valley and Kennedy Meadow. Our trail tops the ridge and begins the somewhat steeper descent to Whitesides Meadow, passing a trail that joins the one mentioned above. Whitesides Meadow is a very long, sprawling, subalpine meadow, with a fringe of lodgepole, silver pine, and mountain hemlock. Its green expanse is broken by the intermittent flow of an unnamed tributary of the South Fork of the Stanislaus River. Our trail parallels this tributary to the west end of the meadow, and then veers away southwesterly to the Y Meadow Dam Lake trail junction. Here our route branches left and proceeds for 1 undulating mile to the fair campsites in the timber fringe at the north end of Y Meadow Dam Lake (8600'). Firewood is plentiful, but the lake is devoid of fish because of severe water-level fluctuations. Anglers may elect to try the waters of Granite Lake (¾ mile south — no trail) for the good fishing for brook (to 13"). There are some poor-to-fair campsites at Granite Lake.

7th Hiking Day **(Y Meadow Dam Lake** to **Gianelli Cabin,** 5 miles) : See 1st hiking day, trip 27.

marmot

The North Boundary Experience

Wherever Sierra mountaineers gather there is sure to be talk of the fabulous "North Boundary Country," and there is just cause for this preoccupation. Here Yosemite boasts its least-visited and wildest back country. In its glaciated canyons and on its granite crests, five generations of hikers, climbers and horsemen have found the solitude, beauty and challenge that they sought. Lying between the Tioga Road (Hiway 120) and the northern edge of the Park, it is a heavily glaciated region of uniform drainage pattern and rounded slopes that appeal to the cross-country wanderer. It is remote because it is large, and because it is isolated by the main stem of the Sierra crest on the east and north, and by the Grand Canyon of the Tuolumne on the south and west.

Too little value is placed on solitude today, and yet, ironically, it is one of the qualities we claim to value most highly. The topography of this region contributes to the feeling of solitude that attends trips taken through it. The terrain is split by no fewer than 11 ridge/valley sequences, all running north to south. One party can be in one drainage and totally oblivious of another party only a few miles distant, with a natural wall of glaciated granite in between. Travelers on the famed Tahoe-Yosemite Trail are aware of another, equally desirable quality that accrues to the ridge-valley sequence. Each ridge encountered and surmounted is sure to reveal a fresh, new valley full of different claims on the visitor's attention.

With the exception of the volcanic rock of the eastern escarpment, this is all granite country, but it is not sterile nor lifeless. Time and evolution are at work here, and mountains are being leveled. You might be misled into thinking that the speed with which this is being done is not such that you might notice it, but the joyous instant a wildflower frantically bursts into bloom is an integral part of the juggernaut process, and the spreading of its petals is as inexorable as the sun's rise, and, in its context, more powerful than an earthquake. One writer put it this way: "Time is the factor. If a butterfly were to brush a wing against the great granite wall of Half Dome in a daily pilgrimage, it would eventually level the mountain." Valleys of the northern part of the Park are full of life that is moving mountains, and if you watch closely you *can* watch it happen.

Aside from the remoteness, perhaps the most appealing thing about the North Boundary Country is the variety of the plant life. The elevation spread of nearly 9000' encompasses almost every kind of Sierran ecological niche. From the digger-pine belt near Hetch Hetchy Reservoir to the whitebark-pined summits of Burro Pass, almost every tree to be seen in the Sierra is represented. Early-summer wildflower displays are nowhere more abundant nor varied, and it is not at all unusual to come across the sunburst yellow of golden brodiaea and the delicate blossom of the alpine-dwelling yellow columbine in the same hiking day. On every hand the hiker sees a vital urgency for life — a living claim for one's right to the sun. Perhaps it is this intense awareness of life frantically renewing itself in a high alpine meadow that man returns time and again to witness. Both a wildflower and a backpacker cram a lot of living into an all-too-short summer. In all cases it is an affirmative celebration of life, and the backpacker, by his personal witness, is a celebrant.

Trails through the North Boundary Country are, understandably, not as well maintained as trails more heavily used and closer to the roads in the Park. However, these officially ignored paths are ways of solitude where one is able to walk for long distances without encountering another living soul. Best-known among the North Boundary trails is the Tahoe-to-Yosemite route. This 180-mile-long trail receives the brunt of the traffic, and the feeder laterals from the east-side trailheads see the least. Most of the routes described in this section begin on the east side of the Sierra. The weekend trips flirt with the Sierra crest, but one should plan at least a three-day trip for any serious penetration of the North Boundary Country.

All kinds of reasons are given for trips into wilderness, but the most commonly given is fishing. For the angler who measures any and all wilderness experiences in terms of the fishing opportunities, the North Boundary Country is a frustrating area to consider—frustrating because the options are so many, the fishery so varied, and the scenery so distracting. Available in the waters of this region are eastern brook, rainbow, brown, golden and some cutthroat trout. The most consistent fish-producing streams are Falls Creek in Jack Main Canyon, Rancheria Creek in Kerrick Canyon, Matterhorn Creek in Matterhorn Canyon and Return Creek in Virginia Canyon. Lakes that are annual "hotspots" include Benson, Smedberg, Peeler, 10 Lakes, the McCabes, and the lakes above Saddlebag Lake. A state fishing license is required within the park for all persons over 16, and both state and federal fishing regulations apply (ask a park ranger for Yosemite's fishing regulations).

All of the west-side trailheads are reached via Hiway 120. Access to the trailhead at O'Shaughnessy Dam (Hetch Hetchy

Reservoir) is by the paved road turning north from Hiway 120 at the San Jose City Camp, or the one turning north at the junction two miles west of the Big Oak Flat Entrance to the Park (both routes merge at Mather). The trailheads at White Wolf, Tuolumne Meadows and Saddlebag Lake are clearly marked turnoffs from Hiway 120, and that at Yosemite Creek is located at the parking area just west of the creek. On the east side of the Sierra all trailheads except Leavitt Meadows are located on clearly marked spur roads branching west from Hiway 395. Leavitt Meadows sits alongside the Sonora Pass road (Hiway 108) midway between Sonora Pass and Sonora Junction.

Mountain lion

34 **Leavitt Meadow to Fremont Lake**

TRIP   From Leavitt Meadow Campground to Fremont
          Lake (round trip). Topo map (15') *Sonora Pass.*
          Best mid or late season; 14 miles.

Grade	Trail/layover days	Total recommended days
Leisurely	2/1	3
Moderate	2/0	2
Strenuous	—	—

HILITES Along this well-traveled route the traveler is intro-
          duced to the contrasts of the North Boundary Coun-
          try. Here the dark rock thrown up by volcanoes
          meets the lighter, more typical Sierra batholith
          granite. Cameras for the photo-bug are a must, and
          the angler can look forward to good rainbow fish-
          ing at Fremont Lake.

DESCRIPTION

1st Hiking Day **(Leavitt Meadow Campground** to **Fremont
Lake,** *7* miles): The trail that parallels the broad, green expanse of Leavitt Meadow leaves the Leavitt Meadow Campground (7120') just north of Leavitt Station via a metal bridge
crossing the West Walker River. The trail and road shown on
the topo map as traversing Leavitt Meadow cross private property (not owned by the pack station), and they should not be
used without permission of the owner. Just beyond the bridge
our trail ascends abruptly, and then traverses the long, dry,
rollercoastering ridge east of the meadow. The rocky trail over
volcanic debris affords constant views of the meadow and the
oxbows of the West Walker River, and it does not take a great
deal of imagination to picture emigrant wagons working their
way westward to Emigrant Pass. Near the south end of the
meadow, the trail descends gently to pass the turnoff to Secret
and Poore lakes. Then, amidst a moderate forest cover of Jeffrey
and lodgepole pine, the trail ascends steadily over a long, dry
summit of a saddle, and finally drops steadily to the north shore
of Roosevelt Lake. The sandy shores of this tiny, algae-bot-
tomed lake are fringed with a moderate forest cover of lodge-

pole and Jeffrey, and the west side of the lake has fair-to-poor campsites near the Forest Service trail register and outhouse.

From the west shore of Roosevelt Lake, the trail undulates over a granite shoulder and fords the outlet creek at the south end of Lane Lake. This outlet usually dries up by midsummer, but the dead lodgepoles southwest of the ford are mute testimony to the flooding earlier in the season. At this point the trail deviates from the trail shown on the topo map. The new trail swings eastward, crossing the rocky white granite saddle south-southeast of Lane Lake, and descends through a sparse-to-moderate mixed forest cover of lodgepole and Jeffrey pine, white fir, aspen and some cottonwood and juniper.

On both sides of the West Walker River valley is evidence of the grand volcanic overlay that once inundated the land. The basic batholith granite on which one walks was re-exposed after the period of volcanic turbulence. As one nears the banks of the West Walker River he encounters large clumps of willow amidst the aspen. Past the willow and aspen the trail fords a small but vigorous tributary (not shown on the topo map), and then rejoins the trail shown on the topo as it continues to ascend gently. This ascent fords another unnamed tributary of the West Walker River, and steepens as the trail crosses a saddle crested with juniper and Jeffrey pine. This saddle offers fine views up the West Walker valley to Forsyth Peak and the Sierra crest. Descending over a sandy trail, our route passes the marked turnoff to Hidden and Red Top lakes, and then resumes its moderate ascent along the east bank of the West Walker River. The rocky stretch of trail alongside the river gives access to many pleasant, granite-bottomed potholes. Here the river tumbles along in a series of small falls and cascades that have carved a narrows through the white granite which typifies the center of the West Walker River drainage. The walls of the drainage are of barren, metavolcanic rock that ranges the color spectrum from black to reds and yellows. As the narrows opens onto a small bench, the trail passes several excellent campsites on both banks of the West Walker River. The topo map shows the trail fording here to the west side of the river; however, a new trail has been made along the east bank for another 1/4 mile to an easier ford upstream. At this ford our route leaves the Piute Meadows trail (this junction is just off the Sonora Pass topo map), branches westward and ascends steeply to cross a saddle topped with juniper and Jeffrey pine. This saddle offers Veed views south to Tower Peak. The trail then descends gently, and 100 yards east of Fremont Lake (8240') passes the trail to Chain of Lakes. The forest cover around this generous-sized lake is moderate-to-dense lodge-pole and juniper, most of it located around the south end of the lake. Here in the timber are fair campsites, and firewood is ample. Lake fishing for rainbow (to 12″) and eastern brook (to 10″) is good.

2nd Hiking Day **(Fremont Lake** to **Leavitt Meadow Campground,** 7 miles): Retrace steps of 1st hiking day.

35 Leavitt Meadow to Cinko Lake

TRIP   From Leavitt Meadow Campground to Cinko Lake (round trip). Topo maps (15′) *Sonora Pass, Tower Peak*. Best mid or late season; 24 miles.

Grade	Trail/layover days	Total recom- mended days
Leisurely	3/1	4
Moderate	3/0	3
Strenuous	2/0	2

HILITES   This interesting route traces the West Fork of the West Walker River to its headwaters cirque beneath the Sierra crestline. From the sagebrush and Jeffrey pine belt it ascends to the Boreal belt, passing through three ecological zones. Of the several trips in this drainage, this offers one of the best exposures to the geological, topographical and biological features of the country.

DESCRIPTION (Leisurely trip)

1st Hiking Day **(Leavitt Meadow Campground** to **Fremont Lake,** 7 miles): See 1st hiking day, trip 34.

2nd Hiking Day **(Fremont Lake** to **Cinko Lake,** 5 miles): After retracing our steps back to the Chain of Lakes junction described in trip 34, the route turns right (south) and ascends

steadily near, but out of sight of, Fremont Lake. This ascent
steepens as it crosses open, granite-sand slopes with only a
few juniper, lodgepole and Jeffrey pine for shade. Near the top
of this ascent one has uninterrupted views to the south of Forsyth and Tower peaks, and one encounters his first silver pines.
The first of the three large granite domes that tower over the
east side of Chain of Lakes comes into view, and the trail crosses
to the north of it. Then, on a gently descending trail through
an increasingly dense forest cover, we pass the marked trail
to Walker Meadows and arrive at the first of these tiny, green,
lily-padded lakes. These lakes reflect the verdant forest cover
that extends to their willow-lined shores, and by late summer
their shallow depths teem with the biota that typifies near-
stagnant waters. Fair campsites for early and mid season, usable
when the water is moving, dot the west sides of all three lakes.

The trail leaves the last and largest of the Chain of Lakes and
ascends gently over sand and duff through a moderate forest
cover of lodgepole and silver pine past the small, unnamed lake
north of Lower Long Lake. A few yards past this lily-padded
lake, the trail veers right around the north side of Lower Long
Lake. The "blancoed" rock in the center of the lake is a favorite
midday resting place for the sandpipers that inhabit the area.
Fishermen seeking the pan-sized rainbow here will enjoy the
sandpiper's low, skimming flight, which seems to trim the fringe
of rushes. Fair-to-good campsites dot the north and west sides
of the lake. More extensive campsites, of the packer variety, are
found a few yards farther up the trail, along the northeast side
of Upper Long Lake. The trail jogs around the lower end of
Upper Long Lake, fords the intermittent outlet stream and
meets the Piute Meadows lateral. Our route turns right past a
picturesque tarn to the banks of the West Fork of the West
Walker River. Here at another junction our route branches left
alongside this tumbling stream. Excellent campsites dot both
sides of the West Fork near the junction, marred only by the
cowflops incident to the Multiple-Use grazing permit for nearby Walker Meadows. Occasional hemlocks with their gracefully
bowed tops occur along this pleasant, granite-ledged, timber-
pocketed ascent. Many wildflowers, including shooting star,
penstemon, bush lupine, aster, pennyroyal, columbine, goldenrod, heather, false Solomon's seal, Mariposa lily, wallflower,
woolly sunflower and fleabane, decorate the stream's edge and
complement the cheerful splashing of the nearby creek. This gentle-to-moderate climb does *not* ford the creek just southeast of
metavolcanic point 9250, as shown on the topo map, but instead continues along the southeast side of the creek to the foot

of the large, white granite dome (topo peak 10010), where it fords to the northwest side of the creek. Contrasts of the dark volcanic rock and the white granite underlayment are nowhere more marked than in this drainage, and the viewer is assailed with dark battlements of multihued basalt, and sheer escarpments of glacially smoothed batholithic granite. William H. Brewer, the head of the Brewer Survey party that passed near here in July 1863, took note of the volcanic surroundings saying ". . . in the higher Sierra, along our line of travel, all our highest points were capped with lava, often worn into strange and fantastic forms — rounded hills of granite, capped by rugged masses of lava, sometimes looking like old castles with their towers and buttresses and walls, sometimes like old churches with their pinnacles, all on a gigantic scale, and then again shooting up in curious forms that defy description."

The ascent takes the traveler to timberline and to alpine climes as the surrounding forest cover becomes stunted and boasts occasional altitude-loving whitebark pines.

At a signed junction our route turns southeast along a clear trail (not shown on the topo map) to Cinko Lake. This short lateral fords the West Fork of the West Walker River and ascends a moderate slope, levels briefly past a charming meadow with a tiny tarn in its upper reaches, and then joins the intermittent north outlet from arrowhead-shaped Cinko Lake. (There is another outlet on the south side of the lake.) The trail emerges on the lake's edge (9200'), adjacent to the north outlet, where there are several good campsites. Firewood is ample, and fishing for rainbow and eastern brook (to 12") is good.

3rd Hiking Day **(Cinko Lake** to **Leavitt Meadow Campground,** 12 miles)** : Retrace steps of 1st and 2nd hiking days.

Leavitt Meadow to Dorothy Lake   **36**

TRIP   From Leavitt Meadow Campground to Dorothy Lake (semiloop trip). Topo maps *Sonora Pass, Tower Peak*. Best mid or late season; 31.5 miles.

Grade	Trail/layover days	Total recommended days
Leisurely	6/1	7
Moderate	4/1	5
Strenuous	3/1	4

HILITES   Touring the headwaters of the West Fork of the West Walker River and the headwaters of Cascade Creek and Falls Creek would be an ambitious undertaking in any one trip, but this trip boasts more. Near Dorothy Lake, the culmination of the trip, the visitor can take in the unusual Forsyth Peak "rock glacier." Because of the cross-country section between Cinko Lake and the Dorothy Lake Pass trail, this trip is recommended for experienced backpackers only.

DESCRIPTION (Moderate trip)

1st Hiking Day **(Leavitt Meadow Campground to West Fork of the West Walker River,** 9.5 miles): See 1st hiking day, trip 34, and part of 2nd hiking day, trip 35.

2nd Hiking Day **(West Fork of the West Walker River to Dorothy Lake,** 8 miles, part cross country): Follow the route to Cinko Lake described in 2nd hiking day, trip 35. From the north outlet of this lake, skirt the east shore and begin the cross-country section at the south outlet (not shown on the topo map). This outlet empties into the unnamed tributary just south of Cinko Lake. Keeping to the north side of this tributary, this route arrives at the small, unnamed lake east of Cinko Lake and west of point 9195. Fording the tributary near the inlet of this lake, our route rounds the granite nose of the ridge to the south, and strikes the Dorothy Lake Pass trail near the two tiny tarns just south of point 9195. Our route turns right (south), following the trail on a gentle ascent through a thinning forest cover of lodgepole, hemlock and whitebark pine. The trail then fords the outlet stream from Bonnie Lake. (An alternative route is to ascend along this outlet stream, round the east side of windy Bonnie Lake, and rejoin the Dorothy Lake Pass trail at the ford of the stream joining Stella and Bonnie lakes.) After this ford the trail ascends more steeply, and becomes rocky after passing island-dotted Lake Harriet. This ascent levels through a meadowy section and fords the outlet stream joining Stella and Bonnie lakes. Ahead, the low profile of Dorothy Lake Pass is fronted by another moderate, rocky ascent, and the trail then levels past the grassy north arm of Stella Lake. At the northeast end of this arm, a ducked cross-country route to Lake Ruth and Lake Helen departs from our route. The long, low saddle on which Stella Lake sits terminates at Dorothy Lake Pass, where there is an excellent view of Dorothy Lake (9400'). To the southeast, the hiker has V-notched views of Tower Peak, and to the south, the granite grenadiers of multi-turreted Forsyth Peak dominate the landscape. From the pass, the trail descends steadily over a rocky slope that is the territory of numerous conies and marmots. As the trail skirts the north side of this beautiful lake, it winds through lush grass and willow patches with spots of color provided by bush lupine, shooting star, lousewort, goldenrod, paintbrush, whorled penstemon, aster, fleabane, pussypaws and false Solomon's seal. This stretch of the north shore was not so lush when the first recorded explorer of this lake walked here. Lt. N. F. McClure, of the 4th Cavalry, came this way in 1894 noting, "Grazing here was poor, and there had evidently been thousands of sheep about." The trail passes three windy campsites along the north shore before arriving at the good campsites at the west end of the lake. Firewood is somewhat scarce near these meadow-fringe sites, but fishing for rainbow and occasional eastern brook is good-to-excellent except during a midsummer slow-down. This lake makes an excellent base-camp location for exploring and fishing the surrounding lakes in the upper Cascade Creek basin, and for viewing the Forsyth Peak "rock glacier."

This phenomenon can be viewed from the unnamed lake south of Dorothy Lake. Seen from here, it is a prominent "river" of rock flowing in a long northwestward-curving arc. This arc begins on the northeast face of Forsyth Peak, then curves down the easternmost ravine and points its moving head toward Dorothy Lake. Composed of coarse rock that tumbled from Forsyth

Peak's fractured face, it hides an underlayment of silt, sand and fine gravel, and when moving it depends upon ice caught between larger boulders for its mobility. Other rock glaciers are found in the Alps, Alaska and the Andes.

3rd Hiking Day **(Dorothy Lake** to **Campsites, Fremont Lake Trail Junction on the West Walker River,** 8 miles) : This route retraces the steps of part of the previous hiking day and continues to descend on the north side of tumbling Cascade Creek. From the subalpine climes of Dorothy Lake one descends to the Hudsonian life zone through an increasingly dense forest cover of lodgepole, hemlock and occasional silver pine. As the trail nears the West Walker River, the moderate descent levels, and then fords near an old corral. After the ford there is a "Y" junction, and our route turns left (downstream). The trail continues north along the east side of the West Walker River, fords an unnamed tributary of the river, and jogs around a meadow before beginning a long, gentle-to-moderate ascent. This ascent crosses and recrosses an intermittent stream that drains a small lakelet near the top of this climb. The sand-and-duff trail then crosses a saddle before descending to ford Long Canyon Creek and the unnamed tributary to the north. At the latter ford, one may ford to the good campsites on the west side of the West Walker River (a few yards beyond the junction with the trail to Fremont Lake). Or one may continue downstream on the east side of the West Walker River (on a trail segment not shown on the topo map) to the good campsites (8000') on the east side of the river. These campsites have an adequate firewood supply, and fishing in the deeper holes of this segment of the river is good for rainbow (to 11″).

4th Hiking Day **(Campsites, Fremont Lake Trail Junction on the West Walker River** to **Leavitt Meadow Campground,** 6 miles) : Retrace steps of most of 1st hiking day, trip 34.

37   Leavitt Meadow to Tower Lake

TRIP   From Leavitt Meadow Campground to Tower Lake
(semiloop trip, part cross country). Topo maps
(15′) *Sonora Pass, Tower Peak*. Best mid or late
season; 37.5 miles.

Grade	Trail/layover days	Total recom- mended days
Leisurely	7/2	9
Moderate	5/2	7
Strenuous	4/2	6

HILITES   The cross-country segment of this trip makes it a
choice for experienced backpackers only. The stren-
uousness of the route guarantees the walker a pro-
portionate measure of solitude, and views of the alpine crestal country seldom seen by anyone except
the cross-countryer.

DESCRIPTION (Moderate trip)

1st Hiking Day (**Leavitt Meadow Campground** to **West Fork
of the West Walker River,** 9.5 miles) : See 1st hiking day, trip
34, and part of 2nd hiking day, trip 35.

2nd Hiking Day (**West Fork of the West Walker River** to **Dorothy Lake,** 8 miles) : Follow the route to Cinko Lake described
in 2nd hiking day, trip 35; then follow the cross-country segment and trail segments described in 2nd hiking day, trip 36.

3rd Hiking Day (**Dorothy Lake** to **Tower Lake,** 5 miles) : From
the campsites at the west end of Dorothy Lake, retrace the steps
of the previous hiking day to Stella Lake, where the ducked
cross-country route to Lake Ruth rounds the northeast end of the
lake. This route ascends over a rock-and-grass ledge system
along the east side of the intermittent stream joining Stella Lake
and Lake Ruth, and arrives at the outlet end of Lake Ruth. Here,
nestled in the sparse whitebark-pine fringe of the lake, are good

campsites that make a fine alternative to the more crowded environs of Dorothy Lake. The route from the outlet skirts the east side of the lake for a short distance and then ascends a long, gentle swale to the southeast. Several small melt-off tarns mark the crossover point to the Lake Helen drainage. Keeping to the south side of this large, granitoid, circular lake, the route fords the tiny but noisy southwest inlet, and then crosses the rocky slope directly south of the lake. At the southeast inlet our route fords and ascends moderately to a lovely grass bench. The remaining ascent to the obvious saddle to the southeast crosses steeper sections, and route-picking is best accomplished on the left (north) side of the cirque wall. This steep pitch brings one to a sparsely dotted whitebark-pine saddle offering incomparable views. Included in the views to the north and west are (from north to west) Wells Peak, White Mountain, Sonora Peak, Stanislaus Peak, Leavitt Peak, Kennedy Peak, Relief Peak and Forsyth Peak. To the east and southeast the view encompasses (from east to south) : Flatiron Butte, Walker Peak, Buckeye Ridge, the Kirkwood Creek drainage, Grouse Mountain, Hunewill Peak, Hawksbeak Peak, Kettle Peak, Cirque Mountain and Tower Peak. From the summit of this saddle one can also see most of the lakes of the Cascade Creek drainage, as well as Tower Lake at the foot of Tower Peak. Tower Peak, the most spectacular peak of the North Boundary Country but not the tallest, is the goal of most climbers in this region. Visible from most of the drainages to the south, it has served mountaineers as a landmark for more than a hundred years.

Descending from the saddle on the southeast side entails crossing rock and scree on a steep descent to a rocky bench, and thence, via a grass and ledge system, to the small lakelet just north of Tower Lake. The route then rounds the south nose of a mafic-intruded granite ridge to the willowed outlet of Tower Lake, where it fords to the fair campsites, centered in the only stand of timber (whitebark pine) found here on the east side of the outlet (9600'). Firewood is scarce, but choosing this spot for a campsite allows one to take advantage of the fair-to-good fishing for the golden (to 11") that inhabit this lake. Good alternative campsites with more wood and cover can be found ½ mile down the outlet stream.

4th Hiking Day **(Tower Lake** to **Campsites, Fremont Lake Trail Junction on the West Walker River,** 9 miles) : From Tower Lake the trail deviates from that shown on the topo map in that it descends over a rocky slope along the south side of the outlet stream from Tower Lake, and then fords to pass just south of the small tarn shown on the topo. This steep, rocky descent affords a view of a dramatic avalanche chute that slices the slope on the northeast side of Kirkwood Creek canyon. To the rear, back toward Tower Peak, the view is dominated by the climactic, phalluslike northern extension of Tower Peak. This classic white-granite pinnacle soon obliterates views of Tower Peak itself, and it stands as mute testimony to the obdurate granite's resistance to glacial erosion. The rocky descent soon reaches timberline, where hemlock and lodgepole pine appear, and then refords the outlet stream in a willowed section at the confluence of the Tower Lake outlet and the tiny stream draining the glacier at the foot of the granite column to the south. The new section of trail from Tower Lake, not shown on the topo map, keeps to the east side of the creek as it descends gently over duff and rock, and fords an unnamed tributary.

Beyond the ford, the new trail rejoins the old trail and the route continues as shown on the topo. Winding through a dense forest cover of lodgepole and hemlock, the trail refords the Tower Lake outlet stream and ascends above the narrowing canyon. These narrows show almost vertical granite walls, between which the stream becomes a plummeting ribbon. Ahead, the valley of the West Walker River (Upper Piute Meadows) can be seen through the trees, and a short, easy descent over a duff trail soon brings us to a trail junction just north of the confluence of the Tower Lake outlet and Kirkwood Creek. Our route turns right, fords the West Walker River, and then skirts the oxbows of the river as it serpentines through Upper Piute Meadows. At the north end of the meadows the sandy trail passes the turnoff to Piute Cabin, a Forest Service trail-maintenance station (emergency services available here), and then veers away from the river as it continues to descend gently. It should be noted that the cattle in Upper Piute Meadows are part of the Forest Service's "Multiple Use" administrative concept. Cowflops have been reported as far away as the head of Thompson Canyon — and it may be logically assumed that they were a result of allowing grazing here. After jogging around a marshy section, the trail again comes within sight of the river, and then joins the trail from Dorothy Lake. From the junction we proceed as described in 3rd hiking day, trip 36.

5th Hiking Day **(Campsites, Fremont Lake Trail Junction on the West Walker River** to **Leavitt Meadow Campground,** 6 miles) : See most of 1st hiking day, trip 34.

Leavitt Meadow to Buckeye Creek   **38**

TRIP   From Leavitt Meadow Campground to Buckeye Pack Station (shuttle trip). Topo maps (15') *Sonora Pass, Tower Peak, Matterhorn Peak*. Best early or mid season ; 38.5 miles.

Grade	Trail/layover days	Total recom- mended days
Leisurely	7/2	9
Moderate	5/2	7
Strenuous	4/1	5

HILITES   Using two major eastside drainages this trip circumnavigates Walker Mountain and Flatiron Ridge, and is about evenly split between the high country and the lower, forested areas. This is a superlative choice for the novice who has a couple of shorter trips behind him, and who is looking for a longer trip with some of the challenge of cross-countrying.

DESCRIPTION (Moderate trip)

1st Hiking Day **(Leavitt Meadow Campground** to **West Fork of the West Walker River,** 9 miles)** : See 1st and part of 2nd hiking day, trip 35.

2nd Hiking Day **(West Fork of the West Walker River** to **Dorothy Lake,** 8 miles, part cross country)** : Follow the route to Cinko Lake described in 2nd hiking day, trip 35, and then follow the cross-country and trail segments described in 2nd hiking day, trip 36.

3rd Hiking Day **(Dorothy Lake** to **Tower Lake,** 5 miles)** : See 3rd hiking day, trip 37.

4th Hiking Day **(Tower Lake** to **Campsites at The Roughs,** 8.5 miles)** : Descend to Upper Piute Meadows as described in 4th hiking day, trip 37, and just below the confluence of Kirkwood Creek and the creek draining Tower Lake, ford to the northeast side and turn right up Kirkwood Creek. Here at the southernmost extension of Upper Piute Meadows our route ascends moderately through a dense forest cover of lodgepole and occasional silver pine that sees the inclusion of hemlock near the top of the climb. This route passes below the spectacular avalanche chute noted on the previous hiking day. On a moderate ascent that steepens as it turns easterly and then northeasterly, the trail rises to the saddle marking the divide between the Walker River and Buckeye Creek drainages. The startling eminence of Hawksbeak Peak to the south vies for the traveler's attention with the rich volcanic reds and blacks of the slopes to the north. After reaching a small pond at the headwaters of Kirkwood Creek, the trail descends moderately over duff and rocky surfaces to the head of the North Fork of Buckeye Creek. This descent through a sparse-to-moderate forest cover of lodgepole, hemlock, and occasional whitebark and silver pine crosses back and forth over the splashing creek. Then, in a final steep descent, the trail drops to "Buckeye Forks," where it meets the trail descending from Buckeye Pass to the south. (Contrary to the topo map, the junction is west of the cabin.) Here at the forks is a meadow-set snow-survey cabin of log-tenon construction. It is believed that this well-made cabin was constructed in 1928, and is the oldest of the U. S. Snow Survey shelters. When built the cabin was surrounded by open meadow, which has since been overgrown with the ubiquitous lodgepole and willow. This dense growth is undoubtedly due to the strong evolutionary contribution of the nearby colony of beavers. As is clearly seen just downstream, these beavers have repeatedly flooded this section between Buckeye Junction and The Roughs, and the consequent buildup of sediments and high water table were conducive to forest reproduction. However, what the beaver giveth he also taketh away. Were this dense forest to be flooded again these healthy trees would be drowned. That happened downstream, where the bleached white ghost snags make skeletal reminders of the beaver's potent niche in the evolutionary cycle. Of the mammals, excepting man, the beaver is far and away the greatest single alterer of the natural environment.

From the cabin the trail continues to descend steadily over alternating duff, sand and rock. On each side, gnawed and fallen aspen show the beaver's dietary preferences, but despite this rodent's industrious efforts (some naturalists would say "because of it") the forest cover along the creek is dense, and it serves as a foraging grounds for all manner of birdlife, including flickers, chickadees, juncos, robins, Williamson's sapsuckers, hummingbirds and nuthatches.

As the canyon narrows between high, glacially polished granite walls, the trail enters the section known as The Roughs. Here, for about a mile, the sometimes swampy trail winds along the left bank of Buckeye Creek (it does not ford to the south side as shown on the topo map), overshadowed by sheer, rounded granite to the north and polished spires to the south. Good campsites with ample firewood can be found at both ends of The Roughs (8240′). Fishing for rainbow and eastern brook (to 9″) is good.

5th Hiking Day **(Campsites at The Roughs** to **Buckeye Pack Station,** 8 miles) : From the lower end of The Roughs, the trail climbs steeply over the black, metasedimentary shale of the north canyon wall to a juniper-topped saddle. A few yards beyond this saddle it fords the vigorous creek draining the basin between Ink Rocks and Hanna Mountain. This segment of trail is not shown on the topo map, and although the location of this new trail is due to engineering necessities, the happy result provides one of the esthetic highlights of the trip. From the wildflower garden surrounding the ford of this unnamed stream, views down the Buckeye Creek drainage are spectacular. The lush grasslands of Big Meadow provide a soft counterpoint to the ruggedness of Flatiron and Buckeye ridges, and the tumultuous sounds of the cascades above and below the ford furnish soul-satisfying background music for a fine rest stop.

From this viewpoint the trail descends over a rocky exposed slope on a long traverse to rejoin the trail shown on the topo map just upstream from the confluence of Buckeye Creek and the tributaries draining the slopes of Hunewill and Victoria peaks. This steady descent is the last of the precipitous terrain, and the remainder of the walk to the pack station is over long, gradual slopes covered with sagebrush, mountain mahogany, bitterbrush and mule ears. Occasional clumps of aspen occur where the trail crosses a tributary or where it veers close to Buckeye Creek, and they provide welcome shade on a hot mid-summer afternoon. In these well-watered sections the traveler also encounters colorful clumps of monkeyflower, goldenrod, lupine, shooting star, paintbrush and penstemon.

Big Meadow itself is a charming two-mile-long grassland replete with Belding ground squirrels and morning-feeding deer. At one time (circa 1870) this meadow rang with the sounds of axes and the whirring of a sawmill blade. Here the Upper Hunewill mill operated to provide mining timber. It was best remembered by the locals for the annual "free for all" fight staged here between rival crews at the Fourth of July picnic. The present "Multiple Use" grazing policy limits cattle to the area downstream from the fence that also marks the Hoover Wilderness boundary. Near this fence the observant passerby can make out the signs of an abortive effort to construct a flume to carry water from Buckeye Creek to Bodie.

Below the fence our trail joins a jeep road and passes through several fine stands of Jeffrey pine. Then it fords an unnamed tributary and continues along the north bank of Buckeye Creek. (This section of trail is not shown on the topo map.) From the washed-out bridge (the topo-map trail crossing) it continues along the north bank for another ½ mile, and arrives at Buckeye Pack Station (7420′).

39   Twin Lakes to Peeler Lake

TRIP   From Twin Lakes to Peeler Lake (round trip). Topo map (15′) *Matterhorn Peak*. Best mid or late season; 16 miles.

Grade	Trail/layover days	Total recom- mended days
Leisurely	—	—
Moderate	2/1	3
Strenuous	—	—

HILITES   Despite a stiff 2400′ climb, this trip makes a fine choice for the city-weary hiker with a "long week-ender" trip-selection problem. An early start will allow the hiker to enjoy the early morning freshness on the steeper uphill parts, and to be in camp soon enough for a pleasurable swim and/or some afternoon angling. Peeler Lake, as a destination, is a delightfully unique Sierra experience in that one camps literally on top of the mountain chain. This lake pours its waters down both sides of the Sierra divide.

DESCRIPTION

1st Hiking Day **(Twin Lakes** to **Peeler Lake,** 8 miles) : The trail leaves from the west end of Mono Village Campground (follow the signs through the private campground to the pack station). There is a fee for parking at the trailhead (7092′) or anywhere on the private property that bounds the west end of upper Twin Lake. Travelers setting out in the fall season should take a few minutes at the outset for a side trip to view the Kokanee salmon spawning run in the shallows of Robinson Creek adjacent to the private campground.

At the pack station a trail register marks the trailhead, from which the sandy trail winds through a moderate-to-dense forest cover of Jeffrey pine, juniper, lodgepole pine, aspen and cotton-wood along Robinson Creek. In late summer the cottony catkins from the latter litter the initial section of trail, leaving the ground surface the gray-white of spring snow. Crossing several tiny tributaries, the trail then ascends gently, and within ¾ mile encounters the first fir.

The forest cover soon opens onto a sagebrush-and-meadow bench, where one can see the headwall of the cirque basin to the west. As one makes his way up this open bench through thigh-high sagebrush, rabbitbrush, chamise and mule ears, he has unobstructed views of Kettle Peak, Crown Point, Cirque Mountain, Victoria Peak and Hunewill Peak. About halfway up this bench the trail passes a "ghost forest" of drowned trees caused by beaver dams downstream. Beaver still share this fine Sierra stream with us. On the right, somnolent marmots are likely to be seen dozing among piles of scree that flow from the feet of the avalanche chutes scarring Victoria Peak ; on the left, the dramatic, unbroken granite wall of Blacksmith Peak at the top of Little Slide Canyon dominates the view. A sign here marks the departure point for the difficult cross-country route up Little Slide Canyon ; the sign also proclaims this area as part of the Hoover Wilderness. Douglas firs just beyond this man-made sign are natural guideposts that announce a steepening of this ascent. On the left, Robinson Creek becomes a willow-lined cascade that is frequently heard but seldom seen. The ascent resolves into switchbacks that ford several small tributaries. Here one encounters monkeyflower, monkshood, red columbine, swamp onion and shooting star scattered among clumps of bracken fern. Along the drier pieces of trail the severity of the rock is alleviated by colorful patches of Indian paintbrush, Mariposa lily, scarlet gilia, yarrow milfoil, whorled penstemon, pussypaws, streptanthus and goldenrod.

The ascent levels out, veers southerly, fords another tributary, and arrives at the outlet point of arrow-shaped Barney Lake. (The trail shown on the topo map as crossing the saddle between Hunewill Peak and Cirque Mountain is no longer maintained and is not signed.) Anglers wishing an interlude of fair-to-good fishing for eastern brook and rainbow trout will want to tarry around the deeper east and northeast shores of this 9-acre gem. The alternatives for the nonfisherman are equally attractive. He may elect to take a cool, quick dip, or merely to lie back and watch the play of the local water ouzels.

The remainder of the trail to the top of the watershed is not marked on the topo map, but is patently clear on the scene. This trail skirts the west side of the lake in a steady, long, hot ascent that takes one high on the canyon wall, well above the "ghost forested" delta inlet to Barney Lake. Once above the wetter sections of the delta, the trail descends to a wildflower-decorated ford of Robinson Creek. Here amidst the willow can be found swamp onion, columbine, tiger lily and monkeyflower. The moderate forest cover now shows the transition to higher climes with the introduction of hemlock, and some silver and whitebark pine. About ¼ mile upstream the trail refords Robinson Creek, and after fording the outlet creek from Peeler Lake just above its confluence with Robinson Creek (there are two magnificent specimens of silver pine at this ford), it rises abruptly by rocky switchbacks to the bench junction with the Crown Lake trail. This junction is ¼ mile northwest of Robinson Lakes (the two tiny lakes downstream from Crown Lake). Our route turns right and ascends moderately for about ½ mile along the outlet from Peeler Lake, and then steeply up the draw just northeast of Peeler Lake to the outlet of the lake. Beautiful Peeler Lake (9500′) sits astride the Sierra crest, contributing water to Robinson Creek on the east and Rancheria Creek on the west. Large (about 60 acres), it has abrupt, rocky shores, and the deep-blue color characteristic of the deeper Sierra lakes. The trail rounds the north side of the lake and arrives at the good campsites along the west side. Firewood is ample, and fishing for eastern brook and rainbow trout (to 14″) is good. These campsites make an excellent base-camp location for exploratory trips to the northwest and southeast.

2nd Hiking Day **(Peeler Lake** to **Twin Lakes,** 8 miles) : Retrace steps of 1st hiking day.

Twin Lakes to Crown Lake

40

TRIP From Twin Lakes to Crown Lake (round trip). Topo map (15′) *Matterhorn Peak*. Best early, mid or late season; 16 miles.

Grade	Trail/layover days	Total recommended days
Leisurely	—	—
Moderate	2/1	3
Strenuous	—	—

HILITES Like the previous trip, this one entails considerable "up," but it is still a good two-day trip selection. This route follows Robinson Creek all the way to Crown Lake, and in its course exposes the traveler to some of the finest east-side scenery available anywhere along the Sierra. Crown Lake itself is set in the heart of the Sierra crest, and consonant with its name, it forms a royal diadem of blue in a regal setting of forest greens.

DESCRIPTION

1st Hiking Day **(Twin Lakes** to **Crown Lake,** 8 miles) : Proceed to the Peeler/Crown Lake junction as described in trip 39. From this junction our route turns south, undulating gently between large outcroppings of glacially polished granite. As the trail ascends moderately below Robinson Lakes (unmarked on the topo map; they are the lakes downstream from Crown Lake) it hooks east, and then crosses the timbered isthmus between the two little lakes. The segment of trail from the junction to Robinson Lakes winds through one near-pure stand of hemlock— unusual for this part of the Sierra. Robinson Lakes are tiny, granitoid lakes with a sparse forest cover of lodgepole pine, silver pine and hemlock. Across the isthmus, the trail rounds the south side of the larger Robinson Lake and then turns south on a steady ascent. This ascent jogs eastward briefly as it fords and refords Robinson Creek just below Crown Lake.

The final few yards to the outlet of Crown Lake (9500′) are accomplished by switchbacks. Excellent campsites are just downstream from the lake along the outlet, where there are ex-·cellent views of Kettle Peak and Crown Point. Firewood is ample, and fishing for rainbow and some eastern brook (to 9″) is fair. The fishery of Crown Lake is unusual in that it is one of the few Sierra lakes claimed by the Department of Fish and Game as self-sustaining.

2nd Hiking Day **(Crown Lake** to **Twin Lakes,** 8 miles) : Retrace steps of 1st hiking day.

41   **Twin Lakes to Upper Piute Creek**

TRIP   From Twin Lakes to Campsites, Upper Piute Creek (round trip). Topo map (15′) *Matterhorn Peak.* Best mid or late season; 23 miles.

Grade	Trail/layover days	Total recommended days
Leisurely	—	—
Moderate	4/1	5
Strenuous	3/1	4

HILITES   This trip is a satisfying one for the hiker who has always viewed the Sawtooth Ridge from the north side only. Following Robinson Creek nearly to the crest of the Sierra, this route circles the west end of Sawtooth Ridge, and then drops down into the scenic upper reaches of Piute Creek. For those who appreciate spectacular mountain scenery of alpine character, this trip is a must.

DESCRIPTION (Moderate trip)

1st Hiking Day **(Twin Lakes** to **Crown Lake,** 8 miles) : See 1st hiking day, trip 39, and 1st hiking day, trip 40.

2nd Hiking Day **(Crown Lake** to **Campsites, Upper Piute Creek,** 3.5 miles) : From Crown Lake's outlet the trail ascends along the west side, offering fine views of the meadowed inlet. The ascent soon steepens as the trail begins a series of short, rocky switchbacks that terminates just east of Crown Point. Here the trail levels out into a willowed meadow section with several small lakelets, and meets the Snow Lake trail just beyond. Our route turns left (south), fords the stream draining Snow Lake, and climbs over an easy talus-and-scree pile. This rocky ascent levels briefly within sight of another small lakelet; then the trail cuts across the bench and ascends steeply by rocky switchbacks. In most years, there is a large snowbank across this slope, well into the summer, and one should exercise some caution here. After one more bench this ascent terminates at a tundra-topped saddle that straddles the divide north of Slide Mountain. Here sparse whitebark pine and hemlock stoop to alpine climes, and the traveler taking a breather at this unnamed pass is likely to hear the scolding of a disturbed cony.

From this pass the trail stepladders down through a series of sandy tundra pockets, serpentining its way north and then east before beginning the long, forested traverse down to Piute Creek. This traverse strikes timberline just below the cross-country turnoff to Ice and Maltby lakes, which is at the ford of the stream draining the swale that gives obvious access to Ice Lake. Fishermen will find the excellent fishing for eastern brook in these two lakes worth the side trip. On the lodgepole and hemlock that line the trail, one will encounter the historic "T" blaze typical of the older trails found in Yosemite National Park—a sign emblazoned on these trails by the U. S. Cavalry in the early part of the century, when it was their responsibility to patrol the Park.

This hiking day terminates at the campsites upstream from the signed turnoff to the cross-country route down Slide Canyon, located on Piute Creek (9600′) along the first ½ mile after the trail comes within sight of the creek. Firewood is abundant, and fishing for eastern brook (to 8″) is fair. This location makes a fine base-camp location for exploratory trips down Slide Canyon or over into Matterhorn Canyon, and it is a traditional base camp for climbers making ascents of Matterhorn Peak and other climbs along the Sawtooth Ridge complex.

3rd Hiking Day **(Campsites, Upper Piute Creek** to **Crown Lake,** 3.5 miles) : Retrace steps of 2nd hiking day.

4th Hiking Day **(Crown Lake** to **Twin Lakes,** 8 miles) : Retrace steps of 1st hiking day.

42   Twin Lakes to Buckeye Creek

TRIP   From Twin Lakes to Buckeye Pack Station (shuttle trip via Peeler Lake and Buckeye Pass). Topo map (15′) *Matterhorn Peak*. Best mid or late season ; 24 miles.

Grade	Trail/layover days	Total recommended days
Leisurely	4/1	5
Moderate	3/1	4
Strenuous	3/0	3

HILITES   Using the alpine reaches of Buckeye Pass, this shuttle trip circles Buckeye Ridge. It visits nearly the entire gamut of Sierran ecology from the sagebrush-scrub of the east side to the subalpine grassland of Kerrick Meadow. In between, it winds through pure stands of hemlock, past water-loving clumps of quaking aspen and amidst windblown, gnarled whitebark pine. In its ecological variety it is indeed an "everything trip for everyone."

DESCRIPTION (Moderate trip)

1st Hiking Day **(Twin Lakes** to **Peeler Lake,** 8 miles) : See 1st hiking day, trip 39.

2nd Hiking Day **(Peeler Lake** to **Campsites at The Roughs,** 8 miles) : From the campsites on the west side of Peeler Lake the trail descends along the west outlet (not shown on the topo map). Crossing and recrossing this outlet as it flows down into the marshy upper reaches of Rancheria Creek, the trail winds into the meadow, where it meets the Kerrick Canyon trail. Our route turns right (north) and ascends a gentle slope through the northern end of the meadow. A moderate forest cover of high-elevation pines lines the rest of the gently ascending sand-and-duff trail all the way to the summit of Buckeye Pass. This pass, which is marked by a small, lodgepole-encroached meadow, is the Park boundary, and a metal Park sign indicates an elevation of 9650'. Then the duff trail drops down on the northeast side of the pass, and winds back and forth northeasterly over the infant rill of Buckeye Creek on a gentle-to-moderate descent. From the pass to where the trail veers north after the ford, this descent threads a series of charmingly meadowed steps situated on the northwest side of the creek. These pockets of grassland have grown rich gardens of flowers whose splashy colors invite the passerby to linger. The wildflowers include aster, goldenrod, paintbrush, penstemon, shooting star, larkspur, monkshood, swamp onion, corn lily, Sierra rein-orchis, knotweed, lupine, forget-me-not, buttercup, columbine, and monkeyflower.

Owls hunt these meadows at night, and the daytime traveler should keep a sharp lookout for large convocations of agitated birdlife. At the core of these gatherings, frequently, is an owl seeking protection in dense foliage.

The series of meadows terminates at a ford where the trail crosses to the east side of the creek. This is the last ford until the trail reaches Buckeye Forks. (The topo map incorrectly shows the trail to be on the west side of Buckeye Creek for about ¼ mile shortly below here.) After the ford, the trail continues to descend moderately through an area where the trees are much avalanche-broken, and then fords an unnamed tributary (not shown on the topo map) that tumbles down from Hunewill Peak. As the canyon narrows, the trail passes several excellent campsites and then descends more steeply to the flats at Buckeye Forks. Here the trail fords the South Fork of Buckeye Creek and meets the Piute Meadows trail west of the snow-survey cabin. (The topo map incorrectly shows this junction east of the cabin.) This is a marshy junction, the result of beavers "doing their thing" downstream, and the early-summer traveler may have to skirt around the meadow just west of the cabin. Beyond the junction, the trail fords the North Fork of Buckeye Creek. From this junction, we continue to the campsites at The Roughs as described in 4th hiking day, trip 38.

3rd Hiking Day **(Campsites at The Roughs** to **Buckeye Pack Station,** 8 miles) : See 5th hiking day, trip 38.

43 Twin Lakes to Kerrick Meadow

TRIP From Twin Lakes to Kerrick Meadow (semiloop trip via Crown Lake and Peeler Lake). Topo map (15') *Matterhorn Peak*. Best mid or late season; 23.5 miles.

Grade	Trail/layover days	Total recom-mended days
Leisurely	5/1	6
Moderate	3/1	4
Strenuous	3/0	3

HILITES To use a business metaphor, this trip gives a great return for a minimum investment. From the outset this route is enveloped in magnificent scenery. Along Robinson Creek, the skyline and the immediate surroundings are those of rugged grandeur, consonant with the physical expenditure of effort required on the uphill. As the trip circles Crown Point, it "levels out" both in physical terrain and in emotional impact. The ruggedness gives way to sweeping meadows and rounded summits, providing the traveler an opportunity to absorb some of the impact of this land of contrasts.

DESCRIPTION (Moderate trip)

1st Hiking Day **(Twin Lakes** to **Crown Lake,** 8 miles) : See 1st hiking day, trip 39, and 1st hiking day, trip 40.

2nd Hiking Day **(Crown Lake** to **Peeler Lake,** 7.5 miles) : Rounding the rocky west side of Crown Lake, the trail rises out of the lake basin by steep, rocky switchbacks that offer fine views back of the white snag "ghost forested" inlet to the lake. This ascent levels out as it crosses a dome-flanked saddle and meets the Rock Island Pass trail just west of a tiny lakelet upstream from Crown Lake. This lakelet and the trail junction are set in a sandy meadowed section, with several small lakelets and tarns hidden in willows near the trail. Our route turns right (southwest) and begins the long, steadily traversing climb toward Snow Lake. This traverse gives way to switchbacks midway up the hill and jogs west under Crown Point before resuming its southward course to the willowed outlet of Snow Lake. Looking back from the top of this climb, we have fine views to the east of the soldier-tipped summit of Kettle Peak and the west end of the Sawtooth complex (called Blacksmith Peak). Snow Lake itself, like Peeler Lake to the north, is a crestal lake perched atop a divide, but in angling circles it is best known for its fishery of golden trout. As the trail rounds the rocky north edge of the lake, we see the meadowy lake fringes, which are most extensive at the southwest end. Here the meadows extend from the lake's edge to overtop the low-profiled saddle that is Rock Island Pass (10150'), a few yards southwest of the lake. From this grassy saddle one can absorb the excellent views of the North Boundary Country to the southwest. These views are dominated by Piute Mountain and Price Peak.

From Rock Island Pass the trail descends into the Rancheria Creek drainage, but those wishing an additional exploration of a nearby watershed may elect to contour south from the pass to the easy saddle above the headwaters of Rock Creek. Views of this barren, treeless basin are sweeping in their grandeur, and sufficient justification (should it be needed) for the detour. From this saddle one can drop down to the unnamed tributary that drains Rock Island Pass and rejoin the trail near the long sandy meadows midway down this tributary's drainage. The descent witnesses a change from sparse whitebark pine to a conglomerate forest of lodgepole, hemlock and silver pine. The "T"-blazed trail here undulates sharply over a sandy ridge and then drops moderately through dense forest cover to the meadowed ford of Rancheria Creek.

On the northwest side of the ford the trail meets the Kerrick Canyon trail, where our route turns right and ascends gently up Kerrick Meadow. Rancheria Creek winds its oxbowing way through these sandy grasslands, and on the right we can see large crestal sand accumulations indicating where the living stream has moved across the meadow floor, leaving its spoor. The meadow bottlenecks briefly into a canyon narrows, where the creek tumbles over a silver cascade, and then opens into a beautiful, open, wetter section near the headwaters. In the middle of this marshy section the trail fords one arm of the creek and meets the Peeler Lake trail, where our route turns right (east). From this junction the trail crosses the open meadow and winds through a broken, moderate forest cover of lodgepole. This route crisscrosses back and forth over the west outlet stream from Peeler Lake and arrives at the good campsites along the west shores of this large and beautiful lake (9500'). These campsites offer fine views to the east of Cirque Mountain, Kettle Peak and Crown Point, and the deep waters near the west shore offer fine bank fishing for eastern brook and rainbow (to 14"). Firewood is ample.

3rd Hiking Day (**Peeler Lake** to **Twin Lakes,** 8 miles) : Retrace steps of 1st hiking day, trip 39.

44   Twin Lakes to Horse Canyon

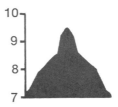

TRIP   From Twin Lakes to Campsites, Upper Horse Canyon (round trip). Topo map (15') *Matterhorn Peak*. Best early, mid or late season; 9 miles.

Grade	Trail/layover days	Total recommended days
Leisurely	2/1	3
Moderate	—	—
Strenuous	—	—

HILITES   This scenic route with its cross-country stretches offers a fine opportunity for the moderately skilled backpacker who wishes to try out his cross-country abilities. The upper stretches of this route demand some bushwhacking and climbing over talus and scree, but the excellent views of the Sawtooth Ridge complex make the necessary slow pace a pleasurable affair. Experienced backpackers will find on this route a choice base-camp location for exploring the north side of the Sawtooth Ridge complex or the class 3 south-face ascent of Matterhorn Peak.

DESCRIPTION

1st Hiking Day **(Twin Lakes** to **Campsites, Upper Horse Creek,** 4.5 miles)** : The trailhead at Mono Village (7092′) is located at the south end of the private campground of the Mono Village complex. There is a fee for parking on this private property. At the south end of the campground, the trail leaves from the peripheral campground road and crosses Robinson Creek via a small wooden bridge. During the fall Kokanee salmon run, this bridge is a fine observation spot from which one can watch the spawning rituals of these colorful fish. Migrating miles downstream in their adulthood, the salmon answer the instinct to reproduce with annual returns to the spawning beds upstream. Their return journeys entail many decisions at forks of the stream, and only recently has the mystery been unraveled of how these fish find their way back to the same spawning beds whence they sprang. Maze studies of salmon and other migrating fishes have shown that they have an uncanny sense of smell, and that they retrace their downstream meanderings by an ancestral memory of the smell of their birthplace.

Leaving the Kokanee salmon behind, the trail veers eastward through dense Jeffrey pine and white fir and fords Horse Creek. A few yards past the ford our trail passes a trail that circles the south shores of the Twin Lakes and begins a long, switchbacking ascent of the lateral moraine to the south. This ascent soon rises above the dense forest cover, and becomes dry on open slopes covered by low-growing manzanita and sagebrush. The glacial till and silt of this hillside are clear evidence of the glacier that carved the valley below; looking east, one can see clearly the path the glacier took as it ground its way northeast, pushing out the debris to either side. Near the top of this ascent the trail traverses a bushy slope that affords excellent views of mulifaceted Horsetail Falls, and then it joins the creek just above the falls. This juncture is marked by two magnificent samples of the silver pine of this region of the Sierra, whose girths indicate that they saw the passage of early pioneers in this area.

After one more dogleg switchback the trail levels out in the hanging valley called Horse Canyon. The first part of this valley has a beautiful stand of lodgepole and silver pine, and several excellent campsites near the meandering stream. About ¼ mile beyond these campsites the trail passes the signed junction to Cattle Canyon and ascends gently past a lovely small snowmelt tarn. Although trail maintenance by the Forest Service stops at the Cattle Canyon junction, climbers using the valley for access to Sawtooth Ridge have made the trail beyond the junction quite clear. The obvious trail disappears, however, as it enters thickets of small aspen and willow mixed with boulders. Bushwhacking here alternates with bouldering along a route on the east side of the creek which is sometimes a trace and sometimes ducked. Ahead, views of Matterhorn Peak and the Sawtooth Ridge complex come into sight, and one can make out such famous climbs as Dragtooth, Doodad, Three Teeth and The Cleaver. Since 1899 climbers have left record of their passage by wearing this unimproved trail into the rock and sod, and each year adds to the number who make the pilgrimage. Our route then climbs steeply over a talus rockslide that descended from the east side of the canyon. This scrambling climb sees the ducked route cross over the stream near the top. There is no ford — the stream being a mere rumble beneath the dry rocks.

At the top of the rockslide, the route continues to ascend moderately through sparse stands of whitebark pine and hemlock. In these stands next to the creek one will find fair campsites, where wood is scarce. Now along the west side of the creek our route continues to ascend in stepladder style over piles of scree and talus, and at each leveling is a stand of lodgepole, whitebark pine and hemlock surrounding a fair-to-good campsite (9520' to 9600'). All these sites offer excellent views upstream of the many-hued peaks making up the north face of Sawtooth Ridge. To the south Twin Peaks stand in dark splendor, footed by the icy blue of glaciers. These glaciers are responsible for the slate-gray color of Horse Creek, as they release glacial silt suspended in the melted ice and snow. Mirrored in the gray of Horse Creek are the upper reaches of Horse Canyon, where those wishing to try the easier class 3 south-face ascent of Matterhorn Peak should plan their access. These campsites in upper Horse Canyon are also ideal base-camp locations for scrambling exploration of the north side of Sawtooth Ridge via Cleaver Col, Avalanche Lake and Glacier Lake.

2nd Hiking Day **(Campsites, Upper Horse Creek** to **Twin Lakes,** 4.5 miles) : Retrace steps of 1st hiking day.

Twin Lakes to Hetch Hetchy

45

TRIP   From Twin Lakes to O'Shaughnessy Dam via Bear Valley (shuttle trip). Topo maps (15') *Matterhorn Peak, Tower Peak, Hetch Hetchy Reservoir*. Best mid or late season; 45.1 miles.

Grade	Trail/layover days	Total recommended days
Leisurely	8/2	10
Moderate	7/2	9
Strenuous	6/2	8

HILITES   Striking through the heart of the North Boundary Country, this trip crosses the Sierra crest at Peeler Lake and thence, with a detour to Pleasant Valley, traces the course of Rancheria Creek from its beginning to the point where it enters the pipeline to San Francisco faucets. The long trans-Sierra crossing endears this trip to the solitude-seeker by virtue of the fact that it is one of the least traveled yet most scenic trails in Yosemite.

DESCRIPTION (Strenuous trip)

1st Hiking Day **(Twin Lakes to Peeler Lake,** 8 miles) : See 1st hiking day, trip 39.

2nd Hiking Day **(Peeler Lake to Arndt Lake,** 5 miles) : Leaving Peeler Lake via the west outlet, the trail drops down gently as it crosses back and forth over the outlet stream. This descent soon leaves the moderate lodgepole-pine forest cover and enters the northern edge of Kerrick Meadow. Crossing these open, rank grasslands, the trail fords an arm of the creek and meets the Buckeye Pass trail, where our route turns left (south). Kerrick Meadow proves a long, gentle descent. The trail stays to the west side of twisting Rancheria Creek and is a narrow, sandy track lined with a wildflower collage of shooting star, penstemon, lousewort, paintbrush, forget-me-not, aster, goldenrod, fleabane, buttercup, lupine, Douglas phlox, blue gentian and pussypaws. In a timber-lined bottleneck the meadows narrow briefly and then reopen. On the left one can see sand banks that were stranded when the oxbowing stream altered course sometime in the geologic past. The broad grasslands are alive with the scurrying and piping of the alarmed Belding ground squirrel.

The trail then passes the Rock Island Pass trail and continues to descend into a second timbered bottleneck. This brief stretch of lodgepole pine opens to yet another long meadow that is flanked on the southwest by the granite heights of Price Peak and, lower down, by the drainage leading down from Arndt Lake. On the descent through this meadow the canyon narrows, and where the Arndt Lake outlet stream joins Rancheria Creek our route leaves the trail.

This short cross-country route strikes out southward, fords Rancheria Creek, and ascends the tundra-lined outlet of Arndt Lake. A good crossing to the north shore of hidden Arndt Lake can be made via the saddle on the granite just east of where the outlet leaves the lake.

One will find good campsites at the outlet and around the north and east shores of Arndt Lake (9600'). Campers will find the firewood ample, and those with a tolerance for cool mountain water will enjoy the swimming off the granite shield that drops into this lake. Views of the polished granite domes flanking the south and east sides of the lake are soul-satisfying, and beckon the explorer to further investigation and discovery. The fishery is unknown.

3rd Hiking Day **(Arndt Lake** to **Upper Bear Valley Lake,** 7 miles): (Note that the Upper Bear Valley Lake referred to here is the lake shown on the topo map beside the label "Bear Valley." The topo's label is a misidentification. Bear Valley is really the next cirque basin south of the one so labeled on the map.) From Arndt Lake our route retraces the cross-country segment of the previous hiking day to the Kerrick Canyon trail, and then continues down through a narrow, rocky canyon just west of Arndt Lake. The unseamed white granite canyon walls in this narrows show the glacial polish, smoothing and sculpting that is the geologic history of the canyon. Rancheria Creek on the left bumps and splashes down through a series of fine potholes offering swimming and fishing spots. Like all the older trails in the Park, this one is "T"-blazed, indicating that it was once a U. S. Cavalry patrol route — a route blazed when the Army was responsible for the integrity of the Park lands.

The sparse-to-moderate forest cover of whitebark, hemlock and lodgepole pine found in the narrows gives way to another meadow as the trail continues to descend. This meadow is surrounded by several magnificent examples of glacial domes — all unnamed. The clean, sweeping lines of the dome to the west are particularly impressive, and the passerby cannot help but feel the awesome power of the natural forces that created it. Near the foot of the meadow, the trail fords to the east side of Rancheria Creek, where it hugs the sheer, water-stained granite wall. Both the trail and the creek make an exaggerated "Z" before straightening out on a westward course and passing the Seavey Pass/Benson Lake trail junction. Beyond this junction the trail undulates along the south wall of Kerrick Canyon. As it passes below the heavily fractured north facade of Piute Mountain, it is sometimes high above the creek and sometimes on the creek's banks. Many tributaries, varying in size from step-across to jump-across fords, break this route segment into lush gardens of monkeyflower, tiger lily, shooting star, bush lupine, corn lily, columbine and goldenrod. (Most of these tributaries are not shown on the topo map.) As the canyon walls open, the trail descends close to the creek and passes the Tilden Lake trail junction. A few steps past this ford and junction our route begins a steep switchbacking ascent up the south wall of Kerrick Canyon. Winding back and forth through a moderate forest cover of lodgepole pine, silver pine and hemlock, the trail near the top affords superlative views to the north and northeast. The panorama includes the hallmark of the North Boundary Country, Tower Peak.

These views behind, the trail tops the canyon wall and emerges suddenly to the dramatic setting of Upper Bear Valley Lake (9200'). Drama at this alpine gem of a lake is provided by a spectacular granite pinnacle on the south side of the lake that spires upward, 600 feet above the lake's surface. Here excellent camping may be found in the timbered swales between the long granite fingers that slide under the north edge of the lake. Firewood is abundant and swimming is excellent. The fishery is unknown.

4th Hiking Day **(Upper Bear Valley Lake** to **Irwin Bright Lake,** 7.5 miles) : The trail from Upper Bear Valley Lake drops down along the outlet, Breeze Creek, and then fords to the east. The descent through a moderate forest cover of lodgepole pine, hemlock, silver pine and occasional whitebark pine passes a marsh-fringed lake, and then climbs over an easy ridge to Bear Valley. This valley, the headwaters of the south fork of Breeze Creek, is a large, circular, sandy meadow with a beautifully whitened silver-pine snag in its middle.

The trail then fords the south fork of Breeze Creek and begins a steep ascent. The trail on this ascent is indistinct in the willowy sections, but the tedium of route-finding is made more tolerable by the fine wildflower displays along this wet slope. Included in these displays are lush stands of red columbine, lupine, aster, fleabane, monkeyflower, paintbrush, tiger lily, currant, lilac, forget-me-not, golden brodiaea, and shooting star. At the top of this long climb the trail levels out on a long, sandy saddle offering spectacular views to the north. Evidence of the ambitious pocket gopher can be seen on every side in the form of its sand castings.

The sandy trail then makes a long, gradual descent across a meadow filled with brilliant fields of lupine, corn lily, whorled penstemon, lousewort, lavender paintbrush and goldenrod, and then re-enters dense timber of lodgepole, hemlock, silver pine and some white fir. Views across the rolling country to the south include Colby Mountain and occasional glimpses of Mt. Clark.

Our trail then fords one fork of an unnamed tributary of Rancheria Creek, and skirts the edge of the meadowed head of another branch of this same tributary. In midsummer this meadow is filled with shoulder-high corn lily and cow parsnip, making the route sometimes difficult to pick out. Fording this branch, the trail winds through dense stands of red fir and lodgepole pine. Some stands of lodgepole have been struck by the needle-miner and are fast becoming ghost forests.

The trail then skirts the west edge of a marshy lake set in dense stands of lodgepole pine, and near the outlet encounters some quaking aspen. Just past this marshy lake one has his first views into the Piute Creek drainage, and these views are impressive in their scope. The steep east wall of the canyon holding Pleasant Valley is deeply scarred with gigantic granite avalanche chutes, while the near wall shows signs of a recent forest fire.

Then, at the crest of a knife-like ridge, the trail comes to the junction with the Pleasant Valley trail, where our route turns left and descends by steep switchbacks into Pleasant Valley. Views along this descent include the Cathedral Range to the southeast and the granite domes up Piute Creek Canyon just below Benson Lake and Volunteer Peak. In Pleasant Valley the trail fords Piute Creek and then it ascends over a rocky saddle to grass-fringed Table Lake. Rounding the south end of this lake, the trail undulates over another rocky divide to the moderately forested south shore of Irwin Bright Lake (7100′).

Good campsites along the south shore and near the outlet provide an excellent base-camp location for exploratory and fishing excursions to nearby Saddle Horse Lake. All three of the lakes in Pleasant Valley hold rainbow, and fishing is good. Firewood is ample.

5th Hiking Day **(Irwin Bright Lake** to **Rancheria Creek,** 11.1 miles) : Retrace steps of 4th hiking day to the top of the ridge and the Hetch Hetchy Reservoir trail, where our route turns left (southwest) toward the dry slopes of Rancheria Mountain. (As the first water is five miles from the starting point of this hiking day, it is suggested that the traveler carry a full water bottle.) From the above-mentioned junction the trail ascends moderately through hemlock, red and white fir and occasional lodgepole. This forest cover gives way to open meadow at the rounded crest of Rancheria Mountain, and the trail winds through fields of mule ears. Beyond the meadow, the trail re-enters timber, crosses the summit, and begins a moderate descent that fords the stream draining the west shoulder of Rancheria Mountain. Near this ford the wildflower fancier will want to linger in the lush clumps of thigh-high lupine and larkspur, and right on the stream banks quaking aspens shade scarlet patches of columbine and rank clusters of the long-leafed corn lily.

The trail veers southward to the next stream before resuming its westward course, and at this second stream it passes an ancient, notched-log cabin built by a trapper before the turn of the century. Crossing the drainage separating the unnamed creek near the cabin and the creek forded earlier, the trail touches the edge of the same forest-fire scars that were seen enroute to Pleasant Valley. Here Jeffrey pine, incense cedar and fir show blackened trunks from the holocaust that swept the mountain. Since the fire, brush has taken over much of the hillside, and it proves a haven for many coveys of quail. Most of the brush is manzanita, mixed with ceanothus. The descent here reflects the drop in altitude as deciduous forest makes its appearance in the form of black oak, and lower-growing conifers, like the sugar pine, appear. Across the reservoir to the south and southwest one can see the perpendicular scars of the avalanche chutes east of Smith Peak, and as the trail nears LeConte Point, Kolana Rock comes into sight.

The trail then ascends gently over the east shoulder of the rounded granite prominence of LeConte Point. On this shoulder the reservoir itself comes into view, and the blue of the water is a cool invitation to the good swimming available at Rancheria Creek. The trail then begins a series of steep, rocky switchbacks down a long slope which terminate at the metal bridge crossing

just above Rancheria Falls. Deep potholes above and below the bridge caught in smooth granite bedrock beckon to the swimmer, and the campsites (4550') a few yards below the falls are a welcome end to this hiking day. Fishing on Rancheria creek for rainbow (to 13") is good, and firewood is adequate.
6th Hiking Day **(Rancheria Creek** to **O'Shaughnessy Dam,** 6.5 miles) : See 1st hiking day, trip 51.

46   Twin Lakes to Benson Lake

TRIP   From Twin Lakes to Benson Lake (round trip). Topo maps (15') *Matterhorn Peak, Tower Peak.* Best mid or late season; 42 miles.

Grade	Trail/layover days	Total recommended days
Leisurely	9/3	12
Moderate	6/3	9
Strenuous	4/2	6

HILITES   This long trip penetrates to the heart of the North Boundary Country. In its course it surmounts the Sierra crest and traces a westside watershed to the Shangri La basin of Benson Lake. Because of its moderate climes and its remote location, this lake is a favorite layover spot for parties traversing the Tahoe-Yosemite Trail, and its popularity is well founded.

DESCRIPTION (Moderate trip)

1st Hiking Day **(Twin Lakes** to **Peeler Lake,** 8 miles) : See 1st hiking day, trip 39.

2nd Hiking Day **(Peeler Lake** to **Arndt Lake,** 5 miles) : See 2nd hiking day, trip 45.

3rd Hiking Day **(Arndt Lake** to **Benson Lake,** 8 miles) : Proceed to the Kerrick Canyon/Benson Lake trail junction as described in the 3rd hiking day, trip 45. At this junction our route turns left (south) and ascends steadily by switchbacks through a moderate forest cover of hemlock. At the top of the first rise Piute Mountain comes into sight, and the trail levels briefly as it wends past a tiny snowmelt tarn. The trail then resumes climbing steeply through an increasingly sparse forest cover of lodgepole, hemlock and silver pine to Seavey Pass (9150′).

From the glacially polished granite setting of Seavey Pass the trail drops past another stately rockbound tarn just below the pass, and finally plummets down over steep, eroded pitches alongside a riotous unnamed stream that feeds the Benson Lake alluvial fan. This descent is rocky going, requiring a "grunt and bear it" attitude of the downhill-weary traveler alleviated only by the fine views of Volunteer Peak across the Piute Creek drainage and of the splashing waterfall springing from the ridge south of Piute Mountain.

As the trail levels out on the valley floor it crosses the sandy alluvial sediments, and witnesses some drastic changes in the flora. The initial contact with the valley floor, with its solitary-standing specimens of Jeffrey pine towering amidst gooseberry, gives the traveler the impression of sandy aridity. Within a few yards, the atmosphere changes as the trail becomes immersed in bracken fern, overflow freshets and dense forest. The trail is sometimes difficult to follow because of the rank growth and quagmire conditions of the valley floor, but some wandering brings one to the junction with the short spur lateral to Benson Lake, just before the ford of Piute Creek. This lateral winds along the northwest bank of Piute Creek through fields of corn lily and bracken fern, with occasional clumps of tiger lily and swamp onion, to the good campsites just beyond the drift fence along the east shore of the lake (7600′). Campers will find the supply of firewood ample, and fishermen can look forward to good fishing for rainbow and eastern brook trout (to 14″). Except in mosquito season, this lake makes a fine spot for a layover day.

4th Hiking Day **(Benson Lake** to **Arndt Lake,** 8 miles) : Retrace steps of 3rd hiking day.

5th Hiking Day **(Arndt Lake** to **Peeler Lake,** 5 miles) : Retrace steps of 2nd hiking day.

6th Hiking Day **(Peeler Lake** to **Twin Lakes,** 8 miles) : Retrace steps of 1st hiking day.

47 **Twin Lakes to Smedberg Lake**

TRIP   From Twin Lakes to Smedberg Lake (semiloop trip via Peeler Lake, Arndt Lake, Benson Lake, Smedberg Lake, Matterhorn Canyon and Burro Pass). Topo maps (15') *Matterhorn Peak, Tower Peak.* Best mid or late season; 52 miles.

Grade	Trail/layover days	Total recommended days
Leisurely	11/3	14
Moderate	8/3	11
Strenuous	5/2	7

HILITES   Making a grand loop through the center of the North Boundary Country, this trip traces three major watersheds, visits six major lakes, and views the finest scenery in the region. Layover days taken on this long route provide the opportunity of visiting any of the nearby lakes, over a dozen, or making side trips into any one of several other watersheds. It is a long trip with many stiff climbs that make it advisable for the hiker to first prepare himself by taking one or more shorter trips.

DESCRIPTION (Moderate trip)

1st Hiking Day **(Twin Lakes** to **Peeler Lake,** 8 miles): See 1st hiking day, trip 39.

2nd Hiking Day **(Peeler Lake** to **Arndt Lake,** 5 miles): See 2nd hiking day, trip 45.

3rd Hiking Day **(Arndt Lake** to **Benson Lake,** 8 miles): See 3rd hiking day, trip 45, and 3rd hiking day, trip 46.

4th Hiking Day **(Benson Lake** to **Smedberg Lake,** 4.5 miles): There is an old saying among those who have visited Benson Lake, "Everywhere from that hole in the ground is up," and one contemplating this hiking day must agree. Retracing our

**Boulder-strewn meadow
above Rock Island Lake**

Karl Schwenke

A rest stop to enjoy the view back over Steelhead and Saddlebag lakes

Don Denison

The matchless Sierra dawn *Don Denison*

Rockslide on Forsyth Peak *Karl Schwenke*

Don Denison

The early riser
may share morning
with a browsing mule deer

A few last casts
before the alpenglow fades to night

Thomas Winnett

The early-season snow plant

Ron Felzer

The Hetch Hetchy,
a drowned counterpart of Yosemite Valley

Don Denison

May Lake, Yosemite

Esther Higgins

**Lodgepoles capture
the soft morning sun**

**Lyell Canyon
of the Tuolumne River**

steps over the short lateral to the main trail, the route then fords Piute Creek and begins a long, steep, dry climb through a moderate forest cover of lodgepole laced with occasional silver pine. Criss-crossing back and forth over the outlet stream from Smedberg Lake, the trail then circles beneath the steep west facade of Volunteer Peak, and finally crosses over the shoulder of this peak just past the first of two trail junctions to Pate Valley. On the north side of Volunteer Peak the trail drops abruptly to the south shore of Smedberg Lake (9220'), where excellent campsites may be found all along the south shore and along the inlet. Firewood is ample, and fishing for rainbow and occasional eastern brook (to 13") is excellent. As a layover point this picturesque, island-dotted lake makes a fine central location for excursions to nearby Surprise and Sister lakes.

5th Hiking Day **(Smedberg Lake** to **Matterhorn Canyon,** 6.5 miles)**: From the narrow valley holding Smedberg Lake, the trail is a steady climb to Benson Pass. It first follows an inlet of Smedberg Lake on a southward, meadowed course, then swings east on a stepladdering climb through moderate forest cover to an upper meadow above the main drainage feeding Smedberg Lake. After this brief respite the trail resumes its steep, rocky, upward course to Benson Pass (10139'). The last climb is over a heavily eroded surface through sparse whitebark pine and hemlock. Excellent views to the north present themselves at the pass, and one can see the complex of pinnacles making up Sawtooth Ridge and the granite divide between Matterhorn Creek and Piute Creek.

The trail leaves Benson Pass on a descent that is at first gentle, later moderate as it drops to Wilson Canyon, and finally steep as it plunges down along the shores of Wilson Creek to Matterhorn Canyon. In this last section the trail winds back and forth over Wilson Creek through an increasingly dense forest cover of lodgepole, with occasional whitebark pine near the top and silver pine near the bottom. On the canyon floor, Matterhorn Canyon Creek is a meandering stream flowing alternately through willowed meadows and stands of lodgepole mixed with silver pine and hemlock. As our trail turns north, it fords to the campsites on the east side of the creek, in the meadows and just upstream. These canyon campsites (8480') have ample firewood, and boast several fine swimming holes just upstream in the granite potholes. They are located at the junction with the Tuolumne Meadows trail. Fishing for eastern brook and rainbow trout (to 12") is good.

6th Hiking Day **(Matterhorn Canyon** to **Campsites, Upper Piute Creek,** 8.5 miles)**: From these campsites on the Tahoe-

Yosemite Trail, our route turns north and leaves that trail behind. The route ascends moderately through alternately sandy and rocky sections, climbing through a series of tiny meadows. On both sides of the canyon, glaciated gray granite shoulders drop to the valley floor, and the black water-staining on their broad surfaces, particularly on Quarry Peak, makes eerie configurations. In a wet section where the trail fords several small tributary runoffs (not shown on the topo map), it winds through wildflower displays that include false Solomon's seal, lupine, lousewort, monkeyflower, paintbrush, goldenrod, aster, fleabane, buckwheat and Mariposa lily. The trail then fords to the west side of Matterhorn Canyon Creek and then refords to follow the east bank through the canyon narrows. At the foot of a meadow it then refords back to the west side.

From this ford the trail keeps to the west side of the creek, winding through meadow and tundra sections on a steady-to-moderate ascent. Ahead, the pointed tops of Finger Peaks come into view, and later the massive granite of Whorl Mountain and Matterhorn Peak. Scattered clumps of lodgepole and hemlock dot the trail as it progresses up to the sky-parlor meadows of the upper cirque basin. Each clump of trees holds a campsite (their protected location is testimony to the wind that often sweeps through the canyon), and the tree clumps are interspersed with stretches of grassland laced with sage, primrose and willow.

The trail passes the last stand of trees, and ascends steadily on a long traverse below Finger Peaks. Views across the barren upper cirque basin of Whorl Mountain are awesome, and its domelike massiveness contrasts sharply with the delicate wildflowers found underfoot as one nears Burro Pass. Here, scattered amongst sparse whitebark pines, one enjoys the spots of color provided by primrose, scarlet penstemon, wallflower and Douglas phlox.

The final climb to the divide is accomplished via rocky switchbacks that terminate on the low saddle of Burro Pass (10560'). Fine views of both the Matterhorn and Piute Creek drainages are to be had, but overshadowing all are the soldier-topped summits of Sawtooth Ridge to the north.

The first recorded crossing of this pass was made by Lt. N. F. McClure in 1894. Today's traveler can compare his observations of the pass and its surroundings with those of McClure, who said, "The route now led for five miles through little meadows on each side of the stream, until a comparatively low saddle was seen to the left of us and near the head of the canyon. Investigating this, I found it was a natural pass. The scenery here was truly sublime. I doubt if any part of the main chain of the Sierras presents a greater ruggedness . . ."

As the trail descends on the north side of the pass, it affords fine views of the tiny, barren lakes at the foot of Finger Peaks. The basin of the pass is usually wet, and sometimes covered with snow, thereby making route-picking an instinctive matter. Here Piute Creek is a far cry from what was seen two hiking days ago. A mere stripling of a stream, it tinkles through meadow grass, and the traveler fords to the north side by an easy step. Beldings pipe one's passage through the grassy tundra stretches, and the call of the marmots on the nearby scree is a cacophonous accompaniment to the gentle descent into the moderate forest cover of lodgepole and hemlock. This hiking day ends at the good campsites (9600') found along that stretch of Piute Creek where the trail touches the creek banks northeast of Finger Peaks. Here fishing for eastern brook (to 8") is fair. Firewood is ample.

7th Hiking Day **(Campsites, Upper Piute Creek** to **Crown Lake,** 3.5 miles) : See 2nd hiking day, trip 41.

8th Hiking Day **(Crown Lake to Twin Lakes,** 8 miles) : See 1st hiking day, trip 40.

Green Creek to East Lake

48

TRIP   From Green Creek Roadend to East Lake (round trip). Topo map (15') *Matterhorn Peak*. Best early, mid or late season ; 7 miles.

Grade	Trail/layover days	Total recommended days
Leisurely	2/0	2
Moderate	—	—
Strenuous	—	—

HILITES   This is a fine beginner's weekend hike. East Lake offers one of the most colorful backdrops to a camping scene to be found in any wilderness. The trilogy

of Gabbro, Page and Epidote peaks are composed of
rocks varying in hue from vermilion reds to ochre,
and these colors are set in metavolcanic blacks for
contrast. Nearby Nutter, Gilman and Hoover lakes
offer good fishing to supplement that found in East
Lake, and the general spectrum of scenery along the
trail rounds out a rich diet indeed.

DESCRIPTION

1st Hiking Day **(Green Creek Roadend** to **East Lake,** 3.5
miles) : The trailhead is just beyond the Green Lakes Pack
Station at the road's end. Here a trail register and a sign indicating that this trail is closed to motorized vehicles mark the
beginning of this hiking day. Amid moderate-to-dense Jeffrey,
juniper, lodgepole and aspen forest cover, the trail ascends
gently to a small step-across spring runoff. A ground cover of
sage, mule ears, serviceberry, western blueberry, wild lilac, lupine, wallflower, paintbrush, pennyroyal and buckwheat lines
the trail in the initial drier stretches, and along the wetter spots
one finds tiger lily, penstemon, shooting star, monkshood, monkeyflower, columbine, rein-orchis and aster. The ascent then
becomes steeper as it crosses an easy rocky ridge, and finally it
begins a long series of steady switchbacks.

Crossing several intermittent runoff tributaries coming down
from Monument Ridge, the trail keeps to the northwest side
of the West Fork of Green Creek. While the creek itself is never
out of hearing, it is often obscured visually by the sheath of
willows that line its bank. Ahead, on the left, one can make
out Gabbro Peak, and on the right the stream that falls from
the hanging valley containing West Lake. Added to the wildflowers to be seen along the trail here are iris, corn lily, cow
parsnip, stickseed, gooseberry, Douglas phlox and pussypaws.

The trail then climbs another dry slope by moderately ascending switchbacks to an old cabin site. Here our trail passes the
trail to West Lake, and then leads through a stand of hemlock
to the east shore of Green Lake. Anglers may wish to tarry here
for the good fishing for rainbow and eastern brook (to 14″).
Green Lake is large (about 50 acres), with a rocky west shore
and a steep southeast shore. A mixed timber cover of lodgepole,
hemlock and occasional silver pine surrounds most of the lake
except for the meadowed inlet delta.

Our route fords the West Fork of Green Creek just below
the lake, and makes a long dogleg to the south before turning
east to ford the outlet stream from East Lake. This outlet stream,
not shown on the topo map, is a vigorous watercourse that fol-

lows the natural ravine shown on the topo just north of East Lake. The trail continues east on another long dogleg, and then turns south to reford the outlet stream. The ascent is sometimes steep as it continues on to the meadowed outlet of East Lake. Here fair-to-good campsites (9440') can be found around the outlet just below the flood-control dam, and around the north shore. Firewood is plentiful, and fishing for rainbow on this 75-acre lake is good. This lake makes a fine base-camp location for forays to nearby Nutter, Gilman and Hoover lakes.

2nd Hiking Day (**East Lake** to **Green Creek Roadend**, 3.5 miles): Retrace steps of 1st hiking day.

Green Creek to Tuolumne Meadows

TRIP From Green Creek Roadend to Tuolumne Meadows (shuttle trip). Topo maps (15') *Matterhorn Peak, Tuolumne Meadows.* Best mid or late season; 25 miles.

Grade	Trail/layover days	Total recommended days
Leisurely	4/1	5
Moderate	4/0	4
Strenuous	3/0	3

HILITES Three quarters of this scenic route travels remote sections of Yosemite National Park that are not frequented by day walkers. The solitude-seeker will find the quiet of upper Virginia Canyon to his liking, and the fisherman wanting a variety of lake and stream fishing for rainbow and eastern brook will pronounce this trip ideal for his purposes.

DESCRIPTION (Moderate trip)

1st Hiking Day **(Green Creek Roadend** to **East Lake,** 3.5 miles) : See 1st hiking day, trip 48.

2nd Hiking Day **(East Lake** to **Campsites, Lower Virginia Canyon,** 9 miles) : From the outlet of East Lake the trail ascends above the lake's waters as it rounds the east shore, affording superlative views of Gabbro, Page and Epidote peaks foregrounded by the deep blue of East Lake. The trail drops briefly across the gentle ridge separating East Lake from the tiny lakelets to the east, and then veers away from East Lake on a gentle ascending traverse before descending gently to the meadow-fringed shores of Nutter Lake. Through a sparse forest cover of lodgepole and hemlock, the trail then ascends to beautiful Gilman Lake. Flanked by the steep west face of Dunderberg Peak, and foregrounded by a meadow and timber cover, this lake is a favorite of photographers. Fishermen may also wish to linger — the better to sample the good fishing for rainbow.

From the west shore of Gilman Lake the trail ascends past several small tarns, fords the stream joining Gilman and Hoover lakes, and then rises steeply to the bench holding Hoover Lakes. These two alpine lakes are set between the dark rock of Epidote Peak and the burgundy-red rock of the magnificent unnamed mountain to the southeast. They are considerably colder than the lakes below, and they have been planted with eastern brook trout. The trail skirts the southeast side of the first, fords the stream between them, and passes by the northwest side of the second. After fording the inlet, it ascends steeply along the stream joining Hoover Lakes with Summit Lake. This rocky ascent through a thinning forest cover of lodgepole and occasional hemlock and whitebark pine meets the Virginia Lakes trail on a small bench, where our route turns right (northwest). This moderate ascent fords the intermediate stream and arrives at aptly named Summit Lake (10160'). Like Peeler Lake to the north, Summit Lake contributes water to both sides of the Sierra. It sits atop the crest in a Veed notch between the dark rock of Camiaca Peak and a lighter ridge extending north from Excelsior Mountain.

The trail rounds the north side of Summit Lake and switchbacks down steeply on the west side. Looking back toward Summit Lake, we can see clearly that the glaciers which had their beginnings below Camiaca Peak on both the east and the west sides met at the present site of Summit Lake. Across the cirque basin of upper Virginia Canyon, the rounded eminence of Grey Butte and the sharply nippled tops of Virginia Peak and Stanton

Peak dominate the views to the west. The descent levels out as it fords Return Creek and continues down canyon. Recent avalanches have made obvious incursions into the sparse forest cover of lodgepole, aspen and occasional red fir and hemlock, and have left broken stubs on every hand.

The trail then fords several tributary streams as it keeps to the west side of Return Creek on a long, moderate descent to a junction with the Matterhorn Canyon trail. At this junction our route turns left, fords Return Creek, and arrives at the good campsites (8600') in the granite ledge system on the east side of the creek. Firewood is ample, and fishing for eastern brook and rainbow is fair to good.

3rd Hiking Day **(Campsites, Lower Virginia Canyon** to **Glen Aulin,** 8 miles) : The trail from the campsites near the ford differs from that shown on the topo map in that it continues southwest along the banks of Return Creek and fords McCabe Creek before beginning the steep ascent of the canyon wall. This gentle descent along Return Creek tours the stream's beautiful bedrock-granite cascades. Dropping into deep, clear potholes, the creek has carved and sculpted the bedrock into smooth, mollescent lines that beg the traveler to run his hands across them. Columbine clustered amidst lupine and whorled penstemon add color to the green mats of swamp onion and gooseberry near the ford. Beyond this ford the trail begins long switchbacks across a slope moderately forested with fine specimens of silver pine, lodgepole and occasional red fir. These rocky switchbacks terminate at the McCabe Lakes trail junction. Our route branches right and descends gently over a duff surface. Birdlife abounds through the moderate-to-dense forest cover of red fir, lodgepole and silver pine, and the hiker is very likely to see chickadees, juncos, warblers, flycatchers, woodpeckers, bluebirds, robins and evening grosbeaks.

Undulating gently past the large, unseamed granite dome called Elbow Hill, the trail levels out into a large open meadow that shows a "pinched waist" owing to the encroachment of lodgepole. In the second widening of the meadow, a lesson in the power of exfoliation presents itself in the form of a large boulder that was pried loose from the west wall of the canyon. As the trail nears the end of the meadow one can make out landmarks of the Cathedral Range to the south, including Cathedral Peak, The Cockscomb and The Unicorn. Beyond the meadow, the trail ascends gently over an open ridge, and then begins a long, steady, rocky descent. This rocky stretch has solitary examples of juniper, cracked boulders and glacial erratics as large as a barn. As the descent levels out, the trail crosses a series of tiny meadows near meandering Cold Creek, and then amid sheets of dark granite the trail begins the final, long series of switchbacks that drop down to Glen Aulin. The final rocky turns of the switchbacks afford views across the canyon to Tuolumne Falls and White Cascade. Their roar carries all the way across the canyon.

This hiking day terminates at the fair campsites across Cold Creek from the Glen Aulin High Sierra Camp in a grove of lodgepole and some incense cedar at the foot of the switchbacks. Firewood is scarce, and the "camp bears" that plague the area are a nuisance. Early-spring hikers should take the side trip down the Tuolumne River to California, LeConte and Waterwheel falls. The last-named is particularly outstanding.

4th Hiking Day **(Glen Aulin** to **Tuolumne Meadows,** 4.5 miles) : From the campsites the trail crosses Cold Creek via a steel bridge, and the Tuolumne River by a low wooden one. From the latter bridge one has fine views of White Cascade and its deep green pool just below. The trail then ascends steeply alongside White Cascade, and one has a close-up look at this turbulence. In the midst of the white froth one can make out granite ledges, thrust out by cracking and heaving, that cause the irregular plunges of the water. The lip of the cascade is one gigantic wave thrust up by a submerged ledge. The spume from this cauldron frequently wets the trail, and on a chilly morning the traveler welcomes the point where the trail levels out and passes Tuolumne Falls.

The trail then recrosses the Tuolumne River by two linked wooden bridges. Here the water seems unbelievably calm as it meanders placidly through dense forests of lodgepole, silver pine and hemlock. As the trail ascends gently along the north side of the river, it presents pleasing views of sweeping bends in the river, and deep holes beckon to the swimmer.

Fording Dingley Creek, the trail then passes the junction of the trail to Young Lakes. Then the trail fords Delaney Creek (Delaney Creek and Skelton Lakes are closed to all fishing) by an upstream log, and ascends a long, dry, sandy ridge northwest of Tuolumne Meadows. From the tiny, reeded lakes on top of this ridge the trail drops down through meadowed pockets to the Soda Springs dirt road. Descending past the meadowed structure marking the springs, this hiking day ends at the parking lot 100 yards beyond the springs (8592').

Green Creek to Virginia Lakes

50

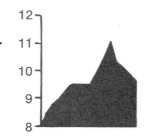

TRIP   From Green Creek Roadend to Virginia Lakes Campground (shuttle trip). Topo map (15') *Matterhorn Peak*. Best mid or late season; 10 miles.

Grade	Trail/layover days	Total recommended days
Leisurely	2/1	3
Moderate	2/0	2
Strenuous	—	—

HILITES   This "U"-shaped trip circles around Kavanaugh Ridge and Dunderberg Peak, and in its passage touches 14 alpine and subalpine lakes. Scenery along this route is mostly of the open alpine variety, and the route is a fine sampling of the majestic Sierra crest. For the beginner or for the experienced backcountry traveler, this trip is an excellent choice for a weekend excursion.

DESCRIPTION

1st Hiking Day **(Green Creek Roadend** to **East Lake,** 3.5 miles) : See 1st hiking day, trip 48.

2nd Hiking Day **(East Lake** to **Virginia Lakes Campground,** 6.5 miles) : Proceed to the Virginia Lakes trail junction as described in 2nd hiking day, trip 49. At this junction our trail turns left (southeast) and climbs steeply up a talus ravine past timberline to a broad, grassy ridge overlooking the headwaters of Virginia Creek and Black Mountain. From the ridge the rocky trail switchbacks down the headwall of the cirque basin on a steep descent, and then levels off as it reaches the sparse whitebark timberline around the shallow, uppermost lake of the Virginia Creek drainage. Frequently there is snow in this upper basin until well into July, and finding the shaley trail as it stepladders down toward Frog Lakes can be a difficult exercise in route-picking. The trail has been altered slightly from that shown on the topo map, now being located farther south where it drops down the tundra steps of Frog Lakes. In Frog Lakes and in the willowed stream between them anglers will find fair fishing for eastern brook and rainbow trout. Just north of Cooney Lake the new trail and that shown on the topo map once more coincide. This granitoid lake, with its willowed inlet and its precipitous outlet, contains thriving populations of eastern brook and rainbow.

Continuing the moderate descent over a rocky ledge system, the trail winds down through sparse clumps of whitebark pine past an active mining claim, and then fords the willowed outlet stream of Moat Lake. In the wetter stretches here, wildflower fanciers will delight in the lush clumps of columbine, swamp onion and shooting star. Under the steep, avalanche-scarred south face of Dunderberg Peak (the second-highest peak in the North Boundary Country), the trail slopes down on a rocky traverse to the outlet of Blue Lake. The broken talus and scree to the north are a haven for marmots and rabbitlike conies, whose scats and hay harvests can be found on and between the rocks next to the trail. Like Cooney Lake, Blue Lake has a fishery of eastern brook and rainbow trout. Past Blue Lake the descending trail is within sight of two more tiny, unnamed lakes. It reaches trail's end at the Forest Service trail register. Following the road as it crosses a gentle, sagebrush-covered ridge, this trip ends at the Virginia Lakes Campground (9760').

51   Hetch Hetchy to Rancheria Creek

TRIP   From O'Shaughnessy Dam (Hetch Hetchy Reservoir) to Rancheria Creek (round trip). Topo maps *Lake Eleanor, Hetch Hetchy Reservoir*. Best early season; 13 miles.

Grade	Trail/layover days	Total recommended days
Leisurely	2/0	2
Moderate	—	—
Strenuous	—	—

HILITES   Early season is the ideal time to view the falls along this route, and eager opening-day anglers will find the good fishing along Rancheria Creek a satisfying culmination to a fine trip.

DESCRIPTION

1st Hiking Day (**O'Shaughnessy Dam** to **Rancheria Creek,** 6.5 miles) : From the trailhead at the south end of the dam, the thunder from the spillway accompanies the traveler as he crosses the 600-foot-long dam. Views to the right (east) across the reservoir waters are flanked by waterfalls on the left and spectacular Kolana Rock on the right. The first 0.7 mile of this route follows the service road to Lake Eleanor. Then the trail branches right and undulates through alternating timbered (digger pine) and meadowed terrain on a long terrace above the reservoir. Grass-pocketed granite slabs where meadow foam blooms in spring at the foot of Tueeulala Falls are a fine place for a breather stop. The trail gets rockier as it approaches larger Wapama Falls, and beneath the rooster-tail spray from the falls it is slippery. This spectacular water drop, little-heralded in Yosemite Park publicity, plummets a total of 1200' in a step-ladder succession of falls, the last step being 200'.

From the bridges across the multibranched creek below the falls, the trail climbs steeply on switchbacks through a bower of bay trees and golden oaks, with here and there some ponderosa pine, incense cedar and digger pine. Leveling out, the trail threads a number of little pocket meadows. After topping a small summit, the trail rollercoasters down and then up, crossing several intermittent runoffs. High points of this segment offer excellent views of the bay into which Tiltill and Rancheria creeks empty. A moderate ascent of another ½ mile takes the hiker to the steel bridge across Tiltill Creek, beyond which the trail climbs steeply for several hundred rocky yards. As one nears Rancheria Creek, he has exciting views of a fine granite bedrock chute over which the creek makes a white ribbon.

Glaciated fields of granite mark the remaining ½ mile of easy climb to the fair campsites (4550') along Rancheria Creek below the falls. These campsites are reached by taking a lateral trail ¼ mile before the junction of the Tiltill Valley trail. Fishing is good for rainbow (to 13″) on Rancheria Creek below Rancheria Falls, and firewood is adequate.

2nd Hiking Day **(Rancheria Creek** to **O'Shaughnessy Dam,** 6.5 miles) : Retrace steps of 1st hiking day.

52   Hetch Hetchy to Tiltill Valley

TRIP   From O'Shaughnessy Dam (Hetch Hetchy Reservoir) to Tiltill Valley (round trip). Topo maps (15′) *Lake Eleanor, Hetch Hetchy Reservoir.* Best early season; 18.6 miles.

Grade	Trail/layover days	Total recom- mended days
Leisurely	4/0	4
Moderate	3/0	3
Strenuous	2/0	2

HILITES   Like the previous trip, this route tours the northern edge of Hetch Hetchy Reservoir. Across the lake the views of Kolana Rock and the sheer granite walls of the Grand Canyon of the Tuolumne provide a majestic accompaniment. The contrasting intimate serenity of Tiltill Valley is a pleasant terminus to this early-season trek.

DESCRIPTION (Leisurely trip)

1st Hiking Day **(O'Shaughnessy Dam** to **Rancheria Creek,** 6.5 miles) : See 1st hiking day, trip 51.

2nd Hiking Day **(Rancheria Creek** to **Tiltill Valley,** 2.8 miles) : From the junction of the Pate Valley/Tiltill Valley trails, the trail to Tiltill Valley climbs steeply 1200′ up to a timber-bottomed saddle. As the trail descends on the north side of the saddle, it traverses a forest of yellow, sugar, and Jeffrey pine with a sprinkling of incense cedar and black oak. When this duff trail emerges at the east end of Tiltill Valley, it meets the trail to Benson Lake. The valley is a long meadow which in early spring is usually quite wet and boggy at the eastern end. Lodgepole pine fringes the meadow, and the valley is flanked by polished outcroppings of granite and by brush-covered slopes. The trail crosses to the north side of the meadow and winds westward to the excellent campsites just south of the Tiltill Creek ford (5600'). These camping places, located in an isolated stand of lodgepole and sugar pine, afford excellent views in both directions down the meadows. Campers have an uninterrupted vantage point from which to watch the large variety of wildlife that make this meadow their home. Fishing on Tiltill Creek for rainbow (to 10″) is excellent in early season. Firewood is plentiful.

3rd Hiking Day **(Tiltill Valley** to **Rancheria Creek,** 2.8 miles) : Retrace steps of 2nd hiking day.

4th Hiking Day **(Rancheria Creek** to **O'Shaughnessy Dam,** 6.5 miles) : Retrace steps of 1st hiking day.

White Wolf to 10 Lakes 53

TRIP From White Wolf Campground to 10 Lakes (round trip). Topo map (15') *Hetch Hetchy Reservoir.* Best mid or late season ; 22 miles.

Grade	Trail/layover days	Total recommended days
Leisurely	4/1	5
Moderate	3/1	4
Strenuous	2/1	3

HILITES This route explores the headwaters of the Middle Fork of the Tuolumne River, crosses to the Yosemite Creek watershed and, near its headwaters, crosses a shoulder to the 10 Lakes Basin (named by John Muir). Wildflower-filled meadows and magnificent stands of lodgepole pine, incense cedar, Jeffrey pine and red fir line this fine route. Fishermen should find the fishing in the 10 Lakes Basin a rewarding climax.

DESCRIPTION (Leisurely trip)

1st Hiking Day **(White Wolf Campground** to **Lukens Lake,** 2.5 miles) : The trail begins at the south entrance to White Wolf Campground (7900') and skirts the meadow just east of White Wolf Lodge. This meadow, like the tinier grasslands that interrupt the lodgepole forest along this route, abounds in wildflowers. The midseason traveler, in particular, cannot help being impressed with the colorful carpet of penstemon, Sierra forget-me-nots, Mariposa lilies, shooting stars, lousewort, and the ever-present lupine. Our route crosses a small rise and descends to cross the Middle Fork of the Tuolumne River. At this point the stream is very small. On the north side of the stream our route intersects the Pate Valley/10 Lakes trail, onto which it turns right (southeast) and continues for ½ mile. At the clearly marked Lukens Lake trail junction, our route branches right (south), and ascends gently to the fair-to-good campsites on Lukens Lake (8200'). Fishing for rainbow (to 12") is fair. Firewood is ample.

2nd Hiking Day **(Lukens Lake** to **10 Lakes,** 8.5 miles) : From Lukens Lake retrace your steps ½ mile to the White Wolf/10 Lakes trail, and turn right (east). This is the beginning of a long, gradual 400' ascent that parallels the Middle Fork of the Tuolumne River almost to its source. In the short 2 miles of gentle uphill grade the traveler passes through healthy stands of lodgepole pine, hemlock and red fir that are inhabited by that noisy fellow, the white-headed woodpecker. Near the spring source of the river, now a jump-across stream, the trail veers southeast and crosses a low saddle to the Yosemite Creek watershed. As one descends on the east side of the ridge there are open views of the glacially formed Yosemite Creek cirque to the northeast and glacially polished granite walls on the western slopes of Mt. Hoffman. Our trail meets the Yosemite Creek/10 Lakes trail, and turns left (northeast). Here it begins a steady ascent that becomes a little steeper just below Half Moon Meadow (8900'). At this altitude springtime arrives later, and hikers frequently see one of the first signs of mountain spring, snowplant, as late as the last week of July. This bright red flower of the heath family lives on decaying organic matter.

At the north end of Half Moon Meadow the trail again ascends steeply, to timberline, and in a meadow near the crest passes the short lateral (not shown on the topo map) to Grant Lakes. The ascent surmounts a rocky ridge separating Yosemite Creek drainage from Tuolumne River drainage, and from this ridge one can survey the surrounding country with a well-earned feeling of omnipotence. Immediately to the east are the blue droplets of the 10 Lakes Basin, each a lake set in its own more intimate basin. To the north, Colby Mountain's east face drops away into the upper reaches of dramatic Muir Gorge. (The gorge is a knapsacker's route travelable *only* during rare years of very low water.) From this crest the trail switchbacks down steeply to the largest and most-used lake in the basin.

Our route branches left (north) along the western shore of this lake and over a low ridge for about ⅓ mile to the fine campsite at the outlet of the northernmost lake (8960′). Here at the foot of Grand Mountain this campsite offers an abundant wood supply, and fishermen will enjoy the good rainbow angling (to 18″). The nearby granite has rain and snow "catch basins" which from early-to-mid July of a typical year make fine, sun-warmed swimming pools.

3rd Hiking Day (**10 Lakes** to **Lukens Lake,** 8.5 miles) : Retrace steps of 2nd hiking day.

4th Hiking Day (**Lukens Lake** to **White Wolf Campground,** 2.5 miles) : Retrace steps of 1st hiking day.

Tioga Road to 10 Lakes   54

TRIP   From Yosemite Creek Trailhead (Tioga Road) to 10 Lakes (round trip). Topo map (15′) *Hetch Hetchy Reservoir*. Best mid or late season ; 13 miles.

Grade	Trail/layover days	Total recom- mended days
Leisurely	2/1	3
Moderate	2/0	2
Strenuous	—	—

HILITES This scenic and instructional tour of the upper reaches of Yosemite Creek also is the easiest and swiftest access to the good fishing in the 10 Lakes Basin. The route includes a 2000' elevation change and provides the traveler with a firsthand look at the forest cover and wildlife in transition between the lodgepole-fir and subalpine life zones.

DESCRIPTION

1st Hiking Day **(Yosemite Creek Trailhead** to **10 Lakes,** 6.5 miles) : From the parking area on the Tioga Road (7500') west of Yosemite Creek, the trail starts out northward across a meadowy section. At first the forest cover is lodgepole pine, but when the level, sandy trail begins to climb, the lodgepole gives way to Jeffrey pine and mountain juniper, and the trail ascends granite slabs. At the top of the first 500' ascent there are sweeping views of Yosemite Creek to the east, flanked by glacially polished granite walls, and in the distance one can make out Mount Hoffman. Continuing northward, the trail levels off and then crosses the west branch of Yosemite Creek. Just before the ford this route meets the Lukens Lake/White Wolf trail; beyond the ford it then veers northeast before beginning the steady ascent to Half Moon Meadow. This meadow, along with Grant Lakes to the east, makes up the headwaters of Yosemite Creek. The present-day trail traveler, like the ones who have gone before, may pause to speculate how long it takes for the water he is looking at to flow the tortuous path to the brink of Yosemite Falls.

From Half Moon Meadow the trail climbs steeply to timberline, and near the crest passes the short lateral (not shown on the topo map) to Grant Lakes. Views are excellent from the point where our route crosses the ridge separating the Yosemite Creek and Tuolumne River drainages. The several lakes making up the 10 Lakes Basin (9 fair-sized ones and numerous tiny lakelets) lie spread out in the basin to the east. Though not all of the 9 lakes are visible from the trail, one can easily make out their individual niches, and can trace their watercourses to where they fall off into the great chasm to the north, the Grand Canyon of the Tuolumne. One gets some idea of the scope of this "gash" by visually following the line of the east face of Colby Mountain into the awesome hole called Muir Gorge.

From this outlook the trail descends by switchbacks that terminate at the largest and most popular lake in the basin. Our route branches left (north) for ⅓ mile over a low ridge to the fine campsite at the outlet of the northernmost of these lakes (8960'). Nearby "catch basins" (meltoff tarns) situated in granite provide excellent, sun-warmed swimming pools from early-to-mid July of a typical year. The campsite here at the foot of Grand Mountain has an abundant wood supply, and angling is good for rainbow (to 18").

2nd Hiking Day (**10 Lakes** to **Yosemite Creek Trailhead,** 6.5 miles): Retrace steps of 1st hiking day.

Saddlebag Lake to McCabe Lakes 55

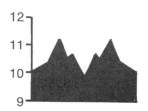

TRIP From Saddlebag Lake to Lower McCabe Lake (round trip). Topo map (15') *Tuolumne Meadows.* Best mid or late season; 11 miles.

Grade	Trail/layover days	Total recommended days
Leisurely	3/0	3
Moderate	2/1	3
Strenuous	—	—

HILITES Alpine from beginning to end, this trip crosses the Sierra crest between the east end of Shepherd Crest and North Peak. High tundra meadows, sparkling clear-water lakes and weathered whitebark pine are hallmarks of this loftily routed excursion. Although the route is not marked as a trail on the topo map, there is either a well-worn trace or adequate duck-on-the-rock markings to delineate the proper route. This is a good trip selection for both novice and advanced backpackers.

DESCRIPTION (Moderate trip)

1st Hiking Day **(Saddlebag Lake** to **Lower McCabe Lake,** 5.5 miles) : Saddlebag Lake (10087′), caught in the barren alpine basin between the Tioga Crest and the main Sierra divide, is one of the largest lakes of the North Boundary Country. About 340 acres in area, it is a long lake to walk around, and hikers may elect to use the boat-taxi that runs the length of the lake from Saddlebag Lake Resort. Rates are reasonable, and the service convenient. However, those who wish to walk should take the mining road that leaves from the east end of the resort area. This road rounds the south end of the lake, and then skirts the rocky, open northeast side of the lake. At various times dating back to the 1880's, it provided access for the numerous mining ventures that occupied the basin above Saddlebag Lake and nearby Lundy Canyon. One claim is still registered as active.

To the east, the gently rounded summits of the Tioga Crest dip to Dore Pass, and hikers with a little imagination can see and hear the struggling men and animals of the winter of 1882 as they "snaked" and hauled 16,000 pounds of mining machinery across this pass on balky skid sleds. Bound for Bennettville, the sleds were lowered to the edge of Saddlebag Lake and run across on the thick midwinter ice.

Near the northwest end of the lake the mining road meets the short trail leading up from the boat-taxi dock, and through a sparse forest cover of stunted lodgepole pine it continues west to the north shore of Greenstone Lake. This rocky lake is backgrounded by the glacier-footed crest of Mt. Conness, and its cold waters hold cutthroat and eastern brook trout. The road then winds gently up through swales in the buckling fields of glacially smoothed granite and past several small tarns to Wasco Lake. The wonderful variety of alpine flora along this gentle ascent sees the appearance of the whitebark pine in the sparse forest cover. Among the predominant wildflowers are primrose, heather, paintbrush (several varieties), wallflower, monkeyflower, penstemon, corn lily, Douglas phlox, alpine columbine and aster.

The road then descends along the gullied stream flowing into Steelhead Lake, and at the south end of Steelhead Lake our cross-country route branches left around the west side of Steelhead Lake. Crossing granite ledges, the route fords Mill Creek, and then veers westerly around the small, unnamed lake to the northwest. At this point, anglers may wish to sample the golden-trout fishing at Cascade Lake before going on. The steep rock-

and-grass-ledge ascent of the crest begins as our route turns northwest beside a flower-lined inlet stream. The course of this tiny rill bends northward, and our route follows it faithfully to the small, unnamed tarn it drains. This tarn, which is frequently snow-covered until late in the summer, lies due southeast of the point on the crestal divide that our route will cross. Following the ducks, our route rounds the east side and ascends very steeply by ledge and diagonal-crevice systems. This zigzag route brings one to the ridge where it meets Shepherd Crest (11210').

Excellent views from here to the northwest include Tower Peak and Saurian Crest. Descending from this ridge, a steep, eroded trail follows the gully northeast of Upper McCabe Lake. This section levels out near some small tarns, and our route continues to the north shore of Upper McCabe Lake. Turning west along the shore, we ford the outlet and then strike out for the low, rock-cairned saddle due west of the outlet. Crossing this saddle, the best route drops past snowmelt tarns (not shown on the topo map) and then winds down through a dense forest cover of lodgepole, whitebark pine and hemlock to the east shore of beautiful Lower McCabe Lake (9850'). The best campsites on the lake are near the outlet. Firewood is ample, and fishing for eastern brook (to 12") is excellent.

2nd Hiking Day **(Lower McCabe Lake** to **Saddlebag Lake,** 5.5 miles) : Retrace steps of 1st hiking day.

56 Saddlebag Lake to Tuolumne Meadows

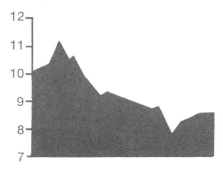

TRIP   From Saddlebag Lake to Tuolumne Meadows (shuttle trip via Lower McCabe Lake, Cold Canyon and Glen Aulin). Topo map (15') *Tuolumne Meadows*. Best mid or late season; 19.0 miles.

Grade	Trail/layover days	Total recom- mended days
Leisurely	4/1	5
Moderate	3/1	4
Strenuous	3/0	3

HILITES   Some hikers may choose this trip for its easy shuttle, but the country that this route tours should be adequate reason in itself. The variety of a trip that is part cross country, part on trail and part over water should appeal to the most jaded mountaineer's appetite. This route does that and more. Crossing the Sierra crestline above Upper McCabe Lake, the trip traverses the long meadows of Cold Canyon, and finishes by touring the splashing cascades and roaring falls of the Tuolumne River.

DESCRIPTION (Moderate trip)

1st Hiking Day **(Saddlebag Lake** to **Lower McCabe Lake,** 5.5 miles) : See 1st hiking day, trip 55.

2nd Hiking Day **(Lower McCabe Lake** to **Glen Aulin,** 9 miles) : From the campsites at the outlet of Lower McCabe Lake the trail descends along the west side of the outlet stream through a moderate-to-dense forest cover of hemlock, lodgepole, whitebark, silver pine and occasional red fir. The trail between Lower McCabe Lake and the place where it veers west is usually very wet and swampy, a soggy condition hospitable to the fields of corn lily that line the way. As the trail veers west it becomes drier, and most of the timber near the trail is lodgepole pine. Flowers indigenous to better-drained soils are found along this section of trail, including wallflower, Douglas phlox, lupine, buckwheat, aster and pussypaws. The descent becomes gentle as the trail passes through a "ghost forest" caused by the needle-miner and crosses an unnamed tributary of McCabe Creek before reaching the junction with the Virginia Canyon trail. At this junction our route turns left (west) and continues to Glen Aulin as described in the third hiking day, trip 49.

3rd Hiking Day **(Glen Aulin** to **Tuolumne Meadows,** 4.5 miles) : See 4th hiking day, trip 49.

Saddlebag Lake to Twin Lakes   57

TRIP From Saddlebag Lake to Twin Lakes (shuttle trip via Lower McCabe Lake, Matterhorn Canyon, Burro Pass, Upper Piute Creek and Crown Lake). Topo maps (15′) *Tuolumne Meadows, Matterhorn Peak.* Best mid or late season ; 34.5 miles.

Grade	Trail/layover days	Total recom- mended days
Leisurely	8/2	10
Moderate	5/2	7
Strenuous	4/2	6

HILITES Of the many crestal routes throughout the Sierra this is one of the most exciting. The scenery is wild and rugged, the six watersheds visited provide excellent fishing, and the route touches some of the most remote country of Yosemite National Park. Most of the campsites mentioned below are situated in central locations that invite side trips, and one is advised to allow sufficient layover days for such trips.

DESCRIPTION (Moderate trip)

1st Hiking Day **(Saddlebag Lake** to **Lower McCabe Lake,** 5.5 miles) : See 1st hiking day, trip 55.

2nd Hiking Day **(Lower McCabe Lake** to **Matterhorn Canyon,** 9 miles) : This is the longest hiking day of the trip, and the prudent hiker will get an early start. From the outlet of Lower McCabe Lake the trail descends to the Virginia Canyon trail junction as described in the 2nd hiking day, trip 56. At this junction our route turns right and descends down the steep switchbacks into Virginia Canyon. The trail along these switchbacks is T-blazed, and the deep layers of bark that have built up around these blazes give the passerby an indication of this trail's age. Blazed by the U. S. Cavalry under the acting superintendency of Captain Abram Epperson Wood in the 1890's, this trail was once used for access to the more remote portions of the North Boundary Country. As the intimidated sheepmen who had been encroaching on Park lands moved their herds northward, it became necessary for the Army caretakers to widen the area of their patrols. The traveler of today, like the mounted cavalryman of yesterday, may pause in wonder at the magnificent specimens of red fir and silver pine along this descent. The trail deviates from that shown on the topo map in that it descends to Return Creek before turning northeast to ford McCabe Creek. Near the ford are magnificent examples of water-sculpting on the granite bedrock of Return Creek, and this bedrock is bordered with colorful patches of columbine, tiger lily and shooting star.

A few yards beyond the ford, the trail passes a packer campsite and there fords to the north side of Return Creek, where it meets the Summit Pass trail. This route turns left (southwest), and ascends moderately across the easy juniper-crowned divide to Spiller Canyon. One's first views of Spiller Creek are those of open granite bedrock, over which Spiller Creek splashes in a series of lovely chutes and miniature falls. The trail ascends along the creek for about $\frac{1}{4}$ mile and then fords.

Through a moderate forest cover that now includes hemlock, the trail then climbs by steady switchbacks. At the hairpin turns one has fine views up Spiller Canyon all the way to the sky-parlor meadows at its headwall, and south across the Return Creek drainage to North Peak and Mt. Conness. The trail then descends briefly through a long, dry, sandy meadow, and then ascends again over a grassy saddle. From the saddle the trail dips gently to beautiful Miller Lake. Foregrounded by a large green meadow, the sparkling waters of this small lake tempt the traveler to stop and rest, but drama lies right around the bend.

From Miller Lake the rutted trail bends north, up a grassy swale to a timbered saddle. The views from this saddle burst upon the traveler as he is suddenly confronted with the chasm of Matterhorn Canyon and the distant teeth of Sawtooth Ridge. This viewpoint marks the beginning of a long, switchbacking descent into Matterhorn Canyon that sees the rocky trail of the descent level off in the sand of the meadowed junction with the Benson Lake trail (8480'). There are good campsites in the meadow and more just upstream, where, at both sites, firewood is ample. Fishing for eastern brook (to 12″) is good in Matterhorn Canyon Creek, and the granite potholes upstream from the junction provide fine swimming in late season.

3rd Hiking Day **(Matterhorn Canyon** to **Campsites, Upper Piute Creek,** 8.5 miles) : See 6th hiking day, trip 47.

4th Hiking Day **(Campsites, Upper Piute Creek** to **Crown Lake,** 3.5 miles) : See 2nd hiking day, trip 41.

5th Hiking Day **(Crown Lake** to **Twin Lakes,** 8 miles) : See 1st hiking day, trip 40.

Saddlebag Road to Green Treble Lake   58

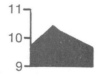

TRIP   From Trailhead on the Saddlebag Lake Road to Green Treble Lake via Bennettville, Fantail Lake, Finger Lake and return via Lee Vining Creek (loop trip, cross country). Topo map (15′) *Tuolumne Meadows*. Best early, mid or late season ; 6.5 miles.

Grade	Trail/layover days	Total recom- mended days
Leisurely	2/0	2
Moderate	—	—
Strenuous	—	—

HILITES   For the beginning knapsacker who desires high alpine scenery and who appreciates pioneer history,
this is an excellent trip selection. Even though it is
a cross-country trip, route-finding is a simple matter, as it follows two watersheds while circling the
large granite island lying between Mine Creek and
Lee Vining Creek. As a bonus, the alpine wildflower displays seen enroute are perhaps the finest
to be seen in the North Boundary Country.

DESCRIPTION

1st Hiking Day **(Trailhead on the Saddlebag Lake Road** to
Green Treble Lake, 3.5 miles, cross country) : The trailhead
for this trip is located on the Saddlebag Lake road ½ mile west
of the junction with the Tioga Road (Hiway 120). There is
a small unmarked parking area in the meadow adjacent to Lee
Vining Creek at the point where the Saddlebag Lake road
ascends away from the creek. From this parking area (9600')
our route fords Lee Vining Creek, and ascends partway up the
opposite hillside to an ancient mining road. Now a mere wide
spot on the hillside, this road once knew the rattle and clamor of
the Bennettville ore wagons making the short but dramatic jour-
ney to Lundy Canyon.

At the mining road our route turns left (south) and ascends
moderately around the granite nose of the ridge to the south.
This ancient track now has head-high lodgepole and whitebark
pine growing between the ruts, and as it crests the ridge it
becomes hard to follow. On the Bennettville side of the ridge,
however, it once more becomes clear, where long sections of it
are built up with native rock. The road descends to the two
solitary cabins above Mine Creek. These two buildings are all
that remain of the once-thriving mining center of Bennettville.
Here the Great Sierra Consolidated Silver Company enjoyed
a two-year boom while it attempted to develop the Tioga gold
mines — a venture that eventually cost them over $300,000 and
bankruptcy. The vein of ore was discovered in 1879, the company was founded in 1882, and it gave up in 1884. While at
this site, the hiker should cross the creek by the old ore-wagon
ford and follow this track to the mine adit on the other side of

the meadow. Spectacular clumps of monkeyflower decorate the runoff from the adit, and from here one can circle back to Mine Creek.

Continuing up the creek's drainage, our route rounds the grassy northeast side of Shell Lake (eastern brook trout), and picks up the faint fishermen's trail along the stream joining Shell and Fantail lakes. Sparse whitebark pines dot the rocky banks of this tumbling creek, and dark spears of swamp onion line the stream. The many-blossomed heads of lousewort make miniature carpets through which lavender-hued flowers of Indian paintbrush poke, and just when one feels he is being glutted by the color, he encounters patches of buttercup salted with lupine, scarlet gilia and penstemon.

Our route then crosses the outlet of Fantail Lake and traverses the rocky south shore to the inlet. Keeping to the left side of the creek joining Spuller and Fantail lakes, the route begins the first steep ascent of the trip. This ascent crosses to the north side of the creek just below Spuller Lake, and crowns the rocky ridge above the lake about 100 yards east of the willowed outlet. Spuller Lake is a rock-fringed lake with a spattering of whitebark pine around the east side. Our route skirts the north side of the lake and ascends the gentle saddle just north of the lake.

From this saddle, the high point of this trip (10300'), the route descends over a field of granite boulders to the granite isthmus between Green Treble Lake and the unnamed lake to the east. Good campsites with grand views of the upper cirque basin of Lee Vining Creek can be found near the outlet (10200') from Green Treble Lake. Firewood is adequate, and fishing for eastern brook (to 9") is fair. For anglers with a little ambition, there is excellent fishing for eastern brook at nearby Finger Lake. The cross-country route to Finger Lake has an additional bonus with the presence of clumps of the rare yellow (alpine) columbine.

2nd Hiking Day **(Green Treble Lake** to **Trailhead on the Saddlebag Lake Road,** 3 miles) : From the campsites at the outlet of Green Treble Lake, our route drops down steeply along the grassy banks of the outlet stream to the large, oxbowing meadow sections of Lee Vining Creek. Thence the route descends along the south bank of Lee Vining Creek via a faint fishermen's trail. Across the creek one can make out the fenced control plots of the Carnegie Institute Experimental Station and the attendant buildings.

Our route occasionally winds away from the stream as it plummets between steep, eroded walls, but then returns to cross long meadow sections as the stream veers southeast. The piping of Belding ground squirrels precedes the hiker as they sound the alarm, and one is likely to see an occasional late-grazing deer or large jackrabbits along these grassy benches. The descent is always gentle, and mostly across open grasslands. Just north of the trailhead our descending route fords a willowed, multitributaried portion of the creek via bridges of old mining timbers. These timbers are placed across the tributaries just upstream from the old mining header that protrudes from the meadow. Following the north bank of the stream on a fishermen's trail, one arrives back at the parking area from whence he began.

59 Tuolumne Meadows to Young Lakes

TRIP   From Soda Springs to Young Lakes (semiloop trip). Topo map (15′) *Tuolumne Meadows.* Best mid or late season; 14.4 miles.

Grade	Trail/layover days	Total recommended days
Leisurely	—	—
Moderate	2/1	3
Strenuous	2/0	2

HILITES The three Young Lakes, cupped under Ragged Peak, offer a large selection of campsites, some in heavy woods and some at timberline. These camps provide a base for exciting excursions into the headwaters of Conness Creek and for climbing Mt. Conness itself.

DESCRIPTION

1st Hiking Day **(Soda Springs** to **Young Lakes,** 7.5 miles) : The first part of this trip follows the Glen Aulin "hiway," a heavily traveled path from Tuolumne Meadows to the High Sierra Camp down the Tuolumne River. From the Soda Springs (8600′) a sandy trail ascends gently through a forest of sparse, small lodgepole pines, and then descends to a log ford of Delaney Creek. The topo map shows the Young Lakes trail turning off to the north some distance east of where it actually does, and our route proceeds west to the new junction, where it turns right (north). From the junction we ascend slightly and cross a broad expanse of boulder-strewn sheet granite. An open spot affords a look south across broad Tuolumne Meadows to the line of peaks from Fairview Dome to the steeplelike spires of the Cathedral Range.

After crossing the open granite, our trail re-enters a tree cover of lodgepole pine before dropping into the shallow valley of Dingley Creek. Beyond the ford of this creek, we begin a long, gradual climb toward the Dog Lake trail junction. First our route ascends on packed dirt and duff under moderate-to-dense lodgepole, to a plateau where we cross a small branch of Conness Creek. The trail then makes a rut through a meadow where we begin to see very graceful specimens of mountain hemlock. From the meadow we cross the tributary, ascend a small slope, and meet the Dog Lake trail coming in from the right. Our route, bearing left, traverses a lush fern glade as it dips through a dense forest of large lodgepoles and hemlocks. Then, emerging from the trees, the trail skirts the north edge of a small, wildflower-filled meadow before surmounting a slight rise and dropping to the west shore of Lower Young Lake (9900′). There are both primitive and well-developed campsites along the north shore of this lake. Firewood is adequate. More secluded campsites may be found on Middle and Upper Young lakes by following one of several ducked trails that lead east from the ford of the outlet of the lower lake. It is about one mile and 400′ elevation gain to the upper lake (10200′), which is the most attractive but has the sparsest wood supply. Fishing on the Young Lakes is fair to good for brook trout (to 12″).

2nd Hiking Day **(Young Lakes** to **Soda Springs,** 6.9 miles)*:* After retracing our steps to the Dog Lake trail junction, we turn left onto the southwest spur of Ragged Peak and make a slight ascent on a sandy, boulder-scattered slope under a moderate lodgepole and hemlock forest cover. As the trail ascends, the trees diminish in density and change in species, to a predominance of whitebark pine, the highest-dwelling of subalpine trees. From the shoulder of Ragged Peak the trail descends through a large, gently sloping meadow. This broad, well-watered expanse is a wildflower garden in season, littered with large boulders, and laced with meandering brooks. Paintbrush, lupine and monkeyflower in the foreground set off the excellent views of the Cathedral Range to the south.

Near the lower edge of the meadow we cross the headwaters of Dingley Creek and descend, steeply at times, some 300' through a moderately dense forest of lodgepole, in which a few red firs appear as the elevation decreases. Then, after some minor ups and downs, we cross Delaney Creek in a large, level meadow, with the reddish peaks of Mounts Dana and Gibbs looming in the east. Signs near the creek tell of the fishing prohibition in both Delaney Creek and the Skelton Lakes at its source. The prohibition is due to a research project on the rare Paiute cutthroat trout. (The Delaney Creek ford is difficult in early season; shallower fords may be found upstream.) Our trail leaves the meadow ascending slightly, then drops once more toward Tuolumne Meadows. Lembert Dome, the "first ascent" of so many visitors to Tuolumne Meadows, can be glimpsed through the trees along this stretch of trail. The trail levels slightly as it meets the .1 mile lateral to Dog Lake. Then it passes a junction with the trail that leads east along the north side of Lembert Dome, and fords the lake's outlet. The 560' rocky-dusty descent from the outlet ford switchbacks under the steep west face of Lembert Dome and comes out onto a dirt service road that terminates at a parking lot a few yards west of the Tioga Road. From here, a level meadow walk of less than a mile west along the Soda Springs road will return the hiker to the spot (8600') where this circuit originated.

Southern Yosemite/Devils Postpile

This region's topography is varied and complex, ranging from the yawning chasm of Yosemite Valley to the snowy heights of the Sierra crest's peaks, some over 13000'. In profile this section of the Sierra rises from west to east like a building wave. It ascends in a long, gentle slope, increasing in height and power until it climaxes at the white-peaked summit. It then drops away suddenly, in an escarpment, to Mono and Long valleys. The more gradual western slope is wrinkled into a complex of lesser crests and valleys that roughly parallel the north-south main crest, and this corrugated surface is broken by drainages of the three major rivers of the area: the Tuolumne, the Merced, and the San Joaquin.

Southern Yosemite National Park provides the grandest scenery in this region. But if Yosemite is first in grandeur, the Devils Postpile area, including the spectacular Ritter Range, is a close second. Combined, these two regions afford some of the best backpacking country in the world.

In all, Yosemite offers the traveler over 700 miles of trail, a figure that does not include the outside-the-Park portions of trails originating in the Park. Because of the number of people traveling the Yosemite back country, the Park Service has now instituted a policy of allowing camping only at designated camping spots, and fire permits issued by a Park ranger are required. These fire permits, unlike the permits issued by the Forest Service, require a detailed trip itinerary — a sound practice, regulations notwithstanding. Forest Service fire permits are required for trips outside the Park. The credit for the well-maintained trails of this area belongs to trail crews of the U. S. Forest Service and of the National Park Service. Backpackers in Yosemite soon become familiar with the international "i" tree blaze of the Forest Service and with Yosemite's distinctive "T". The "T" blaze was first used when the U. S. Cavalry administered the Park. It is claimed that the "T" stood for "tree"—a necessary clarification for raw, "citified" recruits.

The general landforms of the southern Yosemite and Devils Postpile regions are similar because both were created by mountain-building forces followed by erosion by glaciers and rivers. However, anyone who hikes the back country of southern Yosemite and of the Devils Postpile/Ritter Range will see the marked differences between the two areas. In Yosemite, one is struck with the gargantuan scale of the landscape. Vast expanses of solid white granite give a sense of colossal immobility. By contrast, the dark heights of the Minarets of the Ritter Range appear almost like chocolate icing — decorative and ephemeral. The difference between the two areas is in the type of rock, the Yosemite high country being primarily massive, resistant granites, and the Ritter Range being mostly metamorphosed volcanic rocks, alternating with limestone layers. The softer rock of metamorphosed volcanic origin was more easily quarried by the ice and water, allowing the more delicate and fragile sculpting.

This dramatic landscaping is the product of several inundations by glaciers, and evidences of these ancient ice fields are readily seen along trails in both Yosemite and the Devils Postpile/Ritter Range country. The size of some of these glaciers is hard to imagine, for they covered hundreds of square miles. The most impressive was the great Tuolumne glacier, emanating from Mt. Lyell and Mt. Dana, which carved and polished the present Tuolumne and Tenaya basins. Incredible as it may seem, the Tenaya basin was scoured by an incidental overflow from the primary Tuolumne Basin glacier, which was a *mer de glace* that once filled the Grand Canyon of the Tuolumne to its brim! The top of the Devils Postpile, a fascinating columnar basaltic formation, offers mute testimony to the awesome power of the shearing action of these glaciers. Feeder glaciers, like the ones that carved Echo Creek Canyon, Triple Peak Fork Canyon, Chain Lakes basin and Shadow Creek Canyon, are responsible for much of the scenery described in the following trips. Huge deposits of rocky glacial debris (moraines) compose significant parts of the landscape (e.g., the lateral moraines along the descent from Clouds Rest to Little Yosemite Valley). Other glacial manifestations that backpackers will see include domes, U-shaped valleys, glacial polish (rock abraded to a sheen by silt embedded in the moving ice), erratics (boulder flotsam left by receding ice fields), striae (grooves) and hanging valleys (the valleys out of which come the falls of Yosemite Valley are classic examples).

Man on this scene seems almost an afterthought. The first were the Indians of the Mono and Ahwahneechee tribes. Primarily peaceful, seminomadic peoples, they hunted and fished the idyllic Yosemite and Mono regions long before the white man came. Virtually all that remains to mark their occupancy of the land are place names. They carried on some trade and social intercourse with each other (the primary trade route was via Tuolumne Meadows and the present Sunrise Trail) but for the most part they remained isolated.

The Mariposa Battalion of 1851 was the first white party to penetrate the Yosemite Valley, but the trapper, Joseph Walker, first crossed the Park and saw the valley as early as 1833. From 1848 until the 1860's gold fever brought the white man into the Sierra in swarms. By 1853 Lee Vining had made prospecting forays into the Mt. Dana country, and by 1859 a temporary boomtown grew up around Dogtown (Hiway 395 near Conway Summit). After the discovery of the fabulous Comstock Lode east of Lake Tahoe, gold fever subsided in the Yosemite/Devils Postpile region, except for a brief flurry caused by the abortive excitement of the Tioga Mine, and it had all but died by the turn of the century. This speculative mine, although it never opened or mined a ton of ore, was responsible for the building of the old Tioga Road.

In Yosemite Valley a burgeoning tourist trade arose, centering about the natural wonders of the Valley. In 1864 President Lincoln signed an Act of Congress giving Yosemite over to the care of the State of California in the form of a public-land grant. Galen Clark, who established Clark's Station (the current site of Wawona), was appointed Yosemite's first guardian, and served in this capacity until 1879. In 1890 the Yosemite was made a National Park, the grant to be administered by the U. S. Cavalry. This Army administration lasted until 1916, when the National Park Service was established. Short as it was, this interim period of U. S. Army administration based at Wawona saw many "firsts" in the Park. Its boundaries were patrolled to keep out infringing cattle- and sheepmen; fish were introduced to high-country lakes and streams (the new strains included golden, brook, brown, cutthroat, Dolly Varden and grayling); and an exploration and trail-blazing program was carried out that created trails still used today. This was an exciting pioneer period, and today's backpacker can glean a taste of its fascination by visiting the Pioneer Yosemite History Center at Wawona.

The advent of the automobile has (blessedly) not infringed unduly upon this section of the Sierra. The sole trans-Sierra route in this region remains the historic Tioga Road (Hiway 120). Recently widened or rerouted in its steeper sections, this paved road crosses Yosemite National Park via Tuolumne Meadows, and thus provides the trailheads for several trips described below. The east end of this trans-Sierra route is at Lee Vining on U. S. 395. From the west, one reaches Tioga Pass by Yosemite Valley or the Big Oak Flat Road and Crane Flat. Access to the trailhead at O'Shaughnessy Dam (Hetch Hetchy Reservoir) is by the paved road turning left (north) from Hiway 120 at the San Jose Family Camp or the one turning left shortly west of the boundary of the Park (they later merge). The trailhead at Happy Isles is reached via Hiway 41 from Fresno or Hiway 140 from Merced. Trailheads at Bridalveil Creek Campground and Glacier Point are reached by the Glacier Point road, turning east from Hiway 41. The trailheads at Chiquito Creek and Granite Creek Campground and the one on the Strawberry Tungsten Mine road are reached via the thirty-mile dirt road (Road "434") turning east from the Bass Lake Hiway at The Pines. On the east side of the crest, Agnew Meadows Campground is reached from Hiway 395 (at Casa Diablo Hot Springs), via the paved road west to Mammoth Lakes. Just beyond the Mammoth Lakes business area, our signed route branches right and crosses the Sierra Nevada crest at Minaret Summit (panoramic views). The dirt-road descent from Minaret Summit to Agnew Meadows (3 miles) and Devils Postpile (9 miles) is dusty and narrow.

Anglers will find that this region abounds in "hot fishing spots." Some of them are the Merced River east of Little Yosemite Valley, the Royal Arch Lake-Chilnualna Lakes area and the Chain Lakes basin.

Today four species of trout (rainbow, brook, brown and golden) make up the primary fishery of this area, although an occasional catch will be made of a hybrid or a cutthroat. Nearly all the lakes and streams of the high country have been planted, and most of them have fish populations today, sustained either by continued planting or by natural reproduction. The present policy of the California Department of Fish and Game is to introduce the golden trout to more of this region's high lakes.

Fishing on the lakes is best during the first three weeks after the ice has cleared (from late June to the end of July, depending on the altitude) and during the last few weeks of the season before the first snows (late September to mid October). After the streams clear up, fishing is generally good all summer long. Usually they clear up by early July; however, this date can be affected by late rains and by the ground cover on the particular stream's watershed.

Flies are preferred to bait by most backpackers for reasons of sport, esthetics and weight, and the clear waters of the high-country lakes and streams behoove the angler to use fine leader material and a wary approach. Experienced backpacking fishermen use a light-action fly rod (3-5 sections) strung with tapered line and leader. Novice anglers find that the spinning rod with a bubble-fly combination or a metal wobbler is easily mastered, and is effective against blustery afternoon winds on lakes.

Anglers should keep only the fish they will eat. A fishing trip's success is never measured solely by the number of pounds in the creel.

Tenaya Lake to Sunrise Camp **60**

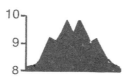

TRIP From Tenaya Lake Walk-In Campground to Sunrise High Sierra Camp (round trip). Topo map (15') *Tuolumne Meadows*. Best mid or late season; 10 miles.

Grade	Trail/layover days	Total recom-mended days
Leisurely	2/1	3
Moderate	2/0	2
Strenuous	—	—

HILITES Although this route is very popular, being within the Yosemite High Sierra Camp network, the superb, unusual scenery of the high country makes this trip a must. The spectacular topography of the Tenaya Canyon and of the serrated northwestern end of the Cathedral Range combine to overcome the most strident objections of the solitude-seeker.

DESCRIPTION

1st Hiking Day **(Tenaya Lake Walk-in Campground** to **Sunrise Camp,** 5 miles):** Beginning at the outlet of Tenaya Lake (8149'), this route skirts the meadowed edge of the lake's walk-in campground, and ascends steadily through a thinning forest cover of lodgepole pine and occasional red fir, white fir, silver pine and mountain hemlock. The trail soon rises above Tenaya Canyon, and from several vantage points one may look back on the emerald blue of the lake and the surrounding polished granite faces. The Indian name for Tenaya Creek, Py-wi-ack ("Stream of the Shining Rocks"), was more apt than the name it has. Tenaya Lake was named for old Chief Tenaya, an honored Ahwahneechee chief. To the southwest Tenaya Canyon stretches away in broad granite steps, and there is no grander view to show the work of the brobdingnagian forces of stream erosion and glacial grinding. This canyon exhibits the largest exposed granite area in the Park, and its shining surfaces are barren except for sporadic clumps of hardy conifers that have found root in broken talus pockets. To the east the canyon is walled in by Tenaya Peak and the granite face of Sunrise Mountain. On the west one can see the cliffs of Mount Hoffman and Tuolumne Peak, and as the trail becomes steeper and begins steady switchbacking, the long, gradual slope falling from the promontory called Clouds Rest comes into view to the south. This slope is a 4500' drop, claimed to be one of the largest continuous rock slopes in the world. The traveler who feels sated by the panorama will find a different world to wonder at, right at his own boot-clad feet, for these slopes are reputed to grow more than 100 different kinds of wildflowers. Among them one finds pussypaws, penstemon, paintbrush, lupine, streptanthus, western mountain aster, larkspur, golden brodiaea and buttercup.

Beyond the steepest part of this climb our route branches left (east) and continues on a more gentle ascent to Sunrise Lakes. This lateral, joining the Forsyth trail to the Cathedral Pass trail, is not marked on the topo map. For the solitude-seeker who would not relish the conviviality of the High Sierra Camp above Long Meadow, the campsites at Sunrise Lakes make a fine alternate for the end of a hiking day. Fishing is fair for rainbow and brook on these lakes (8-13″). Our route continues eastward across a low ridge and descends to the south end of Long Meadow. Here one may choose one of the fair campsites along the creek (poor fishing) or, if advance reservations have been made, the facilities of Sunrise High Sierra Camp (9460′, emergency services available). These campsites have excellent views and easy access to Columbia Finger and Matthes Crest. An easy day's round trip in the other direction takes the base-camping hiker to the top of Clouds Rest and back.

2nd Hiking Day **(Sunrise High Sierra Camp** to **Tenaya Lake Walk-in Campground,** 5 miles) : Retrace steps of 1st hiking day.

61   Tioga Road to Cathedral Lake

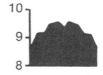

TRIP   From Trailhead on Tioga Road (Tuolumne Meadows) to Cathedral Lake (round trip). Topo map (15′) *Tuolumne Meadows.* Best mid or late season ; 7 miles.

Grade	Trail/layover days	Total recom- mended days
Leisurely	2/0	2
Moderate	—	—
Strenuous	—	—

HILITES Used since the time of the Indians, this trail offers some of the finest views of the Tuolumne Meadows region. Two large granite domes, Fairview and Medlicott, and the foremost landmark of the area, Cathedral Peak, line this route. Because of the relatively short mileage and the high-country scenery, this round trip is an excellent beginner's selection.

DESCRIPTION

1st Hiking Day **(Trailhead on Tioga Road** to **Cathedral Lake,** 3.5 miles) : From the parking area (8560') on the Tioga Road (0.8 mile east of the turnout at the west end of the Meadows, and 1.7 miles west of the Tuolumne Meadows Visitors Center) the trail begins a somewhat steep ascent bearing south from the road. A few yards from the trailhead our route crosses the Tenaya Lake/Tuolumne Meadows trail and continues southwesterly. Near the top of the first rise, the traveler is treated to peephole glimpses, through the lodgepole-pine cover, of granite-topped Fairview Dome on the right. This monolith towers 700' above us, and its polished surfaces remind the passerby of the glacial ices that once filled this basin. During one rest stop the traveler can look back on the basin centering on Tuolumne Meadows, the largest subalpine meadow in the Sierra. Roughly, the basin is 15 miles long by 8 miles wide, and because of the easy east-to-west going, one can readily see why it was a favored Indian trade route.

After the initial 500' climb, the trail levels off, and then climbs again as it rounds the northern base of thrusting Cathedral Peak. The route then descends gently along Cathedral Peak's western wall. Periodically the traveler has westward views of another granite sentry left by the glacial ices, Medlicott Dome, and the observer can easily discern the difference between the rounded, polished tops of the domes and the jagged crest of Cathedral Peak. The domes were completely covered by the ice, whereas the top few hundred feet of Cathedral Peak stood above the grinding glacier, and hence was not rounded and smoothed by the ice. Once more the trail begins to ascend, and our route branches right (west) for about ½ mile of interesting meadows to the fair campsites on the southern shore of lower Cathedral

Lake (9420'). The meadows on the east side of the lake are classic examples of the transition of small glacial lakes to meadows. Firewood is somewhat scarce, and fishing is poor for rainbow and brook (to 9") but swimming is good. The views from these campsites more than make up for their shortcomings, however, for from here Polly Dome, Cathedral Peak, Echo Peaks, Echo Ridge and Eagle Peak provide a rugged glacial setting.

2nd Hiking Day **(Cathedral Lake** to **Trailhead on Tioga Road,** 3.5 miles)** : Retrace steps of 1st hiking day.

62   Tioga Road to Sunrise Camp

TRIP   From Trailhead on Tioga Road (Tuolumne Meadows) to Sunrise High Sierra Camp (round trip). Topo map (15') *Tuolumne Meadows*. Best mid or late season; 16 miles.

Grade	Trail/layover days	Total recommended days
Leisurely	4/1	5
Moderate	3/1	4
Strenuous	2/1	3

HILITES   The Sunrise Trail, of which this is the first leg, is a justly famous and popular route. Superlative views confront the knapsacker on every hand, and the route traverses a nearly complete spectrum of conifers found within the Park.

DESCRIPTION (Leisurely trip)

1st Hiking Day **(Trailhead on Tioga Road** to **Cathedral Lake,** 3.5 miles)** : See 1st hiking day, trip 61.

2nd Hiking Day **(Cathedral Lake** to **Sunrise High Sierra Camp,** 4.5 miles)** : Retrace your steps of the 1st hiking day to the Cathedral Pass trail at the foot of Cathedral Peak. Our route turns right (south) and ascends to Upper Cathedral Lake; the lake is a few yards to the right of the trail. The trail then skirts the east side of the lake and ascends to Cathedral Pass, where views include Cathedral Peak, Tresidder Peak, Echo Peaks, Matthes Crest, Columbia Finger, the Clark Range to the south and Tower Peak far to the north. As the strolling traveler contours around on the south side of Cathedral Pass and then descends past the Echo Creek trail junction, he notices how apropos are the names of some of the nearby peaks. Columbia Finger (the trail crosses its south shoulder) is a columnar pinnacle that looks remarkably like a slender, pointing finger. This aspect is particularly noticeable from Long Meadow. Similarly, the Cockscomb and Cathedral Peak fit their names. These unusual peaks make up the northwest end of the Cathedral Range, and from several vantage points at the foot of Columbia Finger the traveler has unusual "end-on" views of this range. From these vantage points, the trail descends to appropriately named Long Meadow (9480'), and one may choose from the fair campsites along the stream at the south end, or may elect to use the facilities of the Sunrise High Sierra Camp (reservations must be made in advance). The camp is located on a rocky bench slightly above the southern end of the meadow. Firewood is somewhat scarce, particularly in late season (owing to the heavy traffic), and the nearest good fishing is at the Sunrise Lakes (about 1½ miles west).

3rd Hiking Day (**Sunrise High Sierra Camp** to **Cathedral Lake,** 4.5 miles) : Retrace steps of 2nd hiking day.

4th Hiking Day (**Cathedral Lake** to **Trailhead on Tioga Road,** 3.5 miles) : Retrace steps of 1st hiking day.

Clarke nutcracker

63   Tioga Road to Yosemite Valley

TRIP   From Trailhead on Tioga Road (Tuolumne Meadows) to Yosemite Valley (Happy Isles) via the Sunrise Trail (shuttle trip). Topo maps (15') *Tuolumne Meadows, Merced Peak, Yosemite.* Best mid or late season; 24.4 miles.

Grade	Trail/layover days	Total recommended days
Leisurely	5/1	6
Moderate	4/1	5
Strenuous	3/0	3

HILITES   The Sunrise Trail route from the Meadows to the Valley is one of the Park's most famous and most used knapsack routes. Its reputation is an honest one, for these miles contain a magnificent range of flora and fauna, and the trail surveys some of the Park's best-known landmarks. This is a fine trip for the beginning knapsacker who has a couple of shorter trips under his (or her) belt, and has a taste for more.

DESCRIPTION (Leisurely trip)

1st Hiking Day **(Trailhead on Tioga Road** to **Cathedral Lake,** 3.5 miles) : See 1st hiking day, trip 61.

2nd Hiking Day **(Cathedral Lake** to **Sunrise High Sierra Camp,** 4.5 miles) : See 2nd hiking day, trip 62.

3rd Hiking Day **(Sunrise High Sierra Camp** to **Sunrise Creek,** 3.9 miles) : The trail from Sunrise High Sierra Camp continues south through Long Meadow, and undulates gently below the eastern crest of Sunrise Mountain. Paralleling the headwaters of Sunrise Creek, the trail descends steeply by switchbacks down a rocky moraine. This moraine is the largest of a series of ridge-like glacial deposits in this area, and the gigantic granite boulders along their sides testify to the power of the *mer-de-glace* that once filled Little Yosemite Valley and its tributaries. One such "erratic," about the size of a compact car, was found poised on the side of Moraine Dome (to the southwest) and geologists have determined that it came from the slopes of the peaks at the northwest end of the Cathedral Range. The current belief is that there were at least 3 and possibly 4 ice ages that covered the country with glaciers. Because of the glacial moraines, the forest cover (mainly lodgepole pine) occurs in splotchy, broken stands. At the foot of the morainal descent, the trail crosses Sunrise Creek, and then descends on a westerly course to the fair-to-good campsites a few yards north of the multiple junction of the Forsythe, Sunrise, and Merced Lake trails (8080'). Firewood is ample. Those who wish to lay over here may choose to take the Forsythe trail to the north for the famous views to be had from Clouds Rest. This is an arduous 1900' ascent spanning about 8 miles (round trip), but this vantage point offers the awesome spectacle of an unbroken 4500' granite slope into Tenaya Canyon. The stone of this canyon presents the greatest exposed granite surface in the Park. Fishing on Sunrise Creek is poor-to-fair for rainbow and brook (fry).

4th Hiking Day **(Sunrise Creek** to **Little Yosemite Valley,** 6.4 miles) : Our route continues southwestward on a gradual descent that crosses and recrosses Sunrise Creek several times. This trail is bounded on the north by the Pinnacles (the south face of the Clouds Rest eminence) and on the south by Moraine Dome. Francois Matthes, in an interesting "detective story" written in the form of a geological essay (professional paper 160), discusses Moraine Dome extensively. He deduced, using three examples (one was the "erratic" cited above), that the moraines around the dome were the product of at least *two* glacial ages — a notion contrary to the thinking of the time. The morainal till of the last glacial age characterizes the final steep descent (beginning at the point where this route passes the Clouds Rest trail) into Little Yosemite Valley. About ½ mile beyond the Clouds Rest trail junction our route passes the lateral to Half Dome (about 4 miles round trip), and switchbacks down through a changing forest cover. Along this descent one begins to see more of the large cones of the sugar pine and the smaller, more compact yellow pine cone (with out-turned prickle). On the floor of the valley our route strikes the Merced River trail and turns left (east). The sandy trail through the valley proceeds upstream beside the meandering Merced River to the good campsites at the east end of the valley (2 miles, 6100'). Fishing for rainbow, brown and brook (to 10") is fair-to-good and firewood is abundant.

5th Hiking Day **(Little Yosemite Valley** to **Yosemite Valley,** 6.1 miles) : See 1st hiking day, trip 81.

64   Tenaya Lake to Yosemite Valley

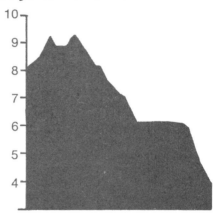

TRIP   From Tenaya Lake Walk-in Campground to Yosemite Valley (Happy Isles) (shuttle trip). Topo maps (15') *Tuolumne Meadows, Merced Peak, Yosemite*. Best mid or late season ; 20.1 miles.

Grade	Trail/layover days	Total recommended days
Leisurely	3/1	4
Moderate	3/0	3
Strenuous	—	—

HILITES   Through an elevation change of over 5000' (mostly down hill) this route covers most of Yosemite's spectrum of life zones. Views from various points above Tenaya Canyon are breathtaking in their panoramic scope. By contrast, a different kind of appreciation is evoked when walking alongside the serene waters of the Merced River as it serpentines across the floor of Little Yosemite Valley. The ever-changing nature of a river is a high-point of this trip — slides, cascades, and earth-shaking water-falls add exclamation points. This route is a fine selection for the intermediate knapsacker who has never had a taste of Yosemite's varied back country.

DESCRIPTION

1st Hiking Day **(Tenaya Lake Walk-in Campground** to **Sunrise Creek,** 7.6 miles) : The trailhead is located at the Tenaya Lake Walk-in Campground parking lot (8149'). From this point the trail crosses the outlet of Tenaya Lake, skirts the meadowed fringe of the walk-in campground, and begins an easy ascent through lodgepole pine. The first part of this trail is lush with wildflowers as late as July, and the hiker can expect to see lupine, western mountain aster, larkspur, golden brodiaea, and buttercup. In the tiny, intimate meadows just south of Tenaya Lake the quiet hiker will more than likely encounter browsing mule deer. The trail begins a series of steep, rocky switchbacks, and then crosses the intermittent outlet streams from Sunrise Lakes. Several vantage points offer excellent views of granite-filled Tenaya Canyon. The plant life along the trail reflects the transition from one life zone to another (Canadian to Hudson-ian). First the forest cover is an agglomeration of lodgepole pine, red fir, white fir and silver pine, but as the trail continues to ascend, more mountain hemlock is mixed with the ubiquitous lodgepole. Underfoot, the rocky hillside harbors different flowers, and the investigating naturalist will find streptanthus (jewel flower), pussypaws, various kinds of paintbrush, lupine and penstemon. It is claimed that these slopes have over 100 varieties of wildflowers, and interested hikers should make room in their knapsacks for a good wildflower identification book (see bibliography).

This ascent passes the lateral to Sunrise Lakes and Sunrise High Sierra Camp, and levels out briefly before beginning a gradual, undulating descent along the western face of Sunrise Mountain. At the Clouds Rest trail junction those who have a little steam left take this short lateral (2½ miles roundtrip) to this lofty prominence. Views from Clouds Rest are among the most spectacular in the Sierra, including a 4500' continuous granite slope stretching all the way down to Tenaya Creek and rising on the other side — the largest exposed granite area in the Park. From the Clouds Rest trail junction the trail drops steeply by switchbacks over a lateral moraine to the fair-to-good campsites on Sunrise Creek (8080'). Firewood is ample. Fishing for rainbow and brook (fry) is poor-to-fair.

2nd Hiking Day **(Sunrise Creek** to **Little Yosemite Valley,** 6.4 miles) : See 4th hiking day, trip 63.

3rd Hiking Day **(Little Yosemite Valley** to **Yosemite Valley,** 6.1 miles) : See 1st hiking day, trip 81.

65   Tuolumne Meadows to Elizabeth Lake

TRIP   From Tuolumne Meadows Campground to Elizabeth Lake (round trip). Topo map (15') *Tuolumne Meadows*. Best mid or late season; 5 miles.

Grade	Trail/layover days	Total recommended days
Leisurely	2/0	2
Moderate	—	—
Strenuous	—	—

HILITES   Few places in Yosemite give so much for so little effort as does Elizabeth Lake. This lovely alpine lake is backdropped on three sides by Johnson Peak, Johnson Ridge and Unicorn Peak, while the open side looks across tundralike meadow to the snow-topped peaks of the Sierra Crest on the north side of Tuolumne Meadows.

DESCRIPTION

1st Hiking Day **(Tuolumne Meadows Campground** to **Elizabeth Lake,** 2.5 miles) : To reach the trailhead, walk to the southeast end of the campground, and pick up the "T" blazed trail at the end of the "group area" parking lot (8600'). A few yards from the trailhead our route crosses the Tenaya Lake/ Lyell Canyon trail (not shown on topo map) and continues a steady southward ascent. The forest cover along this climb is predominantly lodgepole pine, but maverick representatives of almost all the conifer family will be encountered. The trail soon joins Unicorn Creek, and the second half of the trip is accompanied by the music of this dashing, gurgling, cold-water stream. Near the top of the climb, the trail levels out, the stunted lodgepole pines are farther spaced, and the hiker emerges at the foot of a long meadow looking south toward Johnson Ridge. It isn't long before Unicorn Peak, topped with "Cathedral Peak granite," comes into view to the west, and to the southeast one sees a long, shallow cirque bounded on the east by Johnson Peak. From the good campsites on the east and north sides of Elizabeth Lake (9508'), the views across the waters to Unicorn Peak are classic, and one can see why this is a traditional camping place for those wishing to climb this unusual spire. This glacially formed basin is indeed one of the most beautiful in the Tuolumne Meadows region. Fishing is only fair for rainbow (to 9") and firewood is somewhat scarce.

2nd Hiking Day (**Elizabeth Lake** to **Tuolumne Meadows Campground,** 2.5 miles) : Retrace steps of 1st hiking day.

Tuolumne Meadows to Nelson Lake   66

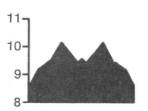

TRIP   From Tuolumne Meadows Campground to Nelson Lake (round trip). Topo map (15') *Tuolumne Meadows*. Best mid or late season; 11 miles.

Grade	Trail/layover days	Total recommended days
Leisurely	—	—
Moderate	2/1	3
Strenuous	—	—

HILITES   This interesting and varied route visits the scenic Elizabeth Lake basin and then crosses the serrated Cathedral Range to Nelson Lake. No trail route offers finer views of those geologic wonders called Unicorn Peak and the Cockscomb. Open, meadow-fringed Nelson Lake makes a pleasantly fitting end to this exciting trip, and anglers can look forward to good brook-trout fishing on the placid waters of this alpine gem.

DESCRIPTION

1st Hiking Day **(Tuolumne Meadows Campground** to **Nelson Lake,** 5.5 miles) : Proceed to Elizabeth Lake as described in trip 65 and then take the meadow trail going south (unmarked on the topo map). This trail at first appears to be leading to the low saddle at the end of a shallow cirque (the southernmost point of Johnson Ridge) but it soon veers off to the right (southwest). The meadow gives way to a moderately dense forest cover of lodgepole interspersed with red fir, and the trail climbs steeply to the low pass (10160') overlooking the northernmost headwaters of Echo Creek. Because of the close proximity of the Cockscomb (about 1 mile due west as the crow flies), the hiker has an excellent view of that knifelike spire. Well-named by Francois Matthes, this slender crest bears clear marks of the highest level reached by the ice of the last glacial episode. Its lower shoulders reveal the rounded, well-polished surfaces that betray glacial action, while its jagged, sharply etched crest shows no such markings. Further evidences of glacial action may be clearly seen on the steep descent into the head of the long, typically U-shaped Echo Creek valley. The shearing and polishing action of the ice mass that carved this rounded valley is evident on the cliffs lining the west side.

As our route descends along exposed, winding Echo Creek for about 2 miles, the valley floor is lush with wildflower growth. During mid season the passerby can expect to see penstemon, lupine, bigelow sneezeweed and swamp whitehead. When the canyon wall on the east falls off abruptly to the south, the hiker should begin looking for the poorly marked (ducked) lateral branching east across a low, rocky ridge to Nelson Lake (9636'). This faint trail's destination becomes apparent as it crowns the ridge, where one surveys the meadowed area surrounding Nelson Lake and its outlet. Excellent campsites may be found on the south-southeast and southwest sides, and firewood is ample. Anglers will find the lake's waters good fishing for brook (7-11").

2nd Hiking Day **(Nelson Lake** to **Tuolumne Meadows Campground,** 5.5 miles) : Retrace steps of 1st hiking day.

Tuolumne Meadows to Lyell Canyon **67**

TRIP

From Tuolumne Meadows Campground to Lyell Base Camp (Lyell Canyon) (round trip). Topo map (15′) *Tuolumne Meadows*. Best early, mid or late season; 18 miles.

Grade	Trail/layover days	Total recommended days
Leisurely	2/0	2
Moderate	—	—
Strenuous	—	—

HILITES

Alpine meadows have a fascination that claims the trail traveler, whether he be novice or hoariest veteran. Campers' descriptions of favorite camping places invariably favor the forested western fringe of a remote meadow (your camp gets the first warming sunlight there). The meadows of Lyell Canyon are the stuff of which such memories are built. Idyllic from beginning to end, this long, gentle grassland with its serpentining river is a delight to travel.

DESCRIPTION

1st Hiking Day **(Tuolumne Meadows Campground** to **Lyell Base Camp,** 9 miles) : The trailhead (marked with a metal sign) is situated ¼ mile into the Tuolumne Meadows Campground (8575′), only a few yards from the south side of the Lyell Fork of the Tuolumne River. In early season the first mile is somewhat soggy, but there are fine views north of Lembert Dome, and of alternately rushing and placid sections of the river. At the junction of the trail leading to the footbridge and the Tuolumne Meadows High Sierra Camp, our trail swings right and skirts a long, lovely section of the meadow. This re-routed trail is relatively new, established because of extensive trail wear and subsequent erosion of the old route. Re-routing is one of several far-sighted Park Service policies that have been adopted to allow areas in the wilderness a "breather" — a chance to recover from overuse. Going through a dense forest cover of lodgepole pine, our route goes past the trail that ascends south to Tuolumne Pass and Vogelsang High Sierra Camp, and then fords Rafferty Creek by a log bridge.

From this point on, the trail traverses alternating meadowed and forested sections as it swings south, and the silent walker is sure to come upon grazing deer in the meadows and an occasional marmot that has ventured from the rocky hillside on the right. Fields of wildflowers color the grasslands from early to late season, but the best time of the year for seeing this color is generally early-to-mid season. From the more open portions of the trail, one has excellent views of the Kuna Crest as it ascends southeast to Kuna Peak. Our route then passes the trail branching southwest to Evelyn Lake and Tuolumne Pass. Beyond this junction the trail fords Ireland Creek, passes below Potter Point, and ascends gently to the good campsites at Lyell Base Camp (9040'). Firewood is somewhat scarce, owing to heavy use, and fishing is poor for rainbow, brook, and occasional brown (mostly fry). This base camp, surrounded on three sides by steep canyon walls, marks the end of the meadowed sections of Lyell Canyon, and is the traditional first-night stopping place for those touring the John Muir Trail beginning at Tuolumne Meadows.

2nd Hiking Day **(Lyell Base Camp** to **Tuolumne Meadows Campground,** 9 miles) : Retrace steps of 1st hiking day.

68 Tuolumne Meadows to Agnew Meadows

TRIP From Tuolumne Meadows Campground to Agnew Meadows Campground via Donohue Pass, Island Pass, Thousand Island Lake, Shadow Lake (shuttle trip). Topo maps (15') *Tuolumne Meadows, Mono Craters, Devils Postpile.* Best mid or late season; 28.8 miles.

Grade	Trail/layover days	Total recommended days
Leisurely	5/1	6
Moderate	4/1	5
Strenuous	4/0	4

HILITES   "Sky parlor" meadows, alpine lakes, clear, icy streams, magnificent peaks — this trip has them all. Except for the last 4 miles, this route follows the well-known John Muir Trail as it tours Lyell Canyon and the view-filled eastern slopes of the Ritter Range. Because of its fame, this trail sees a lot of use, but the incomparable scenery enroute more than compensates for the lack of solitude.

DESCRIPTION (Leisurely trip)

1st Hiking Day **(Tuolumne Meadows Campground** to **Lyell Base Camp,** 9 miles) : See 1st hiking day, trip 67.

2nd Hiking Day **(Lyell Base Camp** to **Rush Creek,** 7 miles) : From Lyell Base Camp, the trail ascends the steep, southern terminal wall of Lyell Canyon along the west side of the Lyell Fork. The trail levels out as it veers away from the stream, and then it rejoins the stream via a wooded section. Just north of the junction of the Maclure Creek tributary of the Lyell Fork, our route crosses the latter to the east side, only to recross briefly farther up. The Lyell Fork and its melt-off tributaries are, at this point, merely "jump-across" rills. The rocky underfooting is pleasantly relieved by superb alpine meadows. Along the first 3 miles of this day's ascent, views of the year-round glaciers on the northern faces of Mt. Maclure and Mt. Lyell are superlative. Those hikers who wish to obtain a more intimate view, or to ascend to these ice fields via the lake-dotted basin at their feet, should take the "duck-on-the-rock" trail that ascends steeply up the canyon to the south-southwest.

Our route turns east, recrosses the Lyell Fork, and climbs steeply up rocky going to Donohue Pass (11056') at the crest of the Sierra. This pass, lying between Donohue Peak (northeast) and Mt. Lyell (southwest), affords majestic views of the Sierra crest, the Cathedral Range and the Ritter Range. From Donohue Pass the trail descends by rocky switchbacks to sparse timber cover on the headwaters of Rush Creek, passing a lateral to Marie Lakes. As the trail levels out somewhat, it joins and then parallels a small unnamed tributary of Rush Creek descending to join the main stream. In the Rush Creek drainage the forest cover of lodgepole and hemlock becomes denser, and the trail fords two tributaries to the "Improved" campsites on Rush Creek (9600'), where our route meets the Rush Creek/ June Lake loop trail. Firewood is adequate, and fishing is good for brook and rainbow (to 10").

3rd Hiking Day **(Rush Creek** to **Thousand Island Lake,** 3 miles): Through a continuing forest cover of lodgepole and mountain hemlock, our route ascends steadily beyond the junction with the trail to Davis Lakes, climbing southeastward to the low saddle known as Island Pass (10200'). Just south of Island Pass the trail passes two small lakes and then veers along the ridge of the divide. (This segment of altered trail route is not shown on the topo map.) Along this ridge trail the hiker will discover a verdant growth of wildflowers, including lupine, lousewort, mustang mint (unusual at this altitude), sulphur flower, Mariposa lily, goldenrod, fleabane, mountain aster, pussypaws, and streptanthus ("jewel flower").

The trail emerges from the lodgepole and hemlock ground cover to a granite slope above the outlet at the east end of Thousand Island Lake. Views from this rocky slope are sweeping. The hiker immediately notices the difference between the predominantly darker rock of the Ritter Range and the lighter granite of the Sierra crest's alpine peaks. Geologically, the Ritter Range is made up of much older rock, volcanic in nature, and the spectacularly jagged skyline from Banner Peak southward attests to the strength of this rock which resisted the massive glaciers that gnawed at the range. As the trail switchbacks down to the outlet of Thousand Island Lake, there are classic views across the island-studded waters to the imposing east facades of Banner Peak and Mount Ritter. Several fair campsites may be found at the outlet and on the north side of Thousand Island Lake (9834'), the better ones being a mile or two west of the Muir Trail and back from the water. All of these sites are somewhat exposed to the wind, but offer unexcelled views. Fishing for brook and rainbow (to 13") is poor-to-fair, and firewood is scarce.

4th Hiking Day **(Thousand Island Lake** to **Shadow Lake,** 6.5 miles): See 2nd hiking day, trip 74.

5th Hiking Day **(Shadow Lake** to **Agnew Meadows Campground,** 3 miles): See 1st hiking day, trip 69.

Agnew Meadows to Shadow Lake 69

TRIP   From Agnew Meadows to Shadow Lake (round trip). Topo map (15′) *Devils Postpile*. Best mid or late season; 6 miles.

Grade	Trail/layover days	Total recom-mended days
Leisurely	2/0	2
Moderate	—	—
Strenuous	—	—

HILITES   Shadow Lake is subject to fairly heavy use, but the intrinsic beauty of this spot warrants consideration even by the hiker seeking solitude. If one needs an example to substantiate the wisdom of the government's setting aside wilderness areas, this high-country jewel is a case in point. This is a fine trip for beginning knapsackers.

DESCRIPTION

1st Hiking Day **(Agnew Meadows Campground to Shadow Lake,** 3 miles): From the trailhead southeast of Agnew Meadows Campground (8335) the trail crosses a small ridge covered with red fir and lodgepole pine, and descends to the San Joaquin River, where a side trail (not shown on the topo map) leads down the river. The initial part of this downslope is interesting in that it incorporates many of the ground-cover changes peculiar to the Mammoth Lakes region. One moment you are in dense pine and fir forest, and the next you are walking on an exposed slope of pumice, manzanita, and abundant wildflowers. (In midsummer, watch for the varieties of paintbrush, delphinium and streptanthus.) This trail re-enters forest cover near the bottom of the canyon as it skirts the northeastern side of tiny, lily-padded Olaine Lake, and then strikes the river amid a stand of quaking aspen and incense cedar. Fishing along the river is fair for rainbow (to 8″).

At the Shadow Lake trail junction our route turns left across the river and then ascends the west side of the canyon via a rocky but well-maintained trail. This path rises steeply for 800′ along juniper- and cedar-dotted switchbacks, and has excellent

views of tumbling Shadow Creek as it falls from the eastern lip
of Shadow Lake. Southeastward from these switchbacks one has
picturesque views of the Mammoth Crest, "Veed" by the steep
San Joaquin River canyon walls. Arrival at lovely Shadow Lake
(8800') is achieved via a granite notch that gives the hiker a
"fish's-eye view" of the lake and the backgrounding Ritter
Range. Good campsites may be found at the outlet, inlet, and
northern edge. Because of heavy use of the lake, firewood is
scarce. Fishing for rainbow and brook (to 10") is fair in mid
season, and excellent in early and late season.

2nd Hiking Day **(Shadow Lake** to **Agnew Meadows Campground,** 3 miles) : Retrace steps of 1st hiking day.

70   Agnew Meadows to Lake Ediza

TRIP   From Agnew Meadows Campground to Lake Ediza
             (round trip). Topo map (15') *Devils Postpile*. Best
             mid or late season ; 12 miles.

Grade	Trail/layover days	Total recom- mended days
Leisurely	2/1	3
Moderate	2/0	2
Strenuous	—	—

HILITES   This is one of the finest routes in the Mammoth
             Lakes region for viewing the spectacular Ritter
             Range, including Banner Peak, Mt. Ritter and the
             Minarets. The pristine, alpine beauty of Sierra lakes
             is nowhere better exemplified than at Lake Ediza,
             where amid towering evidences of glacial and vol-
             canic action, the visitor can readily appreciate the
             colossal natural forces that shaped, thrust, and
             kneaded these natural landforms. Alpine meadows
             at the southeast end of Lake Ediza are often used
             as base camps by parties of mountain climbers who
             are ascending eastern routes on the Minarets. (Note :

inexperienced climbers should not attempt any of these climbs. The often-treacherous rock composition and the ever-unreliable glaciers make these ascents hazardous.)

DESCRIPTION

1st Hiking Day **(Agnew Meadows Campground** to **Lake Ediza, 6 miles)** : See 1st hiking day, trip 69, for the first 3 miles of this route. From Shadow Lake the trail parallels cascading Shadow Creek all the way to Lake Ediza (9300'). Our route skirts the north side of Shadow Lake, meets the John Muir Trail to Devils Postpile at the inlet near the bridge, and follows this famous route for about 1½ miles to a junction where it branches off to Garnet and Thousand Island lakes. From the junction our trail, though heavily used, invites the traveler to stop and rest at one of the several waterfalls. Each has its own deep fishing or swimming hole (late season, when the water has lost most of its chill), and the granite slabs on the water's edge invite sunbathing. At the junction of the Nydiver Lakes trail our route veers left. There are several "packer" campsites near the creek, and others in the meadows at the southeast end of Lake Ediza. Firewood at the lake is scarce. Fishing is fair for brook (to 10") in Lake Ediza.

2nd Hiking Day **(Lake Ediza** to **Agnew Meadows Campground, 6 miles)** : Retrace steps of 1st hiking day.

Agnew Meadows to Devils Postpile **71**

TRIP   From Agnew Meadows Campground to Devils Postpile Campground (shuttle trip). Topo map (15') *Devils Postpile*. Best mid or late season; 15.2 miles (1 mile cross country).

Grade	Trail/layover days	Total recom- mended days
Leisurely	3/0	3
Moderate	2/0	2
Strenuous	—	—

HILITES　For those travelers who like their country high, alpine and remote, this trip is ideal. However, this route is recommended for experienced knapsackers only, because of the steep climb, which is often made more hazardous by late snow melt between Lower and Upper Iceberg lakes. There is no route that offers a finer view of the spectacular and unusual Minarets.

DESCRIPTION (Leisurely trip)

1st Hiking Day **(Agnew Meadows Campground** to **Lake Ediza,** 6 miles) : See 1st hiking day, trip 70.

2nd Hiking Day **(Lake Ediza** to **Minaret Lake,** 3 miles) : The trail climbs south from the southeast end of Lake Ediza over a steep, willow-covered slope. Often the path is almost obliterated by the heavy growth, and some care should be taken when it crosses and recrosses the outlet stream from Lower Iceberg Lake. A memorable view presents itself from the top of the first rise. Below, the glacial cirque that cradles Lake Ediza becomes very clear, and through a notch in the granite to the northwest, Banner and Ritter thrust upward in a side-on view. Immediately to the east, the massive 11501' heights of black Volcanic Ridge dominate the horizon. The trail continues to ascend, winding through tiny alpine meadows covered with the typical lupine, heather, and pussypaws until it emerges at Lower Iceberg Lake (9800'). Both Lower and Upper Iceberg lakes (the topo map calls them "Iceberg Lake" and "Cecile Lake") are favorites of photographers. These granitoid, glacially fed alpine gems are used by lensmen to reflect the towering pinnacles and gray ice sheets of the Minarets.

Leaving the outlet of Lower Iceberg Lake, the foot path becomes somewhat indistinct as it rounds the eastern side and then ascends 500' along the outlet stream from Upper Iceberg Lake. This particular ascent frequently has treacherous, late-melting snow on it, making it a route for experienced knapsackers only. Upper Iceberg Lake (10280') undoubtedly has the choicest views of the Minarets. The trail, undiscernible at this point, rounds the eastern edge of the lake on the broken black rock of Volcanic Ridge. From the southeastern edge of the lake, there are awe-inspiring views of Clyde Minaret, adjoining Minaret Lake, and Minaret Creek canyon. The 500' descent to Minaret Lake is best made over the rock-and-talus slope below this viewpoint, and it may entail some rudimentary rock-climbing. A foot path going east along the northern side of Minaret Lake joins the Forest Service trail at the outlet, and good campsites dot this shore (9800'). Firewood is ample, and fishing in the lake is fair for brook (to 10").

3rd Hiking Day **(Minaret Lake** to **Devils Postpile Campground,** 6.2 miles) : This day is a relatively steady descent of 2200' over a well-maintained but dusty trail. In its upper reaches its dustiness is due to people and stock eroding the decomposing granite; in its lower reaches the dustiness is due to a deep layer of pumice (volcanic ash). From Minaret Lake the trail descends over rocky switchbacks and enters red fir, silver pine, lodgepole pine and mountain hemlock as it nears the highest meadow on Minaret Creek. It then passes the trail to Minaret Mine (not in operation). Just west of this trail junction is a moderately warm lake with good swimming in late season. After switchbacking down a granite slope beside the cascades of Minaret Creek, the trail re-enters timber cover and winds down a pumice slope to Johnston Meadow. This meadow has a magnificent display of wildflowers that usually lasts well into mid season. Part way through the meadow, the trail rejoins the John Muir Trail, and fords Minaret Creek. About ½ mile southeast the route passes the trail to Beck and Holcomb lakes, and from here the now very dusty pumice trail drops steeply to the west edge of a long meadow beside the San Joaquin River, where many Belding ground squirrels are likely to be seen. Beyond the Summit Meadow trail, our route crosses the river via a large bridge at the south end of the meadow, and then turns north to Devils Postpile Campground (7559').

72 Agnew Meadows to Devils Postpile

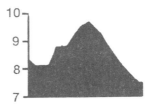

TRIP From Agnew Meadows Campground to Devils Postpile Campground (shuttle trip). Topo map (15′) *Devils Postpile*. Best mid or late season; 11.9 miles.

Grade	Trail/layover days	Total recommended days
Leisurely	—	—
Moderate	2/0	2
Strenuous	—	—

HILITES After crossing the Middle Fork of the San Joaquin, this interesting route ascends to picturesque Shadow Lake. Then, doubling back, it traverses the long, narrow, lake-dotted bench that breaks the slope from Volcanic Ridge to the river. Dense fir forests, intimate, solitary lakes, and good fishing make this an excellent beginner's weekend trip.

DESCRIPTION

1st Hiking Day **(Agnew Meadows Campground** to **Rosalie Lake,** 5.5 miles) : See 1st hiking day, trip 69 to Shadow Lake. At the inlet to beautiful Shadow Lake, this route joins the John Muir Trail and crosses Shadow Creek on a large log bridge. The trail rounds the south side of the lake, and begins a series of 20 switchbacks up a densely forested slope (fir). Breather stops along this 500′ climb afford colorful views of the deep blues and greens of Shadow Lake, and the crest of the ridge is soon topped at a rocky saddle with a meadowy bottom. This saddle leads to the good campsites on the north side of charming Rosalie Lake (9350′). Firewood is ample, and fishing is good for rainbow and brook (to 9″).

2nd Hiking Day **(Rosalie Lake** to **Devils Postpile Campground,** 6.4 miles) : Fishermen who wish to try the many lakes that line the first 3 miles of this day's route will want to get an early start. The trail circles the east side of Rosalie Lake, and

climbs over the southeast ridge that flanks the lake. When passing Gladys Lake (known locally as Vivian Lake) the trail affords views out over the San Joaquin River canyon. To the
west, the black, recrystallized volcanic rocks of Volcanic Ridge
dominate the skyline, and to the east the rock drops away into
the San Joaquin and rises on the far side to red-topped San
Joaquin Mountain and the distinctive Two Teats. From here
the route drops down into the Trinity Lakes basin. These tiny,
meadow-fringed lakes have fair-to-good fishing for rainbow
and brook (to 8″). Access to Castle and Emily lakes is via a
short, steep foot trail that takes off from the western side of the
trail, and fishing at these lakes is about the same as above. From
the lowest of the Trinity Lakes, the trail descends steeply via
dusty trail to Johnston Meadow, where it joins the trail from
Minaret Lake. Follow this trail as described in the 3rd hiking
day, trip 71.

Agnew Meadows to Garnet Lake 73

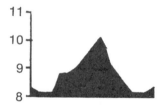

TRIP From Agnew Meadows Campground to Garnet
Lake (loop trip). Topo map (15′) *Devils Postpile.*
Best mid or late season; 13.1 miles.

Grade	Trail/layover days	Total recom- mended days
Leisurely	3/1	4
Moderate	3/0	3
Strenuous	2/0	2

HILITES Employing about a 4-mile stretch of the well-known
John Muir Trail, this trip surveys some of the
northern Sierra's most dramatic country. In the region east of the jagged Ritter Range are some of
the area's most vivid alpine lakes and spectacular
landforms. This route traverses a section of this
country in visiting Shadow and Garnet lakes.

DESCRIPTION (Leisurely trip)

1st Hiking Day **(Agnew Meadows Campground** to **Shadow Lake,** 3 miles) : See 1st hiking day, trip 69.

2nd Hiking Day **(Shadow Lake** to **Garnet Lake,** 4.5 miles) : At the inlet to Shadow Lake, this route joins the John Muir Trail and ascends westerly for 1.1 miles through Shadow Creek canyon before turning north. The trail suffers heavy use, and is likely to be dusty, particularly in late season. The dust, however, settles as the trail emerges from the fir and lodgepole ground cover and tops the 1100' climb from the Shadow Creek Trail junction to the rocky ridge above Garnet Lake. This is an excellent place from which to appreciate the view of the lake itself, Ritter and Banner, and Mt. Davis to the west. The traveler will also note the striking change in the countryside. From the heavily timbered slopes of Shadow Creek canyon, the landscape, except for scattered stands of stunted hemlock and lodgepole, is now predominantly glacially polished rock. From this viewpoint the trail descends 500' to the outlet of Garnet Lake (9680'). Fair campsites may be found near the outlet and on the north side of the lake, but firewood is somewhat scarce. Fishing for brook and rainbow (to 10") is only fair.

3rd Hiking Day **(Garnet Lake** to **Agnew Meadows Campground via the River Trail,** 5.6 miles) : The lateral leading to the River Trail branches from the main trail on the south side of the outlet of Garnet Lake. It is a narrow foot path that descends steeply over a very rocky section in the spray from Garnet Falls. Three-fourths mile northeast it strikes the River Trail, where our route turns right (southeast). The River Trail from this junction is a heavily timbered stretch of trail that passes the Agnew Pass trail lateral and winds down the canyon. The sound of cascading San Joaquin River is a pleasant accompaniment to this dusty descent, and the river is seldom more than a few yards away. Fishing on the San Joaquin for rainbow and brook (to 9") is only fair, and swimming, even in late season, is likely to be somewhat chilly. This route meets the Shadow Lake trail 2 miles from Agnew Meadows Campground, whence it retraces part of the 1st hiking day.

Agnew Meadows to 1000 Island Lake 74

TRIP From Agnew Meadows Campground to Thousand Island Lake via the River Trail (loop trip). Topo map (15′) *Devils Postpile*. Best mid or late season; 16.6 miles.

Grade	Trail/layover days	Total recom- mended days
Leisurely	3/1	4
Moderate	3/0	3
Strenuous	2/0	2

HILITES The climax of this trip is Garnet and Thousand Island lakes. Settings of alpine grandeur make these large lakes favorites of lensmen and naturalists alike. Although this trip can be made in a weekend, the superlative scenery warrants a slower pace. Almost half of this route follows the scenic John Muir Trail.

DESCRIPTION (Leisurely trip)

1st Hiking Day **(Agnew Meadows Campground to Shadow Lake,** 3 miles): See 1st hiking day, trip 69.

2nd Hiking Day **(Shadow Lake to Thousand Island Lake,** 6.5 miles): For a description of the route from Shadow Lake to Garnet Lake (4.5 miles) see 2nd hiking day, trip 73. Beyond the outlet of Garnet Lake, care should be exercised when crossing the 500′ talus-covered ridge that separates Garnet and Thousand Island lakes. This section of trail, though well-maintained, is rocky and treacherous. Enroute, the trail circles the east shore of dramatic Ruby Lake, and then drops down past colorful Emerald Lake to the outlet of Thousand Island Lake (9834′). The island-dotted lake's wind-swept surface reflects the imposing facade of Banner Peak and the more sharply etched Mt. Ritter. Several exposed campsites (subject to a great deal of wind) may be found around the outlet and on the north side of the lake, the better ones being a mile or two west of the Muir Trail and back from the water. Fishing for rainbow and brook (7-13″) is particularly good in early and late season. Firewood is scarce.

3rd Hiking Day **(Thousand Island Lake** to **Agnew Meadow Campground** via the River Trail, 7.1 miles) : This route leaves the John Muir Trail at the meadowy outlet of Thousand Island Lake, and proceeds northeast past several small snow tarns. The alpine setting is soon left behind as the trail re-enters forest cover, fords the infant San Joaquin River, and ascends the far bank. Our route then veers southeast to a junction with the High Trail, branches right at this junction, and slants down through dense lodgepole and fir to the Garnet Lake lateral, whence it proceeds as described in 3rd hiking day, trip 73.

75   Agnew Meadows to 1000 Island Lake

TRIP   From Agnew Meadows Campground to Thousand Island Lake via the High Trail (loop trip). Topo map (15′) *Devils Postpile*. Best mid or late season; 16.6 miles.

Grade	Trail/layover days	Total recom-mended days
Leisurely	3/1	4
Moderate	3/0	3
Strenuous	2/0	2

HILITES   The San Joaquin River drainage provides this trip with a fascinating contrast. The imposing scenery viewed from the west side of the drainage below the Ritter Range has already been described, but few travelers have taken in the altogether different beauty of the slopes of San Joaquin Mountain. Here on the east side of the canyon the trail traveler passes through an entirely different kind of ground cover and he has unbroken views of the Ritter Range. A first assessment would indicate that this hillside was a scrubby, arid stretch, but it is not. Many streams (even in late season) interrupt the trail, and wildflowers line the route.

DESCRIPTION (Leisurely trip)

1st Hiking Day **(Agnew Meadows Campground** to **Shadow Lake,** 3 miles) : See 1st hiking day, trip 69.

2nd Hiking Day **(Shadow Lake** to **Thousand Island Lake,** 6.5 miles) : See 2nd hiking day, trip 74.

3rd Hiking Day **(Thousand Island Lake** to **Agnew Meadows Campground,** via the High Trail, 7.1 miles) : Proceed from Thousand Island Lake to the High Trail junction as described in 3rd hiking day, trip 74. From this trail junction, the route ascends past meadowy Badger Lakes and past a secondary lateral to Agnew Pass. On this first slope the trail emerges from the dense forest cover, and then it winds up and down through a ground cover that, except for a few scattered stands of pine, is sage, bitterbrush, willow, and some mountain alder. When the trail descends to one of the many tributaries of the San Joaquin River, the traveler should observe the lush growth of wildflowers, including larkspur, lupine, shooting star, columbine, penstemon, monkeyflower, scarlet gilia and tiger lily. Views are excellent of the Ritter Range to the west; particularly impressive is the "Veed" view of Shadow Lake directly across the San Joaquin River canyon. From this viewpoint the trail drops sharply to a bench just above Agnew Meadows, and on this slope it returns to forested country. The last mile of severe descent is made via dusty, eroded switchbacks to the road just south of Agnew Meadows Campground.

76   Chiquito Creek to Chain Lakes

TRIP   From Chiquito Creek Trailhead to Upper Chain Lake (round trip). Topo map (15′) *Merced Peak*. Best mid or late season; 16 miles.

Grade	Trail/layover days	Total recommended days
Leisurely	2/1	3
Moderate	2/0	2
Strenuous	—	—

HILITES   This round trip has several interesting route alternatives that will appeal to the experienced knapsacker who is looking for a moderate weekend trip. Granite-bound Chain Lakes are a superlative high-country setting for a base camp, whether the purpose be angling, photography, hiking, or just communing.

DESCRIPTION

1st Hiking Day (**Chiquito Creek Trailhead** to **Upper Chain Lake,** 8 miles) : The trailhead is at a bend in a dirt road (not shown on the topo map) that goes up Chiquito Creek canyon from the major dirt road ("434") leading from Bass Lake to Jackass Meadow. From the trailhead (7300′) the trail immediately begins its 650′ ascent to Chiquito Lake (8010′). This duff segment of trail switchbacks through one of the most magnificent forests of red fir, sugar, yellow and Jeffrey pine remaining outside Yosemite National Park. However, at this writing, "harvesting" of this stand was underway, and knapsackers may well mourn the loss of these trees. Just before arriving at the Yosemite Park boundary at Chiquito Pass, the trail passes marshy Chiquito Lake (poor fishing). A few yards past the north end of the lake, an unmaintained but passable foot path veers off to the northeast, leading to Spotted Lakes. (Later in this trip experienced knapsackers will find this path an interesting alternative route by which to loop back from Upper Chain Lake.)

After crossing the pass and passing the Buck Camp trail junction, our route climbs gently north along the slope of the South Fork of the Merced River. Occasional eastward glimpses may be had of vermilion-capped Red Top Peak and the chalky-white granite of Sing and Gale peaks. Many of the large red firs and lodgepole pines that line this section of trail looked down on the U. S. Cavalry patrols which worked this part of the Park around the turn of the century. Immediately after fording the outlet creek of Chain Lakes, our route branches east along the creek, and it is an easy climb to the lower of the Chain Lakes. Fishing is excellent for brook (9-14″), subject to midsummer slowdown. Swimming, particularly in late season, is good though brisk, and good camping sites may be found at all three lakes. Wood is abundant around the two lower lakes, scarce at the upper lake (9280′). (Note that the figure "8800" just north of Spotted Lakes on the topo map should be 9200.) However, many hikers who prefer the intoxicating atmosphere of a high-country, granitoid lake will overlook the scarcity of wood. If you plan layover days, these lakes make an excellent base camp for cross-country side excursions to Spotted or Breeze lakes, where fishing is good-to-excellent for brook (9-14″) with a midsummer slowdown. (Note: the cross-country route from Upper Chain Lake to Breeze Lake may entail some rock-climbing, and should be undertaken only by experienced knapsackers.)

2nd Hiking Day (**Upper Chain Lake** to **Chiquito Creek Trailhead,** 8 miles) : Retrace steps of the 1st hiking day, or loop to Chiquito Lake via Spotted Lakes (1½ miles cross country, and 4 miles by poor foot trail).

Ouzel

77   Chiquito Creek to Rutherford Lake

TRIP
From Chiquito Creek Trailhead to Trailhead on the Strawberry Tungsten Mine Road (shuttle trip). Topo map (15′) *Merced Peak*. Best mid or late season; 24.7 miles.

Grade	Trail/layover days	Total recom- mended days
Leisurely	—	—
Moderate	3/1	4
Strenuous	3/0	3

HILITES
Rarely does a knapsack trip of 3 days' duration offer such a wide choice of recreational opportunities. Fishing on either side of Fernandez Pass is good-to-excellent, and alternative cross-country routes add a dash of spice for the more adventurous hiker. Scenery along the trail varies from dense red fir forests to the wide-open vistas of high, alpine, glaciated lakes.

DESCRIPTION

1st Hiking Day **(Chiquito Creek Trailhead** to **Upper Chain Lake,** 8 miles)**: See 1st hiking day, trip 76.

2nd Hiking Day **(Upper Chain Lake** to **Rutherford Lake,** 8.5 miles): This route, via Moraine Meadow, begins at 9280′, and descends along the Chain Lakes outlet stream to the trail junction (8500′) of the Buck Camp and Fernandez Pass trails. The section extending north to Moraine Meadow ascends gradually on a "duff" trail largely composed of lodgepole pine needles. Shortly after fording the Merced River, the trail strikes the Merced Pass trail, and at this point our route turns east for a mile, and then re-fords the Merced. Fishing is fair-to-good for rainbow and brook (to 9″). At this point the trail turns southerly and ascends 400′ to two unnamed lakes fed by the outlet stream from Breeze Lake. Fishing at these lakes is fair-to-good for brook and rainbow (to 8″) but anglers will probably wish to bypass these lakes and take the short (0.7 mile) side trail to Breeze Lake for a try at the larger brook (9-14″). Breeze Lake, scooped out of the north face of Gale Peak, is a large (35-acre) granitoid, glacial lake that has an honest claim to its name. The large granite wall bordering the east side gives way to a long, glacially polished scoop on the southeast that acts as a flue to channel the wind across the blue surface of the lake.

From the Breeze Lake side-trail, it is but another 600′ by short, rocky, eroded switchbacks to Fernandez Pass (10200′). This pass, and the lakes of the same name 1 mile east, were named for Sgt. Joseph Fernandez, U.S. Cavalry. Fernandez was among the members of the Benson exploration party seeking the headwaters of the Merced River in 1895-97, and he was later instrumental in planting the first fish in this section of the Park. Views from Fernandez Pass are splendid of both the San Joaquin and Merced River drainages, and on a clear day one can see Banner, Ritter, and the Minarets to the east. Fernandez Pass marks the Park boundary. After you descend 680′ over the steep and rocky switchbacks, you arrive at the marked trail junction to Rutherford Lake. From here it is but 1 steep mile 400′ up to the lake. Rutherford Lake (9760′) is a large (28-acre) lake, nestled in a rocky basin at timberline. A difference in the policies of the National Park Service and the Forest Service is immediately evident in the Forest Service "Improved" campsites, on the east side of the lake. Fireplaces and toilets will be present at most campsites for the rest of this trip. Fishing at the lake is fair (with the notorious midsummer slack period) for golden and brook (to 16″). Firewood is ample.

3rd Hiking Day **(Rutherford Lake** to **Trailhead on the Strawberry Tungsten Mine Road,** 8.2 miles) : After retracing the 1 mile to the Fernandez Pass trail, our route turns east along the main trail that follows Fernandez Creek. This route descends through a dense lodgepole forest that occasionally gives way to extensions of the large meadow on the south side of Fernandez Creek. These breaks in the timber cover offer splendid opportunities for the early-rising and silent knapsacker to observe the wildlife that grazes the meadow and drinks from the creek. Fishing along the creek is good for the abundant, but small, brook. This duff trail passes the junction of the Post Peak Pass trail and veers southeast. The lodgepole pine begins to give way to red fir in the vicinity of Twin Lakes (no fishing, but perhaps the warmest swimming on this trip). As the trail crosses the easy rocky shoulder southeast of Twin Lakes, there are good views of the Gale Lakes basin and of Gale and Sing peaks as seen from the eastern side of the range. Here the trail becomes somewhat dusty, owing to the heavy summer-graze stock traffic (Forest Service "Multiple-use" program). The going becomes somewhat steeper as the trail descends 700' to Madera Creek (log crossing) and then climbs 500' to the junction of the Vandeberg Lake trail. From this point it is an easy downhill amble through a changed forest cover of lodgepole, sugar, Jeffrey and yellow pine to the marked trailhead on the Strawberry Tungsten Mine Road.

78   Chiquito Creek to Bridalveil Creek

TRIP   Chiquito Creek Trailhead to Bridalveil Creek Campground (shuttle trip). Topo maps (15') *Merced Peak, Yosemite*. Best mid or late season; 30 miles.

Grade	Trail/layover days	Total recommended days
Leisurely	4/1	5
Moderate	4/0	4
Strenuous	3/0	3

HILITES   This is a shuttle trip that crosses some of the more scenic southern Yosemite National Park boundary country. Some of the finest fishing in the Park is found along this route at Chain and Royal Arch lakes, and bonus angling spots can be explored on layover days at Breeze, Spotted, Johnson and Crescent lakes. The gigantic, sweeping effects of glacial action are seen throughout this trip. The resulting cirques, U-shaped valleys, jagged ranges, and polished granite are a constant source of awe and delight to the traveler.

DESCRIPTION (Leisurely trip)

1st Hiking Day (**Upper Chiquito Creek Campground** to **Upper Chain Lake,** 8 miles) : See 1st hiking day, trip 76.

2nd Hiking Day (**Upper Chain Lake** to **Royal Arch Lake,** 9 miles) : Retrace the route of the 1st hiking day to the junction with the Fernandez Pass trail. A few yards to the northwest the Buck Camp trail branches west and follows the outlet creek from Chain Lakes as it falls to rendezvous with the South Fork of the Merced. This route fords the South Fork and swings southwesterly over a lodgepole covered slope. Views of the South Fork canyon may be had from this slope. The depth of the U-shaped, glacially formed slopes gives a good account of the forces that were at work when the ice flow originating in the Clark Range to the north was in its heyday. After fording Givens Creek the trail crosses a ridge, where it meets the Moraine Meadow/Merced Pass trail, and then drops down into the Buck Creek drainage. At Buck Camp Yosemite National Park has a trail-maintenance station, and emergency services may be obtained. From Buck Camp the trail ascends via switchbacks to the junction with the Buena Vista trail. From this point it is but 0.7 mile to Royal Arch Lake (8700'). Large, black, rainbow-arched striations across the eastern wall of polished granite gave this picturesque lake its name. These distinctive markings are the result of water discoloration due to centuries of seepage. They make a magnificent backdrop to the excellent fishing for brook and rainbow (8-14") and anglers may well regard this relatively small (18-acre) lake as the high point of the trip. Numerous good campsites are on the northern and western shores, and this lake makes an excellent base camp for scenic and angling excursions to nearby Buena Vista, Johnson and Crescent lakes. Swimming is good in late season and wood is plentiful.

3rd Hiking Day (**Royal Arch Lake** to **Turner Meadows,** 6.5 miles) : See 2nd hiking day, trip 82.

4th Hiking Day (**Turner Meadows** to **Bridalveil Creek Campground,** 6.5 miles) : See 1st hiking day, trip 82.

79 Granite Creek Road to Rutherford Lake

TRIP   From Trailhead on the Strawberry Tungsten Mine Road to Rutherford Lake (semiloop trip). Topo map (15′) *Merced Peak*. Best mid or late season; 19.7 miles.

Grade	Trail/layover days	Total recommended days
Leisurely	3/1	4
Moderate	3/0	3
Strenuous	2/0	2

HILITES   The lake-filled area east of Gale and Sing peaks provides a choice trip for the angler. Except for a midsummer slack period, these lakes are good producers of brook, rainbow, and even golden trout. Add to this benefit the dramatic peaks that lie to the west, and the 35-mile views to the south, and every hiker will find cause for visiting this country. This trip is the answer for the hiker with a short time for travel who wishes to get into the spectacular south boundary country.

DESCRIPTION (Leisurely trip)

1st Hiking Day **(Trailhead on the Strawberry Tungsten Mine Road** to **Vandeberg Lake,** 4 miles) : The trailhead, on a rough dirt road ("434"), is located 32 miles from The Pines on Bass Lake. It is 4.5 miles beyond the turnoff to Clover Meadow. The trail leaves the road and bears northwesterly for a steady uphill climb of 900′ through a forest of red fir, and lodgepole, Jeffrey, yellow and sugar pine. Bird fanciers will find this stretch of trail of particular interest because of the large variety of birdlife. Early-season hikers should listen for the distinctive pulsating "whump-whump-whump" mating call of the ventriloquist grouse. The "chirrr" of the white-headed woodpecker may be heard at any time of the season, and the monotonous cry of the junco

will dog one's footsteps for the entire trip. Other birds one encounters are the white-crowned sparrow, chickadee, and olive-
sided flycatcher.

As the trail crosses the ridge into the Madera Creek watershed, there are views through the thinning timber of Banner
Peak, Mt. Ritter and the Minarets to the northeast. Southward
one has views across the canyon of the Middle San Joaquin to
Kaiser Ridge, up the canyon of the South San Joaquin, and down
the main river to the sides of Mammoth Pool. Here our route
enters the Mount Dana-Minarets Wild Area. The trail branching left to Vandeberg Lake is not marked on the topo map; it is
a new, signed section turning left from the Fernandez Pass trail
just beyond this boundary. The trail climbs gently west through
aspen meadows to Vandeberg Lake (8700'). (The trail is faint
on the last rise before the lake.) Here beneath the brooding
black granite of Madera Peak, Vandeberg and Middle and Upper
Lady lakes provide good fishing for brook (to 9") except in
midsummer. There are Forest Service "Improved" campsites
with woodwork and rockwork by campers on the north shore
and at the inlet of Vandeberg Lake.

2nd Hiking Day **(Vandeberg Lake to Rutherford Lake,** 7.5
miles): The route to the Fernandez Pass trail is unmarked on
the topo map. This day offers many possible stopping places to
fish, eat, look, or just sit. The trail ascends the right side of the
lake inlet to the sign marking a turn to the right to Stanford
Lakes, a mile away over a low crest. Named after an old Fresno
family, they lie on the Shirley Creek tributary of the west fork
of Granite Creek. Anglers will find brook (to 9"). From Stanford Lakes one has a choice. He may (1) choose the signed trail
to Lillian Lake, taking off from the upper end of the main Stanford Lake, or (2) take the unmarked trail up Shirley Creek to
little (5-acre) Shirley Lake (9200'), which is situated in a
shallow granite basin at timberline (good fishing for brook to
12"). Anglers may want to cross the granite shoulder south
from Shirley Lake to Chittenden Lake, for the excellent fishing
for brook (to 12"). The basin in which these lakes lie affords
good views westward of Sing and Gale peaks, remnants of a
Pleistocene ice age. Then, great ice masses formed on the then-
much-rounder slopes of the peaks, and the jagged tops that remain are the "islands" that escaped the plucking and grinding of
the glaciers. If the hiker chooses to go via Shirley Lake, he can
then reach Lillian by crossing a slight divide toward the east
(cross country) and following the inlet stream. Lillian Lake is
the largest lake (35 acres, 8885') in the Granite Creek basin, and
has fair fishing for brook and rainbow (to 11"), best in early

and late season. It is a natural lake, but a flow-maintenance dam was added in 1953, and today it controls the level of the lake and the flow in the outlet stream. Cut timber along one side intrudes on the wilderness feeling of this lake.

From Lillian Lake a well-marked trail leads east to the junction with the Rainbow Lake trail, and thence to the basin of Rainbow and Ruth lakes (good fishing for brook — no rainbow, despite the name). From Ruth Lake the route goes cross country ¼ mile northwest to the Fernandez Lakes chain (good fishing for brook) and down that valley to Fernandez Creek and the Fernandez Pass trail. Here our route turns left (west) on a steep climb to the signed Rutherford Lake turnoff. Thence our route turns right (north) and climbs steeply above timberline to 28-acre Rutherford Lake (9800′). There are fair-to-good Forest Service "Improved" campsites on the west side of the lake south of the outlet. Firewood is ample, and fishing is fair for golden and brook (to 16″).

3rd Hiking Day **(Rutherford Lake** to **Trailhead on the Strawberry Tungsten Mine Road,** 8.2 miles). See 3rd hiking day, trip 77.

80   Granite Creek Road to Isberg Lakes

TRIP   From Trailhead on the Strawberry Tungsten Mine Road to Granite Creek Campground (shuttle trip). Topo map (15′) *Merced Peak*. Best mid or late season; 29 miles.

Grade	Trail/layover days	Total recommended days
Leisurely	5/1	6
Moderate	4/1	5
Strenuous	3/1	4

HILITES   This is a challenging hike, with an altitude change
of over 3000'. Scenery varies from the cloisters of
dense forests and the intimacy of small meadows to
the overwhelming panoramas from two high passes.
Fishing is best in early or late season, and ranges
from fair to excellent.

DESCRIPTION (Leisurely trip)

1st Hiking Day **(Trailhead on the Strawberry Tungsten Mine
Road** to **Vandeberg Lake,** 4 miles) : See 1st hiking day, trip 79.
2nd Hiking Day **(Vandeberg Lake** to **Fernandez Creek Meadow,** 6.5 miles) : Proceed to Lillian Lake as described in 2nd day,
trip 79. The trail from Lillian Lake goes east over gentle slopes
through a mixed forest cover to a ford of the North Fork of
Madera Creek. It then rises slightly to meet the Fernandez Pass
trail, where our route turns left (northwest). After a short
climb the trail passes between the Twin Lakes (no fish, but a
good chance of warm swimming). Heading toward the divide
that is the border of Yosemite National Park, the trail comes
to a meadow with good campsites at the junction of the Fernandez Pass trail and the Isberg Pass/Post Peak Pass trail. Small
brook trout are plentiful on pleasant Fernandez Creek.
3rd Hiking Day **(Fernandez Creek Meadow** to **Isberg Lakes,**
7.8 miles) : Two passes, both over 10500', are the reward for
this day's efforts. The Isberg Pass/Post Peak Pass trail turns
eastward along Fernandez Creek for about ½ mile, fords the
West Fork of Granite Creek, and climbs gently to Post Creek
(9040'). Fishing on the creek is good for brook (to 8"). The
first 3 miles traverse red fir and some hemlock and silver pine.
Then the trail switchbacks steadily up exposed granite to 1-acre
Porphyry Lake (10100'), where fishing is fair for brook and
rainbow. This deep, rocky lake was named for the porphyritic
granite that surrounds the area. A breather here is well-earned,
and the scenery makes it a good choice for a break.

From Porphyry Lake it is 1.5 miles to the highest point on
this route, Post Peak Pass (10700'). The pass marks the divide
between the Merced and San Joaquin drainages. Our route recrosses this divide 1.5 miles farther on at Isberg Pass (10500').
From this section of trail the hiker has views of the Clark
Range to the west, the Cathedral Range to the north and the
tops of Banner, Ritter and the Minarets to the east. This route
was discovered and named by a military expedition in 1895
under the command of Lt. N. F. McClure. From Isberg Pass
the trail descends 1 mile on the southeast slope to Upper Isberg
Lake, and ½ mile beyond to Lower Isberg Lake (9800'). Fish-

ing on these lakes is fair-to-good for brook and rainbow (to 8″) but swimming is poor. There are a few fair campsites at the lower lake, and ample firewood.

4th Hiking Day **(Isberg Lakes** to **Cora Lakes,** 5.7 miles — 6.7 miles by cross country to East Fork of Granite Creek) : From Lower Isberg Lake the trail soon re-enters timber, and about a mile beyond skirts the side of Sadler Lake (9345′). Named for another member of the McClure expedition of 1895, Sadler Lake today affords excellent fishing for brook (7-10″) in early and late season. The lodgepole pines cluster on the south shore, leaving the north, west and east sides open to alpine meadows. These meadows are a splash of wildflower color in early season. From Sadler Lake the trail passes through scattered stands of hemlock and silver pine as it descends steadily southward, and then passes the Timber Creek lateral to Joe Crane Lake. This trail segment parallels the East Fork of Granite Creek, and fishing for brook (some rainbow and brown) is good (to 10″) on the stretches just below Sadler Lake and above Detachment Meadow. However, many anglers will pass up the stream fishing for the slightly larger trout of Cora Lakes (8400′). The largest of the three Cora Lakes is Middle Cora (16 acres), where the best camping may be found. This lake is heavily timbered, and firewood is abundant.

The hiker who is seeking an alternative route and a camping place away from the trail, and whose feet do not balk at a 2-mile cross-country walk, may elect to turn right (west) at the south end of Middle Cora Lake. This unmarked route crosses an easy rocky ridge, veers southwest, and descends to the secluded streamside campsites along the East Fork of Granite Creek. The deep pools and one dashing water slide make this a pleasant night's stop. To join the route described for the 5th hiking day, this cross-country route continues down the East Fork of Granite Creek and it meets the Cora Lakes/Granite Creek Campground trail at the foot of Green Mountain.

5th Hiking Day **(Cora Lakes** to **Granite Creek Campground,** 5 miles) : Within a mile of Cora Lakes the trail rejoins the East Fork of Granite Creek, and follows it closely as far as the rocky west shoulder of Green Mountain. The trail then veers away from the creek and descends rapidly for 2.2 miles before rejoining the stream just north of Granite Creek Campground. This 1000′ descent is marked by the reverse order of the ground-cover change noted in the 1st and 3rd hiking days. The ford of the West Fork of Granite Creek (quite wide at this point) is at a log bridge at the southern end of the campground.

Yosemite Valley to Merced Lake

81

TRIP   From Yosemite Valley (Happy Isles) to Merced Lake (round trip). Topo maps (15′) *Yosemite, Merced Peak*. Best early season; 26.8 miles.

Grade	Trail/layover days	Total recommended days
Leisurely	4/0	4
Moderate	3/0	3
Strenuous	2/0	2

HILITES   An early season trip (low altitude, early melt), this route offers all the scenic grandeur of the Valley attractions, plus the intimate knowledge of the back country that only the knapsacker can have. Fishing is good during early season on the Merced River and at Merced Lake. Swimming is poor during the early season, owing to the chilly waters, but photographers and naturalists will find an exciting area of geologic spectacle and history.

DESCRIPTION (Leisurely trip)

1st Hiking Day **(Yosemite Valley to Little Yosemite Valley,** 7.1 miles): This trip is graded as leisurely, but any hiking day that includes an elevation change of 2200′ must entail some strenuous exertion. The strenuous climb is hereby granted. However, this ascent is not too rough if undertaken during the cool of the morning. The trail begins at Happy Isles and climbs steadily around Sierra Point to the Vernal Fall Bridge (junction with the Mist Trail). If one hits the trail early enough, he will see the rising sun's rays haloing in the mist of Vernal Fall. The sight is a memory to sustain one over the steady slog to the switchback from which there is a fine view of the 370′ Illilouette Fall. Then, passing a short lateral trail to the top of Vernal Fall (a

worthwhile sidetrip), the switchbacks continue to the junction
with the Panorama trail. From here it is but a short distance
to the top of Nevada Fall. The Merced River here takes its
mightiest plunge (594') and its roar signals what to expect
long before the traveler arrives at its edge. The view from the
brink of Nevada Fall is unforgettable — the cauldron of flying
water stands in stark relief to the serenity of the trail, and the
barren solidity of Liberty Cap (7076') is a reassuring reminder
of the solid rock on which the viewer stands. A rest stop is
probably in order here. The camp (6100') in Little Yosemite
Valley is a pleasant 3-mile jaunt away over almost level, sandy
trail. The forest cover is open, with large, mature yellow, Jeffrey,
sugar and lodgepole pine. The trail winds along close beside
the now-serene Merced River, and the green depths invite a
fishing line. Ahead, the granite valley walls close in, and the
hiker comes upon the marked camp. Fishing here is fair-to-good
for rainbow, brown and brook (to 10"). There are several
campsites, and firewood is scarce.

2nd Hiking Day **(Little Yosemite Valley** to **Merced Lake,** 6.3
miles) : On the trail one is immediately aware of the relation
between the narrowing valley and the river. As the trail winds up
the easy 200' ascent to Lost Valley, it passes by silent, swift-run-
ning chutes and roaring cascades. By contrast, once in Lost
Valley, the Merced regains its placid appearance. As this route
enters Lost Valley, a sign points out the extreme fire hazard
of the valley. Heavy "fall" and channeled winds make this short
stretch of trail a fire threat, and the smoker should postpone
his cigarette break until well past this dangerous area. At the
end of Lost Valley the trail begins an 800' climb along the Bunnell Cascade. The early part of this climb brings the traveler
above the timber, and it is time well spent to stop and look back
at the granite domes that flank the trail. On the north side
Moraine Dome (8055') dominates the skyline, while on the
south loom Mt. Starr King (9092') and Bunnell Point (8193').
Ahead the trail climbs above the channeled gorge of the now-
writhing, twisting, tormented river. Once over the shoulder of
Bunnell Point, the trail starts down, recrossing the river at
the foot of Echo Valley. Our route passes the Echo Creek trail
junction, and continues on the gradual ascent to Merced Lake
(7216'). The High Sierra Camp is located at the eastern end
of the lake. (Advance reservations are necessary.) Firewood
is ample in early season, and fishing is good for rainbow and
brook (to 9").

3rd Hiking Day **(Merced Lake** to **Little Yosemite Valley,** 6.3
miles) : Retrace steps of 2nd hiking day.

4th Hiking Day **(Little Yosemite Valley** to **Yosemite Valley,** 7.1 miles) : Retrace steps of 1st hiking day, or take the "Mist Trail" from Nevada Fall. It should be noted, however, that part of the latter route is extremely steep, and the section of trail just below Vernal Fall is slippery. (For the Mist Trail, see 5th hiking day, trip 84.)

Bridalveil Creek to Royal Arch Lake   **82**

TRIP   From Bridalveil Creek Campground to Royal Arch Lake (round trip). Topo map (15′) *Yosemite*. Best early-to-mid season; 26.4 miles.

Grade	Trail/layover days	Total recommended days
Leisurely	4/0	4
Moderate	3/0	3
Strenuous	2/0	2

HILITES   In early season this trip route is lush with wildflowers of every variety, and color film is a must for the photographer. Anglers will find few lakes within the Park to rival the fishing at Royal Arch Lake. The easy grade of the topography makes this an excellent early-season choice.

DESCRIPTION (Leisurely trip)

1st Hiking Day **(Bridalveil Creek Campground** to **Turner Meadows,** 6.5 miles) : From the clearly marked trailhead at the campground, the trail begins winding southeasterly along meandering Bridalveil Creek. The grade is gentle as the trail winds through the dense lodgepole and red fir forest. Periodically, the thick undergrowth gives way to intimate, mountain-bluebell-filled meadows. Near Lost Bear Meadow the trail veers southerly beside one of the larger tributaries of Bridalveil Creek. It crosses this tributary twice, and each fording is heralded by banks covered with shooting stars. The second crossing marks the beginning of an easy 400' climb over the ridge that separates the Bridalveil Creek watershed from the Chilnualna Creek watershed. In early and mid season this ridge is colorfully decked out in lush pink and white fields of pussypaws and Douglas phlox. From the top of this ridge, it is a short walk to Turner Meadows and the campsites at the southern end. The cabin site at the head of the meadows (indicated by the rock fireplace) is all that remains of Bill Turner's pioneer abode. He occupied these grasslands while running cattle around the turn of the century. Firewood is plentiful, and there is good stream water.

2nd Hiking Day **(Turner Meadows** to **Royal Arch Lake,** 6.7 miles) : Before leaving Turner Meadows, one should take the opportunity to study the wildlife that frequents the meadows, particularly in the early morning. Within a mile from Turner Meadows, the trail passes the Wawona trail, which branches south, and a mile farther it passes the Chilnualna Lakes trail branching east. These trails were used by U. S. Cavalry patrols at the turn of the century. Their purpose was to facilitate administration of the Park, which at that time meant keeping the poachers, cattlemen, and sheepmen out. Along this stretch the ground cover of red fir gives way to lodgepole pine.

Once past the second trail lateral to Wawona, the trail climbs 450' to Johnson Lake (8300') via Grouse Lake (off the trail to the right) and Crescent Lake, where fishing is poor-to-fair for brook. Johnson Lake, however, affords good fishing for brook and rainbow (9-13"). Johnson Lake was one of the Park's last acquisitions of private property within its boundaries, and two crumbling cabins remain to remind us of our homesteading era. The area around the lake is now reverting to its primitive state. The mile to the junction of the Royal Arch Lake trail is a 400' ascent over a lodgepole-covered slope. Our route leaves the Buck Camp trail to Chiquito Pass and turns north for a relatively level walk through a dense forest cover. Royal Arch Lake (8700') is small (about 15 acres) but it is deep and it supports an excellent, self-sustaining fishery of brook and rainbow (8-14"). Its dramatic name derives from the blackened granite streaks that rainbow across the steep eastern face of the lake basin. Numerous good-to-excellent campsites are on the north and west shores, and firewood is plentiful.

3rd Hiking Day **(Royal Arch Lake** to **Turner Meadows,** 6.7 miles) : Retrace steps of 2nd hiking day.

4th Hiking Day **(Turner Meadows** to **Bridalveil Creek Campground,** 6.5 miles) : Retrace steps of 1st hiking day.

Bridalveil Creek to Glacier Point

83

TRIP From Bridalveil Creek Campground to Glacier Point (shuttle trip). Topo maps (15') *Yosemite, Merced Peak*. Best early-to-mid season; 29 miles.

Grade	Trail/layover days	Total recommended days
Leisurely	5/1	6
Moderate	4/1	5
Strenuous	3/0	3

HILITES This long circle trip covers some of the more scenic portions of the southern part of the Park, and has the advantage of a very short shuttle between the beginning and ending points. Anglers have a wide choice of lake and stream fishing which is among the best in Yosemite. Despite the attractions, the route is not heavily traveled, and those seeking some solitude will find it on this trip.

DESCRIPTION (Leisurely trip)

1st Hiking Day **(Bridalveil Creek Campground** to **Turner Meadows,** 6.5 miles) : See 1st hiking day, trip 82.

2nd Hiking Day **(Turner Meadows** to **Royal Arch Lake,** 6.7 miles) : See 2nd hiking day, trip 82.

3rd Hiking Day **(Royal Arch Lake** to **Edson Lake,** 5.6 miles) : The 2½-mile ascent from Royal Arch Lake to Buena Vista Lake (9100') is an easy one across granite dotted with stands of lodgepole and hemlock. At Buena Vista Lake anglers can expect to unlimber their rods for good fishing for brook and rainbow (9-13"). Those fishermen desiring a change of scenery (or luck) will elect to continue ½ mile to the Buena Vista summit and the junction with the trail to Chilnualna Lakes. It is only another 0.7 mile, but a 500' descent, to Upper Chilnualna

Lake (8500'). Fishing on this small (7-acre) lake is excellent for brook (8-14"). From Buena Vista summit our trail drops down into Buena Vista Creek drainage, and then climbs abruptly back onto the shoulder of Horse Ridge. At this point lensmen may wish to try to capture the sweeping view. From north to southeast, the view encompasses the granite domes above Yosemite Valley; the Cathedral Range; the Clark Range; and Gale, Sing and Madera peaks. This awesome vista narrows as the trail traverses down to the unmarked junction with the footpath (not on the topo map) to Edson Lake (8160'). Fair campsites may be found on the eastern shore and firewood is ample. Fishing at the lake is only fair for rainbow.

4th Hiking Day **(Edson Lake** to **Illilouette Creek,** 6.7 miles) : The first segment of this trail is a long, steady descent of 1000' along dusty, rocky trail. From Buena Vista Creek the 700' descent to Illilouette Creek is sandy. The dense red fir forest is often interrupted by "ghost forests" of dead lodgepole pine, and the contrast is much like stepping from a cathedral into the adjoining graveyard.

Periodically, the fir cover opens to give peephole views of the granite domes to the north and northeast. Mt. Starr King stands out above all the rest. The junction with the Mono Meadow/Merced Pass trail marks the campsites on Illilouette Creek. Fishing on the creek is fair for rainbow (to 8").

5th Hiking Day **(Illilouette Creek** to **Glacier Point,** 3.5 miles) : The trail descends gently beside Illilouette Creek for about 1½ miles before beginning to climb. As it ascends past the junction with a trail down to Illilouette Fall, each foot of altitude gain improves the view, giving the trail here its meaningful name, the Panorama trail. From this trail, on a clear day (and it is clearer in the morning), one can look across the vast chasm of the Merced River, and with the aid of binoculars see hikers on the summit of Half Dome. Nearer at hand, we can see the work of avalanches that have thundered down from the heights, carrying rocks, trees and soil across the trail. The view from Washburn Point (named after one of the original Wawona settlers) includes Nevada Fall, Vernal Fall, Half Dome, Mt. Starr King, and the high peaks of eastern Yosemite. The last half mile to Glacier Point (7214') is accomplished by switchbacks that rise through a fine stand of red fir.

Bridalveil Creek to Yosemite Valley 84

TRIP   From Bridalveil Creek Campground to Yosemite Valley (Happy Isles), (shuttle trip). Topo maps (15') *Yosemite, Merced Peak*. Best early-to-mid season; 32.8 miles.

Grade	Trail/layover days	Total recom-mended days
Leisurely	5/1	6
Moderate	4/1	5
Strenuous	3/0	3

HILITES   This route traverses some of the finer forest stands in Yosemite, crosses the Buena Vista Crest, and concludes via the famous Panorama and Nevada Fall trails into the Valley. A feeling of remoteness from the start, combined with excellent fishing on several lakes, makes this a fine early-to-mid season trip.

DESCRIPTION (Leisurely trip)

1st Hiking Day **(Bridalveil Creek Campground** to **Turner Meadows,** 6.5 miles) : See 1st hiking day, trip 82.

2nd Hiking Day **(Turner Meadows** to **Royal Arch Lake,** 6.7 miles) : See 2nd hiking day, trip 82.

3rd Hiking Day **(Royal Arch Lake** to **Edson Lake,** 5.6 miles) : See 3rd hiking day, trip 83.

4th Hiking Day **(Edson Lake** to **Illilouette Creek,** 6.7 miles) : See 4th hiking day, trip 83.

5th Hiking Day **(Illilouette Creek** to **Yosemite Valley,** 7.3 miles via the John Muir Trail, or 6.1 miles via the Mist Trail) : From the Mono Meadow/Merced Pass trail junction, the route follows Illilouette Creek for about 1½ miles. At the first trail junction branching north a bridge crosses Illilouette Creek and our route turns right across this bridge toward Panorama Point. Views from this trail section include Illilouette Fall, Illilouette Gorge and Nevada Fall. This route skirts the sheer Panorama Cliff and then switchbacks down 500' to the lip of Nevada Fall, joining the John Muir Trail on this descent. One of the finest falls in Yosemite, Nevada Fall drops 594' in one vertical plunge. Other falls in the Valley drop greater distances, but none has the volume of water that the Merced River has. The result is a thunderous roar that can be heard for miles. As the viewer stands facing out over the fall, the granite dome on his right is Liberty Cap; directly ahead and slightly above him is Glacier Point. Unfortunately, a shelf of the slope on the left hides the 370' Illilouette Fall. However, should the traveler determine to conclude this day's hike via the more gently switchbacking descent along the John Muir Trail (requiring a short retracing of steps to the last junction) he will have the opportunity to see this natural wonder.

The more spectacular route, however, is the Mist Trail. As this route is spectacular, it is also quite difficult, owing to its steepness. The Mist Trail begins 0.2 mile northeast of the top of Nevada Fall. Progress down the Mist Trail is easily measured in relation to Nevada Fall, since the trail at one point comes down to the very base of the fall. At this point the immense power of the fall makes itself known. This route imposes an unforgettable humility on all those who tread it, for no sooner is Nevada Fall left behind than one is at the man-made railing on the brink of Vernal Fall. This site is a point of contrasts. Emerald Pool, just above the fall, is a placid flow of water that elicits a feeling of calm. Ten seconds away, the same water is catapulted with a roar into the misty chasm below. It is into this same chasm that the trail winds. On this trail section the trail's name gains meaning, and one emerges from the cloud of mist 800' lower with clothing damp and ears ringing with the sound of crashing water. At the Vernal Fall bridge the Mist Trail rejoins the John Muir Trail, and then descends slowly to Happy Isles and the Valley floor.

Bridalveil Creek to Royal Arch Lake   **85**

TRIP   From Bridalveil Creek Campground to Royal Arch Lake (semiloop trip). Topo map (15′) *Yosemite.* Best early-to-mid season; 27.6 miles.

Grade	Trail/layover days	Total recommended days
Leisurely	5/1	6
Moderate	4/1	5
Strenuous	3/0	3

HILITES   For the first-timer, exploring Yosemite's south boundary country is a memorable experience, and this loop trip provides an exciting route. Angling on the many lakes around Buena Vista Peak is excellent, particularly in early season, and the easy access and return recommends this trip as an early-season "warm up."

DESCRIPTION (Leisurely trip)

1st Hiking Day **(Bridalveil Creek Campground** to **Turner Meadows,** 6.5 miles) : See 1st hiking day, trip 82.

2nd Hiking Day **(Turner Meadows** to **Upper Chilnualna Lake,** 4.9 miles) : From Turner Meadows the trail continues southeasterly. One half mile from the campsites at the south end of the meadow our route passes the Wawona Trail, and the same distance later it turns eastward along Chilnualna Creek. This junction marks the beginning of a long, easy ascent that is pleasantly accompanied by the creek. Fishing along this cascading stream is fair (small brook and rainbow) ; most anglers will keep their lines dry until they reach Chilnualna Lakes (8480′). Here, all except the lowest lake provide excellent fishing for brook and rainbow (7-12″). Small (7-acre) Upper Chilnualna Lake, alongside the trail, has several good campsites on its northern side. Firewood is abundant.

3rd Hiking Day **(Upper Chilnualna Lake** to **Royal Arch Lake,** 3.0 miles) : From the north side of the lake the trail climbs steeply up the 400', densely forested slope to the junction with the Buena Vista trail. Our route turns right (southeast) and climbs the ridge to beautiful Buena Vista Lake (9100'). On this granitoid lake fishing is good for rainbow and brook (9-13") and anglers may wish to tarry. The remaining 2 miles to Royal Arch Lake is a gentle descent across granite that exhibits a sprinkling of lodgepole pine and hemlock. Royal Arch Lake (8700') is a fine fishing lake (excellent angling for brook and rainbow to 14"). There are numerous good-to-excellent camp-sites on the north and west shores, and firewood is plentiful. The lake's name is well-suited, deriving from the blackened granite streaks that rainbow across the sheer eastern facade of the lake basin.

4th Hiking Day **(Royal Arch Lake** to **Turner Meadows,** 6.7 miles) : See 2nd hiking day, trip 82.

5th Hiking Day **(Turner Meadows** to **Bridalveil Creek Camp-ground,** 6.5 miles) : See 1st hiking day, trip 82.

86   Glacier Point to Merced Lake

TRIP   From Glacier Point to Merced Lake (round trip). Topo maps (15') *Yosemite, Merced Peak.* Best early season ; 29.8 miles.

Grade	Trail/layover days	Total recom-mended days
Leisurely	4/1	5
Moderate	4/0	4
Strenuous	3/0	3

HILITES   This early-season excursion has all the scenic ad-vantages of the Yosemite-Valley-to-Merced-Lake trip (trip 70) without the 2000' climb from Happy

Isles to Nevada Fall. Mild elevation change and solid mileage make this route a fine choice for the hiker who wants to shake winter's kinks out of early-season muscles.

DESCRIPTION (Leisurely trip)

1st Hiking Day **(Glacier Point** to **Little Yosemite Valley,** 8.6 miles) : From Glacier Point the trail switchbacks down through a heavy stand of red fir. This section of trail affords good views of Nevada Fall, Mt. Starr King and the Illilouette Creek drainage. At the Illilouette Creek bridge our route turns left (east) across the bridge, and then skirts the north side of Panorama Point along Panorama Cliff. From this trail section lensmen may wish to take advantage of the views of Illilouette Gorge and Nevada Fall. Beyond the Mono Meadow trail junction this route switchbacks down 500' to the John Muir Trail, and then levels off to the top of Nevada Fall. This waterfall drops 594' in a single leap, and it is one of the most popular in Yosemite, owing to its tremendous volume of water. A break at this point will reward the traveler facing out over the fall with views of Liberty Cap on the right and Glacier Point and the gorge of the Merced River straight ahead. From the lip of Nevada Fall the route crosses a small rise, and then winds through Little Yosemite Valley along a pleasantly level 3-mile stretch of sandy trail. The forest cover on the valley floor is open, with superb examples of large, mature sugar, yellow, Jeffrey and lodgepole pine. Winding beside the now placid and green waters of the Merced River, the trail arrives at the signed campsite at the eastern end of Little Yosemite Valley (6100'). Firewood is abundant, and fishing on the river is fair-to-good for rainbow, brown and brook (to 10").

2nd Hiking Day **(Little Yosemite Valley** to **Merced Lake,** 6.3 miles) : See 2nd hiking day, trip 81.

3rd Hiking Day **(Merced Lake** to **Little Yosemite Valley,** 6.3 miles) : Retrace steps of 2nd hiking day.

4th Hiking Day **(Little Yosemite Valley** to **Glacier Point,** 8.6 miles) : Retrace steps of 1st hiking day.

87   Glacier Point to Rutherford Lake

TRIP

From Glacier Point to Rutherford Lake (loop trip). Topo maps (15') *Yosemite, Merced Peak.* Best in mid or late season ; 68.8 miles.

Grade	Trail/layover days	Total recommended days
Leisurely	11/2	13
Moderate	10/2	12
Strenuous	7/2	9

HILITES

Designed for the experienced knapsacker, this trip offers a combination of excellent fishing and superlative vistas. Almost a dozen angling lakes, most of them in high-country settings, also provide swimming to alleviate the trail dust. Three major passes challenge the most ambitious hiker, and the wide variations in plants and wildlife will satisfy the most discriminating naturalist.

DESCRIPTION (Moderate trip)

1st Hiking Day **(Glacier Point** to **Little Yosemite Valley,** 8.6 miles) : See 1st hiking day, trip 86.

2nd Hiking Day **(Little Yosemite Valley** to **Merced Lake,** 6.3 miles) : See 2nd hiking day, trip 81.

3rd Hiking Day **(Merced Lake** to **Triple Peak Fork Meadow/ Red Peak Pass Trail Junction,** 9.5 miles) : The first mile or so of this trail is level, passing the Merced Lake Ranger Station (emergency services available here), and then the trail ascends steadily (300') to Washburn Lake (7600'). Here fishing is good, particularly in late season, for rainbow, brook and brown (to 9"). Washburn Lake (45 acres) is almost as big as Merced

Lake, but shallower. The trail skirts the northeast side of the lake, and then ascends 260′ in 2 miles to the Lyell Fork footbridge. From this point it is a steep but scenic climb along cascading Merced Peak Fork and then up its canyon wall to Triple Peak Fork. Partway up this climb the route crosses the cascades on a metal footbridge. It was in these upper reaches of the Lyell Fork canyon that the Merced glacier began, and the polished granite on every hand is a constant reminder of its presence. The trail fords the stream twice before reaching the northern edge of Triple Peak Fork Meadow. Fishing along Triple Peak Fork is good for brook and rainbow (to 9″) and the views to each side of the valley are excellent. The best campsites in the upper part of the canyon are along the trail at the southern end of Triple Peak Fork Meadow, near the trail junction with the Red Peak Pass trail. Firewood is ample.

4th Hiking Day **(Triple Peak Fork Meadow/Red Peak Pass Trail Junction** to **Post Creek,** 7.2 miles)**:** One should check in advance whether the snow has melted on the north side of Post Peak Pass (yes, even in late season). The section of trail between Isberg and Post Peak Pass is often rough due to late runoff, and it is a steep climb of 1600′ past the trail lateral to Isberg Pass and on to Post Peak Pass (10700′). This ascent is not without compensation, however, for the views from the trail are among the most outstanding in the South Boundary country. From this divide between the Merced and the San Joaquin River drainages, the traveler has views of the Clark Range to the west, the Cathedral Range to the north and the tops of Banner Peak, Mt. Ritter and the Minarets to the east. Post Peak Pass was named for a U. S. Cavalry soldier who was part of an 1895 military party seeking a route from the Merced River to the Minarets region. At this point our route leaves Yosemite, and later recrosses the boundary at Fernandez Pass — 6 miles away. The trail descends 600′ to little Porphyry Lake (10100′), where the fishing is fair for brook and rainbow, and then descends 1060′ more to Post Creek (9040′). This descent is marked by a re-entry into timber, and there are good campsites and ample firewood along the creek. Fishing along the creek is good for brook (to 8″).

5th Hiking Day **(Post Creek** to **Rutherford Lake,** 3.9 miles)**:** From Post Creek the trail crosses a small rise, passes 2 small, unnamed lakelets (no fish), and fords the West Fork of Granite Creek. Shortly beyond, the trail fords Fernandez Creek and strikes the Fernandez Pass trail. Our route turns right (west) along a level, densely timbered stretch that offers fine views across Fernandez Creek beyond. This route then passes the

signed trail branching left to the Fernandez Lakes basin, and
ascends steeply 350' up a rocky slope to the junction with the
Rutherford Lake lateral. Here our route turns right (north) and
climbs steeply to the granitoid cirque nestling 28-acre Rutherford Lake (9800'). There are fair-to-good Forest Service "Improved" campsites on the west side of the lake south of the
outlet. Views from these sites are excellent, and firewood is
ample. Fishing is fair for brook and golden (to 16").

6th Hiking Day **(Rutherford Lake** to **Chain Lakes,** 8.5 miles) :
See 2nd hiking day, trip 77.

7th Hiking Day **(Chain Lakes** to **Royal Arch Lake,** 9 miles) :
See 2nd hiking day, trip 78.

8th Hiking Day **(Royal Arch Lake** to **Edson Lake,** 5.6 miles) :
See 3rd hiking day, trip 83.

9th Hiking Day **(Edson Lake** to **Illilouette Creek,** 6.7 miles) :
See 4th hiking day, trip 83.

10th Hiking Day **(Illilouette Creek** to **Glacier Point,** 3.5 miles) :
See 5th hiking day, trip 83.

88   Glacier Point to Granite Creek

TRIP   From Glacier Point to Granite Creek Campground
(shuttle trip). Topo maps (15') *Yosemite, Merced
Peak.* Best mid or late season; 40.3 miles.

Grade	Trail/layover days	Total recom-mended days
Leisurely	7/2	9
Moderate	6/2	8
Strenuous	4/1	5

HILITES This route traverses the very heart of Yosemite's south boundary country, and crosses the divide of the Merced and San Joaquin River watersheds at Isberg Pass. Fishing on the lakes and streams is fair-to-excellent, and the life zones range from Canadian to Arctic-Alpine. Remoteness and panoramic vistas beckon the traveler to choose this trip.

DESCRIPTION (Moderate trip)

1st Hiking Day **(Glacier Point** to **Little Yosemite Valley,** 8.6 miles) : See 1st hiking day, trip 86.

2nd Hiking Day **(Little Yosemite Valley** to **Merced Lake,** 6.3 miles) : See 2nd hiking day, trip 81.

3rd Hiking Day **(Merced Lake** to **Triple Peak Fork Meadow/ Red Peak Pass Trail Junction,** 9.5 miles) : See 3rd hiking day, trip 87.

4th Hiking Day **(Triple Peak Fork/Red Peak Pass Trail Junction** to **Isberg Lakes,** 4.9 miles) : Isberg Pass often has snow on its northern slope until quite late in the season. Travelers should check beforehand to see that the pass is clear. Because of the late run-off this section of the pass is often rough. From Triple Peak Fork Meadow the trail crosses the river and climbs steeply to meet the old Isberg Pass/Lyell Fork trail. Views from this point are some of the finest in Yosemite's south boundary country. Below the granite crest of Isberg Pass our route passes the Post Peak Pass trail and then ascends very steeply to Isberg Pass (10500'). From this summit, which divides the Merced River and San Joaquin River drainages, there are fine views of the Clark Range, the Cathedral Range and portions of the Ritter Range. From Isberg Pass the trail descends by switchbacks to rocky Upper Isberg Lake, and then more gradually to Lower Isberg Lake (9800'). Fishing in these lakes is fair-to-good for brook and some rainbow (to 8"). There are a few fair campsites at Lower Isberg, and firewood is ample.

5th Hiking Day **(Isberg Lakes** to **Cora Lakes,** 6 miles) : See 4th hiking day, trip 80.

6th Hiking Day **(Cora Lakes** to **Granite Creek Campground,** 5 miles) : See 5th hiking day, trip 80.

Fish Creek/Mono Creek

Surmounting Duck Pass from the north, one looks south across Cascade Valley to the Silver Divide. In the light of midday, the bleached granite of the divide imparts a glowing crown to the whole range and the impression is one of a royal diadem. Views such as this make the region a special place — a favorite to which one must return time and again lest a nuance of memory be lost. Since most of the region is now part of the John Muir Wilderness, its Sierran tranquility is assured.

The Silver Divide country, composed of the Fish and Mono Creek watersheds, lies southeast of the Devils Postpile. It is bounded on the north by the Mammoth Crest, on the east by the Sierra crest, and on the south by the Mono Divide. Both Fish Creek and Mono Creek drain west from the Sierra crest, and their flow is augmented by feeder streams emanating from pocket lakes and cirque lakes of the Mono Divide, the Silver Divide and the Mammoth Crest. These feeder streams plunge and splash down from their alpine settings to the densely forested canyon floor. The forest carpet in the canyons contrasts sharply with the barrenness of surrounding peaks, like Red Slate Mountain, Mt. Morgan, Mt. Mills, Mt. Gabb and Mt. Hilgard, all over 13000'.

Glacially wrought, the Fish and Mono Creek canyons exhibit typical "hanging valleys," broad expanses of polished granite, amphitheater cirques, and arc-shaped moraines. An outstanding example of a terminal moraine may be seen when one looks back toward Long Valley from the eastern ascent to McGee Pass. The glacier that once filled this canyon was one of the Sierra's most ancient, and it is fitting that it was eroding the oldest rocks in the Sierra. Recent fossil identification has dated these rocks at four hundred million years. Nowhere in the Sierra is the birthplace of a glacier more vividly portrayed than in the Little Lakes Valley on the east side of Mono Pass. Backed by Mts. Mills, Abbot and Dade and Bear Creek Spire, this charming valley has the typical U-shaped profile. Lateral moraines pushed to the sides of the valley by the ebb and flow of ice are now topped by tiny lakelets.

The Indians were the first to appreciate the charm of highcountry retreats like the Little Lakes Valley. On the east side, it was the Mono Indians who sought the high country in summertime. This country provided a plentiful natural larder, but the Indians, like us, also fled to the heights to escape the midsummer valley heat.

Prospectors, following the lure of "that one big strike," soon penetrated into the high country, but most of their efforts were confined to the area around Mono Lake. The first recorded visit to Mono Pass and the San Joaquin River was by the famous Brewer party in 1864. Let by an army cavalryman who claimed that he had once pursued Indians over the pass, this tiny survey team topped the Sierra crest and followed the descent of the present Mono Creek trail to Vermilion Valley (now covered by man-made Lake Thomas A. Edison). Using the valley as a base camp, they made an unsuccessful attempt at ascending Mt. Goddard before returning to Yosemite.

The Brewer party journals do not indicate the quality of fishing available in the area at the time. However, it is difficult to imagine much better angling than is offered there today. The appropriately named Fish Creek boasts a varied fish population of brook, rainbow and some golden trout — as does Mono Creek. On the Fish Creek side of the Silver Divide some of the better fishing spots are Cascade Valley, Tully Hole, Helen Lake and Warrior Lake. The Mono Creek watershed possesses equally fine angling at Grinnell Lakes, Graveyard Lakes and Laurel Lake, and on the upper reaches of Mono Creek. State fishing licenses are required.

There are numerous entries into this fine country. Four of these entries are used in the following trip descriptions. Three access points are on the east side of the Sierra crest: Coldwater Campground (Mammoth Lakes), the McGee Creek roadend, and Mosquito Flat (Rock Creek). The only western-slope trailhead is Vermilion Campground on Lake Edison.

89　Lake Edison to Graveyard Meadows

TRIP　From Vermilion Campground (Lake Thomas A. Edison) to Graveyard Meadows (round trip). Topo maps (15') *Kaiser Peak, Mt. Abbot.* Best mid season; 10.4 miles.

Grade	Trail/layover days	Total recom- mended days
Leisurely	2/0	2
Moderate	—	—
Strenuous	—	—

HILITES　The grail at the end of this quest is a pretty, meadowed campsite within the boundaries of the John Muir Wilderness Area. This route travels densely forested country abounding in wildlife, and tops a crest offering superlative views.

DESCRIPTION

1st Hiking Day **(Vermilion Campground** to **Graveyard Meadows,** 5.2 miles) : Vermilion Campground (7650') is located at the end of an alternately oil and dirt road 26 miles northeast of Huntington Lake off Hiway 168. The first, heavily timbered mile from the trailhead is partly on a Forest Service access road and partly on sandy trail. Beginning in dense stands of Jeffrey pine, the road and then the trail wind eastward along the northwest side of Lake Edison. This artificial body of water created by the Southern California Edison Company fills Vermilion Valley. The lower, lake-fringed areas teem with birdlife and squirrels, and travelers can enjoy well-spent time observing the fauna. Our trail passes the trail that forks left (north) to Devils Bathtub, crosses the bridge over Cold Creek, and then branches left (north) at the Goodale Pass trail junction. This ascent is at first gradual but soon becomes more sudden. As the elevation increases the forest cover consists more of lodgepole pine and red fir, and as the trail veers easterly at the crest of the climb, there are several fine vantage points looking into the country to the south and east. Among the landmarks visible from these points are Mono Divide, Recess Peak, Mt. Abbot,

Mt. Dade and Mt. Mills. From the crown of the climb it is a short ½ mile to the point where the trail rejoins Cold Creek at the foot of Graveyard Meadows (8800'). Around the fringe of this long meadow are several inviting campsites with an abundant firewood supply. The camping places at the south end of the meadow provide titillating views north to the Silver Divide, and serve as excellent watching places from which to observe the variety of wildlife that frequents the grasslands, especially in early morning. Fishing along Cold Creek is only fair for brook and rainbow (to 8").

2nd Hiking Day (**Graveyard Meadows** to **Vermilion Campground,** 5.2 miles) : Retrace steps of 1st hiking day.

Lake Edison to Graveyard Lakes   90

TRIP   From Vermilion Campground (Lake Thomas A. Edison) to Lower Graveyard Lake (round trip). Topo maps (15') *Kaiser Peak, Mt. Abbot.* Best mid or late season; 16.8 miles.

Grade	Trail/layover days	Total recommended days
Leisurely	4/1	5
Moderate	3/1	4
Strenuous	2/1	3

HILITES   The California Department of Fish and Game has never been called overly creative, but it named the lakes in the Graveyard Lakes chain well. Beneath tombstone-granited Graveyard Peak lie lakes with DF&G names like Vengeance, Murder, Phantom, Headstone, Spook and Ghost. This country is worth investigating if for no other reason than to satisfy one's curiosity about these names. The truth is that this particular lake basin is one of the loveliest and most regal in the Silver Divide country.

DESCRIPTION (Leisurely trip)

1st Hiking Day **(Vermilion Campground** to **Graveyard Meadows,** 5.2 miles) : See 1st hiking day, trip 89.

2nd Hiking Day **(Graveyard Meadows** to **Lower Graveyard Lake,** 3.2 miles) : From the south end of Graveyard Meadows, the trail winds the length of this subalpine meadow along the east side of meandering Cold Creek. Bird-lovers should keep an eye out for the Brewer blackbird, white-crowned sparrow, Cassin finch, robin and sparrow hawk that inhabit this high-mountain field. At the north end of the meadow, the trail fords the tiny outlet stream from Arrowhead Lake, and re-enters a forest cover of lodgepole and red fir. This forested, duff trail ascends the narrowing Cold Creek valley, fording the creek in two places to emerge at the south end of Upper Graveyard Meadow. Smaller than Graveyard Meadows, this rolling grassland shows a forest fringe more alpine in character : mountain hemlock, lodgepole pine, and occasional silver and Jeffrey pine. In the middle of Upper Graveyard Meadow our route branches left (west), and then climbs the steep, rocky, western slope of Cold Creek valley. The lodgepole pine and mountain hemlock at the top of this 600' ascent give way to lush meadows at the eastern fringes of beautiful Lower Graveyard Lake (9900'). Excellent campsites may be found in the lodgepole stands where the trail first meets the lake, or along the east side of the lake between this point and the inlet stream.

From any of these places, the camper has marvelous views of Graveyard Peak and the tumbled granite cirque wall that surrounds the entire Graveyard Lakes basin. It is easy to derive the logic behind the name, "Graveyard Peak." Tombstone-makers have for years shown a preference for this particular kind of salt-and-pepper granite. These campsites along the east side of Lower Graveyard Lake make an excellent base camp from which to fish and explore the remaining five lakes in the basin. Firewood is plentiful around Lower Graveyard Lake, but the other lakes are all high, montane, glacial, and above timberline. Fishing is good on Lower Graveyard Lake for brook (to 13″) and fair-to-good on the upper lakes, due to poor spawning waters. This glacially formed basin is a barren but scenic paradise for a base-camping hiker.

3rd Hiking Day **(Lower Graveyard Lake** to **Graveyard Meadows,** 3.2 miles) : Retrace steps of 2nd hiking day.

4th Hiking Day **(Graveyard Meadows** to **Vermilion Campground,** 5.2 miles) : Retrace steps of 1st hiking day.

Rock Creek to Chickenfoot Lake

91

TRIP   From Mosquito Flat (Rock Creek) to Chickenfoot
Lake (Little Lakes Valley) (round trip). Topo
maps (15') *Mt. Tom, Mt. Abbot*. Best mid or late
season; 6 miles.

Grade	Trail/layover days	Total recom- mended days
Leisurely	2/0	2
Moderate	—	—
Strenuous	—	—

HILITES   Majestic scenery dominates this short, popular trip.
Because of its moderate terrain and high country
"feel," this route through the Little Lakes Valley
has been a long-time favorite of the beginning hiker,
and the varied and good fishing for brook, rainbow
and brown makes it also an excellent angling choice.

DESCRIPTION

1st Hiking Day (**Mosquito Flat** to **Chickenfoot Lake,** 3 miles) :
The trailhead (10250') is located at the end of an 11-mile paved
mountain road that branches southwest from Hiway 395 at
Toms Place. This trailhead marks the beginning of the John
Muir Wilderness (no motorized vehicles allowed). The trail
starts southwest, passes the 1-mile trail lateral to Eastern
Brook Lakes, and crosses a low, rocky ridge to the west side of
Mack Lake. Here it passes by the Mono Pass trail, which
branches to the right, and then skirts the western tip of Marsh
Lake. Anglers will wish to try their luck for the good fishing for
brown and brook in Marsh Lake and in the lagoon areas of
Rock Creek. While fishing on the numerous lakes and streams of
Little Lakes Valley, one has views south into the long glacial
cirque — a long-time favorite of lensmen. Flanked by Mt. Starr
(12870') and Mt. Morgan (13748'), the valley terminates in
the omnipotent heights of Mts. Mills, Abbot, Dade and Julius
Caesar, and Bear Creek Spire, all over 13000'. Still-active glaciers on the slopes of these prominences are reminders of the
enormous forces that carved this valley eons ago, and the visitor
cannot help feeling contrasting reactions of exhilaration and
humility.

From the meadowed fringes of Marsh and Heart lakes the trail ascends gently past the western side of Box Lake to the eastern periphery of aptly named Long Lake. For the angler with a yearning to try different waters, the three unnamed lakes on the bench just to the east offer good fishing for brook and rainbow. Beyond Long Lake the trail ascends through a moderately dense forest cover to the fair campsites at the western edge of Chickenfoot Lake (10761'). Overall, this lake does indeed look like a chicken's foot, but any further reference to domesticity in describing this high, glacial lake would be inappropriate. As in the streams and lakes in the north end of the valley, the fishing is good for brook, brown and rainbow (to 15"). Firewood is ample, and the views are magnificent. The close proximity of the Sierra Nevada crest makes Chickenfoot Lake a popular base camp for climbers.

2nd Hiking Day **(Chickenfoot Lake** to **Mosquito Flat,** 3 miles) : Retrace steps of 1st hiking day.

92 Rock Creek to Ruby Lake

TRIP   From Mosquito Flat (Rock Creek) to Ruby Lake (round trip). Topo maps (15') *Mt. Tom, Mt. Abbot.* Best mid or late season; 5 miles.

Grade	Trail/layover days	Total recommended days
Leisurely	2/0	2
Moderate	—	—
Strenuous	—	—

HILITES From the Little Lakes Valley upward to the heights of the Ruby Lake cirque, the traveler gains an appreciation of glacially formed country. One can almost see the main trunk of the glacier flowing northeast through the valley and being joined by the feeder glacier from the cirque that now holds Ruby Lake. The terminus of this trip, Ruby Lake, dwells

amidst the barren peaks of the awe-inspiring Sierra
Nevada crest.

DESCRIPTION

1st Hiking Day **(Mosquito Flat** to **Ruby Lake,** 2.5 miles) : Proceed to the Mono Pass trail junction as described in 1st hiking
day, trip 92, where our route branches right (west) and then
ascends steeply via somewhat rocky switchbacks. The forest cover is moderately dense stands of whitebark and lodgepole pine
along a rocky slope. Views from this slope are excellent, both
of the Little Lakes Valley and of the Sierra Nevada crest. The
majestic skyline includes six landmark peaks, all over 13000',
and three glaciers. The peaks are: Mt. Mills (13468'), Mt.
Abbot (13715'), Mt. Dade (13600+'), Mt. Julius Caesar
(13196'), Bear Creek Spire (13713') and Mt. Morgan
(13748'). From the cirque created by these peaks the main
glacier flowed northeast in the direction of the present flow of
Rock Creek, and the direction of our trail parallels the feeder
glacier that emanated from the Ruby Lake cirque. As the trail
crosses the meadow just below Ruby Lake it nears the outlet
creek from Ruby Lake. Several good campsites with ample firewood are available here, or the traveler may elect to choose
one of the more exposed campsites (windy, but with views of
the basin) near the outlet of Ruby Lake (11100'). Firewood
around the lake camping sites is scarce. The sheer granite walls
of the cirque tower 1500' and more above the lake surface, and
their crest on the west side is a series of spectacular pinnacles.
To the north the low notch marks Mono Pass, and from the
lake one can watch the antlike progress of pack trains and backpackers as they switchback up the precipitous, barren talus of
the south ridge of Mt. Starr. Anglers will find fair fishing for
brook, rainbow and brown in Ruby Lake and its outlet stream,
and the average length is about 9".

2nd Hiking Day **(Ruby Lake** to **Mosquito Flat,** 2.5 miles) : Retrace steps of 1st hiking day.

93   McGee Creek to Steelhead Lake

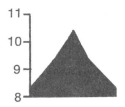

TRIP   From McGee Creek Roadend to Steelhead Lake (round trip). Topo maps (15') *Mt. Morrison, Mt. Abbot*. Best mid or late season; 9 miles.

Grade	Trail/layover days	Total recom- mended days
Leisurely	2/1	3
Moderate	2/0	2
Strenuous	—	—

HILITES   Travelers new to east-escarpment entry to the Sierra will find the ascent to Steelhead Lake a route of fascination and frustration. Frustratingly, one cannot at the same time take in the views to the rear (east) and the majestic heights of the Sierra crest to the front (west). However, the go-and-return nature of this trip allows the hiker to have the views of the Sierra crest before him when trekking in, and the wide vistas of the east-side foothills and flatlands spread out ahead upon returning.

DESCRIPTION

1st Hiking Day **(McGee Creek Roadend** to **Steelhead Lake,** 4.5 miles) : The trailhead (8300') is located at the end of a dirt road, about 2 miles beyond the McGee Creek Pack Station. This road branches right (southwest) from Hiway 395 about 8 miles southeast of the Mammoth Lakes road junction at Casa Diablo Hot Springs, at the resort area overlooking Crowley Lake. From the parking area at the end of the road, the trail ascends a short distance to a Forest Service gate, where a sign proclaims the eastern boundary of the John Muir Wilderness. On the topo map this trail is labeled a jeep trail, but wilderness seekers will be reassured to know that at this writing the mining road to the Scheelore Mine on Mt. Baldwin appeared unused. The signs of motor traffic have all but disappeared and the area is reverting to its primitive state. The route through McGee Creek canyon traverses the north and then the west slope as the trail ascends southerly. The canyon, for the most part, is sage and rabbit-brush covered, but close to the creek cooling shade may be found under thriving black cottonwood, water birch, rare copper birch, and quaking aspen. Dense willow thickets line the very lip of the creek and make fishing for the brown and rainbow (to 12″) very difficult but rewarding. Like all the eastern-escarpment creeks, McGee Creek is a tumbling, riotous, cold-water stream, and as the traveler winds steadily upward through the canyon, the green-lined stream bed snakes a parallel course below. Views from the trail are excellent back over the Owens River Valley, and vie for attention with the awe-inspiring sky-line to the west. The trail fords the tiny watercourse emanating from the springs above Horsetail Falls, and jogs back and forth over McGee Creek below the beaver dam. Early-season high water makes these fords somewhat hazardous.

A short distance beyond the beaver dam, the trail crosses McGee Creek via a large felled log, and ascends more steeply through a narrowing canyon. Occasional juniper begins to appear, mixed with lodgepole, whitebark and limber pine. The trail traverses the eastern side of a long lagoon section of McGee Creek, and then refords the stream. As the trail loops westerly, it becomes steeper and enters a moderately dense lodgepole forest. Via alternately rocky and dusty, duff sections, the trail reaches the Steelhead Lake lateral, where our route branches left (east). Fording McGee Creek, this lateral climbs steeply by switchbacks along the north side of the outlet stream from Grass Lake. Fishing from the meadowed fringes of little Grass Lake is poor-to-fair for rainbow and brook. From Grass Lake the trail once more switchbacks up an abrupt, timbered slope, and ends at the good camping sites at the north end of fairly large (about 25 acres) Steelhead Lake (10350′). Views from these campsites take in the granite grandeur of Mt. Stanford and Mt. Crocker to the south and west, and rust-and-buff-colored Mt. Baldwin to the north. Firewood is ample. Fishermen will find the angling for rainbow and brook excellent (best in early and late season). They will also find the name "Steelhead" Lake a misnomer, though an understandable error. Over the years, catches of rainbow trout from this lake have exhibited pale, faded-out markings, giving an appearance much like their silvery cousins of coastal waters.

2nd Hiking Day **(Steelhead Lake to McGee Creek Roadend,** 4.5 miles)** : Retrace steps of 1st hiking day.

94   McGee Creek to McGee Lake

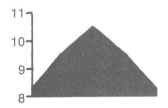

TRIP   From McGee Creek Roadend to Big McGee Lake (round trip). Topo maps (15') *Mt. Morrison, Mt. Abbot.* Best mid or late season; 13 miles.

Grade	Trail/layover days	Total recom- mended days
Leisurely	2/1	3
Moderate	2/0	2
Strenuous	—	—

HILITES   In an alpine setting close under the Sierra crest, Big McGee Lake shares a large granite basin with three other fishable lakes. This beautiful spot nestles under the sheer, colorful walls of Red and White Peak, and close to impressive Mt. Crocker.

DESCRIPTION

1st Hiking Day **(McGee Creek Roadend** to **Big McGee Lake,** 6.5 miles) : Proceed to the trail intersection with the Steelhead Lake lateral as described for the previous trip, where the trail continues, climbing steeply westward over a forested, rocky slope. This ascent borders wildflower-lined McGee Creek, and passes by several "packer" campsites. The trail swings away from the creek, wends through a pleasant lodgepole and mountain hemlock forest cover, and circles a small tarn before ascending steeply to the rocky open slopes just below Big McGee Lake (10480'). Good campsites may be found along the northern shore, but firewood supply is somewhat limited. Fishermen will enjoy the fair-to-good fishing for rainbow and brook (to 13″) on Big McGee Lake, and, if time and inclination allow, will want to explore the equally good fishing at nearby Little McGee Lake, Crocker Lake, or picture-book Golden Lake. Those who wish to try their luck for the famous Sierra golden trout can take the faint trail branching left (south) around Big McGee Lake to Upper Hopkins Lakes via Hopkins Pass (southwest from Big McGee Lake). This is a side trip that should be taken only if one has a layover day.

2nd Hiking Day **(Big McGee Lake to McGee Creek Roadend, 6.5 miles)**: Retrace steps of 1st hiking day.

McGee Creek to Lake Edison 95

TRIP From McGee Creek Roadend to Vermilion Campground (Lake Thomas A. Edison) (shuttle trip). Topo maps (15') *Mt. Morrison, Mt. Abbot, Kaiser Peak*. Best mid or late season; 31.6 miles.

Grade	Trail/layover days	Total recommended days
Leisurely	7/2	9
Moderate	5/2	7
Strenuous	4/2	6

HILITES This trans-Sierra route is one of the finest in the northern Sierra. Two scenic passes, both over 11000', cross the Sierra crest and the Silver Divide. Between them the route visits alpine lakes and streams offering excellent fishing for rainbow, brook and golden trout. Pristine meadows, spectacular peaks, and dense forest mark this trip as a must for any serious wilderness traveler.

DESCRIPTION (Leisurely trip)

1st Hiking Day **(McGee Creek Roadend to Big McGee Lake, 6 miles)**: See 1st hiking day, trip 94.

2nd Hiking Day **(Big McGee Lake to Tully Lake, 4.5 miles)**:

With the colorful and majestic heights of Red and White Mountain to the left (southwest) the route ascends by a rocky, winding trail to Little McGee Lake. Fishing at this granitoid lake is fair for rainbow and brook. From Little McGee Lake, the route ascends more sharply through a rocky side canyon to the shaley heights of McGee Pass (11900'). An interesting turn-of-the-century legend has it that two Indian sheepherders running sheep around the headwaters of McGee Creek were returning from the high country. Enroute, a pack on one of their mules shifted, and they jury-rigged a large rock to balance the shifting action. Upon their reaching their destination, they unloaded the jury-rigged balance and discovered that the rock felt abnormally heavy. As in all good gold legends, the rock assayed rich, and, ostensibly, neither the two Indians nor subsequent treasure-seekers have found the lode from which the rock was taken.

Views from the rarified heights of this lofty saddle are excellent of Red Slate Mountain to the north, Red and White Mountain to the south, and the broad, sweeping, high-country meadows at the headwaters of Fish Creek at the foot of the slope to the west. The vivid reds of the surrounding heights are the product of iron staining of granite and slate, and the buffs and tans are ancient rocks introduced by buckling and folding of the landscape. From the pass our route descends to Fish Creek via a series of switchbacks built by the Sierra Club and the Forest Service. The upper basin giving drainage to Fish Creek is a long, open, grassy meadow of the type some people call "sky-parlor meadows." The trail follows the meandering course of the creek through these grasslands, and at the point where the outlet stream from Tully Lake meets Fish Creek, our route turns south on the short fishermen's lateral to Tully Lake. Those wishing to camp on Fish Creek will find several excellent "packer" campsites a few yards downstream, where the trail encounters the first sparse timber cover. The lateral to Tully Lake is a gentle ascent along the south side of the outlet stream. Good campsites may be found on the meadowed fringes along the northeast side of the lake; firewood is somewhat scarce. Tully Lake (10400') is a small (about 10 acres), granitoid, high-country lake that sustains fair-to-good fishing for golden and brook (to 13"). Anglers will want to try the nearby waters of Red and White Lake, about 1 mile over the ridge to the east. Fishing here is also fair-to-good for rainbow that often run to 16". Those wishing stream fishing can find abundant but smaller rainbow, brook and some golden along meandering Fish Creek.

3rd Hiking Day **(Tully Lake** to **Tully Hole,** 2.5 miles) : This short trail day allows the traveler who admires wild back-country scenery to absorb the primitive beauty of this area. Anglers, particularly fly fishermen, will find the leisurely pace along Fish Creek satisfying. From Tully Lake retrace the route to the main Fish Creek trail, where it turns left (west). The trail now follows the south bank of Fish Creek (the topo map shows it on the north bank) as it descends below treeline. After crossing Fish Creek the trail offers fine views of the Silver Divide to the south before descending abruptly to the meadows of Horse Heaven. This descent parallels cascading Fish Creek, and the trail is dusty. The open grasslands of the meadows abound in wildflowers, particularly in early season, and the idyllic, cold-watered Fish Creek provides good-to-excellent fishing for brook, rainbow and some golden (to 12″). From Horse Heaven to Tully Hole the trail is a gradual descent along the north bank of Fish Creek. Like the meadows at Horse Heaven, the grasslands of Tully Hole (9500′) are also rife with wildflower color. The stream is sometimes bowered with willows, but the long, swirling, curved line of Fish Creek is for the most part an open, pleasant stretch of water with grassy, overhung banks and several deep holes. Good campsites at the northwestern edge of the meadow near the John Muir Trail junction take advantage of the fine views up the meadow, and firewood is abundant.

4th Hiking Day **(Tully Hole** to **Lake of the Lone Indian,** 5 miles): The route at this point joins the John Muir Trail, and leaves Tully Hole by a gentle descent. From the trail, the traveler has splendid views and access to the numerous small falls and holes that characterize nearby Fish Creek. Where the trail crests the rocky ridge above the head of Cascade Valley, there are good views across the valley to the Silver Divide. As the trail switchbacks down, the muted roar of now-tumbling Fish Creek sounds from the left, and the hiker gets a parting glimpse of this memorable stream's last plunge when crossing the bridge at the foot of the descent. The trail then passes the junction with the Cascade Valley trail and climbs steeply over a densely forested slope on the east side of the outlet stream from Helen Lake. Midway up this climb the trail passes several campsites situated in a picturesque meadow on the right (west), and then begins the final, long, steep climb to Helen Lake. This section of trail is rocky and eroded as it passes through a spectrum of changing timber cover: silver pine and lodgepole, concentrations of mountain hemlock and, finally, thinning lodgepole. From the final switchbacks just below Helen Lake the trail affords instructive views of the U-shaped glacial valley that the route has traversed.

As the trail tops the granite brink of the cirque containing tiny Helen Lake (a sign at the lake and the DF&G call this lake "Squaw Lake") the traveler is struck with the awesome scale of the ice mass that began here and in the nearby cirque (containing Bobs Lake) about ½ mile over the steep granite slope to the southeast. Anglers will wish to fish these two lakes, which offer good-to-excellent fishing for brook (to 9"). The trail rock-hops across the outlet of Helen Lake and veers westerly past two small tarns. Near these isolated waters our route leaves the John Muir Trail, and continues west to the foot of barren, granitoid Papoose Lake. This small lake (under 5 acres) affords good fishing for brook, as does Warrior Lake, up the granite slope to the east. At the outlet of Papoose Lake our route branches north, and then descends over a long dusty traverse to the good campsites in the grassy pockets at the southwest end of Lake of the Lone Indian (10200'). Firewood is ample around this alpine, granitoid lake, and angling is good for brook and rainbow (8-14").

5th Hiking Day **(Lake of the Lone Indian** to **Lower Graveyard Lake,** 5.2 miles) : Retrace steps of the previous day to the Goodale Pass trail at the foot of Papoose Lake. Our route then turns right (southwest) and switchbacks up a steep rocky ridge to a long, grass-bottomed swale below Goodale Pass. This is high alpine country. Barren except for heather and occasional clumps of stunted lodgepole, the exfoliating, rocky slopes of the Silver Divide show the usual signs of glaciation — polish, rounding and striation. The whistling of marmots that inhabit the jumbled slopes accompanies the traveler as he climbs the last abrupt, switchbacking leg to the summit of Goodale Pass (11000' on the topo map, though the sign there says 11467'). Panoramic views extend as far north as the Ritter Range, and south over the San Joaquin River watershed to the peaks beyond the Mono Divide. The initial descent down the south side of Goodale Pass, like the ascent on the north side, is rocky and sudden. As the switchbacking trail progresses it offers fine views of the nearby cirque that feeds Cold Creek. The trail levels out somewhat and stepladders down through a series of charming, green pocket meadows. To the west the traveler can see Graveyard Peak and the basin that nestles on its near side. The trail enters forest cover and winds back and forth across still-tiny Cold Creek, and emerges at the north end of Upper Graveyard Meadows. The short lateral to Lower Graveyard Lake (9900') turns off midway through the meadow, where our route branches right (west) onto it, as described for the 2nd hiking day, trip 82.

6th Hiking Day **(Lower Graveyard Lake** to **Graveyard Meadows,** 3.2 miles) : See 2nd hiking day, trip 90.

7th Hiking Day **(Graveyard Meadows** to **Vermilion Campground,** 5.2 miles) : See 1st hiking day, trip 89.

Rock Creek to Lake Edison

96

TRIP From Mosquito Flat (Rock Creek) to Vermilion Campground (Lake Thomas A. Edison) via Mono Creek (shuttle trip). Topo maps (15′) *Mt. Tom, Mt. Abbot, Kaiser Peak.* Best late season; 21.4 miles.

Grade	Trail/layover days	Total recommended days
Leisurely	4/1	5
Moderate	3/1	4
Strenuous	2/1	3

HILITES Taking this trans-Sierra crossing in late season gives the traveler three distinct plusses: First, the luxuriant aspen groves along Mono Creek take on their golden hue about this time. Second, the mid-season fishing slump usually ends as the weather cools off. Last, this popular route sees heavy foot and animal traffic during early and mid season, but this activity tapers off (ironically) when the leaves begin to turn.

DESCRIPTION (Leisurely trip)

1st Hiking Day **(Mosquito Flat** to **Ruby Lake,** 2.5 miles) : See 1st hiking day, trip 92.

2nd Hiking Day **(Ruby Lake** to **Fish Camp,** 7.8 miles) : From Ruby Lake the trail ascends steeply over the rocky switchbacks on the south slope of Mt. Starr to Mono Pass (12000'), a notch in the cirque wall just west of Mt. Starr. Views from the pass are excellent, but those wishing a panoramic outlook on the spectacular Sierra crest should ascend the granite shoulder of Mt. Starr, an easy climb to the east. From this vantage point one has a complete perspective of Pioneer Basin and Mts. Stanford, Huntington, Crocker and Hopkins, and Red and White Mountain to the north. To the south one has an "end-on" view of Mts. Abbot and Dade, Bear Creek Spire, and Mt. Humphreys. From Mono Pass the trail descends over granite slopes past barren Summit Lake (poor fishing), and then drops more severely as it veers westerly above Trail Lake (poor-to-fair fishing for brook). Our route then turns northward and fords Golden Creek. Following the north side of the stream in a moderately dense forest cover, the trail passes by the lateral to Pioneer Basin (north) and the lateral to Fourth Recess Lake (south). Anglers may elect to try their luck at the good fishing for brook (8-14") at Fourth Recess Lake, ½ mile south over a gentle climb.

Our route continues to descend, fording the outlet streams from Pioneer Basin and paralleling the westward course of Mono Creek. As the Mono Creek valley opens up beyond Mono Rock, the trail passes by the steep lateral to Third Recess Lake (south), and, about a mile farther, descends past the turnoff to Lower Hopkins Lake and the Hopkins Lake basin. Anglers will find the many fine holes that interrupt dashing Mono Creek good fishing for the brook, rainbow and occasional golden (to 12"). In late season the groves of quaking aspen that line the stream's banks are an incomparably colorful backdrop to an otherwise steady conifer green. Owing to heavy traffic, this segment of trail becomes somewhat dusty where it passes the Grinnell Lake lateral and descends to Fish Camp (8500'). This traditional camping place marks the junction of the Mono Creek trail with the Second Recess lateral, and travelers will find good campsites (Forest Service "Improved") on both the north and south sides of the creek (access to the latter via a bridge). Firewood is ample.

3rd Hiking Day **(Fish Camp** to **Quail Meadows,** 5 miles) : As this day's route descends along the north side of Mono Creek, the rich yellows of the aspen groves accompany the stream. Occasionally the traveler has views of the stern northern face of Volcanic Knob to the south, and from several spots along the trail one looks up the long, chutelike valley of the First Recess to the granite-topped heights of Recess Peak. Fishing for the brook, rainbow and occasional golden is much like that of the previous day, but the stream is somewhat less accessible from the trail. About 2½ miles below Fish Camp the trail turns right, away from the narrowing canyon, and climbs by rocky switchbacks to the crown of a ridge, where it joins the John Muir Trail. Thence it descends a short distance on the east side of the North Fork of Mono Creek, and fords the North Fork just above its confluence with Mono Creek. From the ford to the edge of Quail Meadows is a gentle downhill walk through dense forest cover. Fair-to-good campsites with abundant firewood can be found on the forested fringe of Quail Meadows (7760'), a few yards down our trail from the point where the John Muir Trail branches left (south) and fords Mono Creek.

4th Hiking Day **(Quail Meadows** to **Vermilion Campground,** 6.1 miles)** : Our route leaves the John Muir Trail at Quail Meadows and proceeds westerly on a level stretch. Mono Creek now cascades over a series of granite-bedrocked holes (fine swimming in late season) before flowing into the northeast tip of Lake Edison. This man-made, granite-edged lake dominates the views to the south for the remainder of this trip. A boat-taxi service operates the length of the lake, based at a resort adjoining Vermilion Campground, but advance inquiry should be made about length of operating season and ferry schedule. (Write to Vermilion Valley Resort/Mono Hot Springs/California 93642.) The ferry lands at the northeast tip of the lake, and the unmarked footpath giving access to this point can be seen from the trail.

The newly constructed trail along the upper reaches of the north side of Lake Edison undulates severely over alternately rocky and dusty stretches. At some points the trail crosses granite ridges 600' above the lake surface, and from these ridges the traveler has fine views of heavily timbered Bear Ridge across the lake. The forest cover reflects the lower altitude, as Jeffrey pine and red fir mix with ever-present lodgepole. This forest becomes quite dense as our route passes the trail going right (north) to Graveyard Meadows and Goodale Pass. A faint trail to the left (south) leads to another landing point, on a nearby bay. Our route continues westward, crosses the bridge over Cold Creek, and passes the trail lateral to Devils Bathtub. Beyond this junction the hiker leaves the worst of the dust behind as the trail winds through a dense stand of Jeffrey pine to the Forest Service access road. This sandy road descends gently to the eastern edge of Vermilion Campground (7650').

97 McGee Creek to Rock Creek

TRIP From McGee Creek Roadend to Mosquito Flat (Rock Creek) via McGee Pass, Red and White Lake, Grinnell Lakes and Fish Camp (shuttle trip). Topo maps (15') *Mt. Morrison, Mt. Abbot, Mt. Tom*. Best late season; 31.8 miles.

Grade	Trail/layover days	Total recom- mended days
Leisurely	6/2	8
Moderate	4/2	6
Strenuous	3/1	4

HILITES For experienced knapsackers only, this rugged route (some cross-country) offers excitement and challenge sufficient to satisfy the most jaded appetite. High-country lakes surrounded by rampartlike peaks characterize this colorful route, and the fishing is good-to-excellent.

DESCRIPTION (Leisurely trip)

1st Hiking Day **(McGee Creek Roadend to Big McGee Lake,** 6.5 miles) : See 1st hiking day, trip 94.

2nd Hiking Day **(Big McGee Lake to Tully Lake,** 4.5 miles) : See 2nd hiking day, trip 95.

3rd Hiking Day **(Tully Lake to Grinnell Lake,** 3.5 miles cross country) : From the east shore of Tully Lake our route ascends the grassy swale that lies due east of the lake. At the outlet stream from Red and White Lake our route turns right (southeast) and follows this stream to the lake itself. Fishermen will wish to try these icy, clear, blue waters for large rainbow (to 18″). Red and White Lake offers an excellent vantage point from which to take in the spectacular and aptly named heights of Red and White Mountain. The saddle that this day's route traverses is clearly discernible on the lowest point of the right shoulder of Red and White Mountain, and the easiest route to the saddle takes the traveler around the rocky east shore of the lake. The steepest part of the ascent is over treacherous shale, and the climber is well-advised to take it slow and easy. Rope should be carried and used, especially if ascending the west side of the pass.

From the top one obtains a well-deserved and exciting view of the surrounding terrain. To the north the immediate, dazzling blue of Red and White Lake sets off the buff browns and ochre reds of the surrounding rock. Beyond this basin the meadowy cirque forming the headwaters of Fish Creek is a large greensward that contrasts sharply with the austere, red-stained eminence of Red Slate Mountain, and the distant skyline offers sawtooth profiles of the Ritter Range, with its readily identifiable Minarets, and the Mammoth Crest. To the south, the barren, rocky shores of the Grinnell chain of lakes occupy the foreground, and, just beyond, the green-sheathed slopes of the Mono Creek watershed drop away, rising in the distance to the Mono Divide. Like the ascent of this saddle, the descent should be taken with some care. The sudden, shaley drop terminates in a large "rock garden," a jumble of large boulders, just above Little Grinnell Lake. Our rock-hopping route takes us along the east shore of this tiny lake to the long, grassy descent leading to the western side of Grinnell Lake (10800′). Midway along this side, where the most prominent peninsula infringes on the long lake, our route strikes the marked fishermen's trail that veers southwest down a long swale to tiny Laurel Lake. There are several fair campsites at this junction which offer excellent views due to their situation on a plateau above the lake. Fishermen will find Grinnell Lake fair-to-good fishing for brook and rainbow (8-14″). Firewood, however, is somewhat scarce. Alternative good campsites can be found along the meadowy fringes of Laurel Lake (10300′), which is about 1 mile southwest. Fishing on this lake is excellent for brook (to 10″) and firewood is abundant.

4th Hiking Day **(Grinnell Lake** to **Fish Camp,** 4.5 miles) : The fishermen's trail from Grinnell Lake to Laurel Lake descends via a long, scooplike swale to the grassy meadows forming the headwaters of Laurel Creek. The trail, though very faint from

Grinnell to Laurel Lake, becomes clearer as it descends gently along Laurel Creek. At this point the creek is still a "jump-across" stream, but a careful approach along the banks will reveal an abundance of brook (to 9″), and fly fishermen who favor stream angling will find this tiny watercourse a delight. The gradual descent along the creek becomes somewhat steeper just above the larger meadows. The pleasant, timber-fringed grassland is divided by the serpentine curves of Laurel Creek. The trail across the meadow is difficult to follow, and the traveler who loses it should cross to the west side of Laurel Creek and look for the trail in the vicinity of the campsites at the south end of the meadow. The dense lodgepole cover at the end of the meadow soon gives way to manzanita thickets and occasional clumps of quaking aspen as the trail reaches the steep, switchbacking descent above Mono Creek. These switchbacks are unmaintained, and are subject to heavy erosion. However, the difficult going is more than compensated for by the excellent views across the Mono Creek watershed into the Second Recess. Particularly impressive are the heights of Mt. Gabb and Mt. Hilgard, which guard the upper end of this feeder canyon. When our route strikes the Mono Creek trail, it turns right (west) for a gently descending ½ mile to the several good campsites at Fish Camp (8500′). Several additional campsites are located across Mono Creek, via the bridge, alongside the lateral to the Second Recess. Firewood is ample, and fishing is good for brook and rainbow (to 12″) on Mono Creek.

5th Hiking Day (**Fish Camp** to **Ruby Lake,** 10.3 miles) : See 2nd hiking day, trip 96.

6th Hiking Day (**Ruby Lake** to **Mosquito Flat,** 2.5 miles) : See 1st hiking day, trip 92.

98   Mammoth Lakes to Purple Lake

TRIP   From Coldwater Campground (Mammoth Lakes) to Purple Lake (round trip). Topo map (15′) *Mt. Morrison.* Best late season ; 16 miles.

Grade	Trail/layover days	Total recommended days
Leisurely	3/1	4
Moderate	2/1	3
Strenuous	2/0	2

HILITES   The rewards for crossing a mountain pass amount to more than the views that are presented. Most experienced knapsackers know that passes have a way of separating the day-hikers from overnighters. So it is with this trip across the Mammoth Crest. Those seeking a modicum of solitude, along with the satisfaction of seeing what lies beyond the top of the hill, will find this hike a worth-while choice.

DESCRIPTION (Moderate trip)

1st Hiking Day (**Coldwater Campground** to **Purple Lake,** 8 miles) : From Coldwater Campground (8960') the Duck Pass trail ascends on an alternately sandy and rocky section along a moderately forested slope. The initial portion of this trail, from the road end to Barney Lake, receives a good deal of day-hiker and fisherman use, so by mid season the trail is fairly dusty. As the going levels off, after the first rise, Arrowhead Lake is visible off to the left (east). Then the trail ascends again to Skelton Lake. The lake was named for the brothers Skelton, who, during this mining area's heyday, established and maintained a stamp mill at the lower end of the lake. Owing to heavy fishing pressure on these lakes, the angling is only fair. As our route crosses the rolling terrain to the south of Skelton Lake, the barren canyon walls along the Mammoth Crest show the scouring action of the ancient glaciers that once covered the land. From the rocky shores of emerald-green Barney Lake the steep ascent to Duck Pass is easily seen. The switchbacks ascending this steep slope leave hemlock and silver pine behind, and except for an occasional stunted lodgepole this climb is barren and exposed.

At Duck Pass (10790') there are views of Mammoth Creek watershed and the Mammoth Crest to the northwest. Beyond, the skyline is dominated by the distinctive spires of the Ritter Range. To the south and southwest Pika and Duck lakes occupy the basin immediately below; and these blue, still waters are flanked by the green depths of Cascade Valley. Across the valley the Silver Divide's rocky peaks occupy the horizon. The short descent to the rocky shores of large Duck Lake passes a faint fishermen's trail to Pika Lake. The boulder-strewn west shore of Duck Lake is rugged going, and one has plenty of time during rest stops to admire the pure blue of the deep waters. Except for a few gnarled whitebark pines, the jumbled slopes and rocky crags surrounding the lake are barren and austere. From Duck Lake our route crosses the outlet and descends to join the scenic John Muir Trail. It then turns left (south), rounds a rocky, granite shoulder, and veers eastward to the several good campsites near the outlet at the south end of Purple Lake (9860'). Firewood is somewhat scarce, but fishing is fair-to-good for rainbow and some golden and brook (8-13″). Purple Lake's partly timbered, rocky shoreline gives way to meadow at the northeast end of the lake. The rocks above the meadow give this lake its name; they have a rosy tint during the day, but around sunset they turn purple and violet.

2nd Hiking Day (**Purple Lake** to **Coldwater Campground,** 8 miles): Retrace steps of 1st hiking day.

99　**Mammoth Lakes to Lake Edison**

TRIP　From Coldwater Campground (Mammoth Lakes) to Vermilion Campground (Lake Thomas A. Edison) via Cascade Valley and Goodale Pass (shuttle trip). Topo maps (15') *Mt. Morrison, Mt. Abbot, Kaiser Peak.* Best late season; 29.9 miles.

Grade	Trail/layover days	Total recommended days
Leisurely	6/1	7
Moderate	5/1	6
Strenuous	4/1	5

HILITES　This trans-Sierra route explores two watersheds, ascends two passes, and offers a world of fine fishing along the way. About one fourth of the route follows the famous John Muir Trail, and high, alpine scenery alternates with intimate, friendly meadows, fast-running streams, and lonely, placid lakes. Long mileage and stiff climbs make this a trip for the hiker who prepared himself with a couple of early- or mid-season warm-ups, but the rewards, in views and fishing, repay him for the required effort.

DESCRIPTION (Moderate trip)

1st Hiking Day **(Coldwater Campground** to **Purple Lake,** 8 miles) : See 1st hiking day, trip 98.

2nd Hiking Day **(Purple Lake** to **Cascade Valley/Fish Creek ford,** 3.5 miles) : From the outlet of Purple Lake our route branches right (southwest) from the John Muir Trail and descends, gently at first, parallel to Purple Creek. The forest cover along this switchbacking descent is primarily lodgepole pine, giving way to Jeffrey pine and incense cedar near the valley floor. Manzanita is the main shrub on the steeper part of the descent. The hiker has fine views of the Silver Divide across the valley. The long switchbacks of this steep descent terminate in a large meadow on the floor of Cascade Valley. Here our route strikes the Cascade Valley trail and turns left (east) along Fish Creek. The fairly level going along the valley floor gives the angler ample opportunity to test the good fishing for brook and rainbow (to 9″). California's DF&G *Anglers' Guide* says about Cascade Valley: "One of the finest trout streams left in the High Sierra; meandering and scenic with splendid campsites and forest cover." As the hiker works his way up the valley, Fish Creek rushes and then meanders on his right, and open meadow fringes beckon. Where this trail crosses Fish Creek via a wading ford, this hiking day ends at one of the many campsites (8560′). Firewood is ample and fishing is good, as noted above.

3rd Hiking Day **(Cascade Valley/Fish Creek ford** to **Lake of the Lone Indian,** 4.8 miles) : Beyond the ford of Fish Creek the trail ascends somewhat more steeply over rocky stretches. Fish Creek, now on the left, changes as the canyon narrows. The water is faster and the creek becomes a riotous tumble of waterfalls and tiny holes. Just below the point where our route rejoins the John Muir Trail, the canyon wall on the north side of the valley becomes a sheer, dramatically polished granite surface. Our trail crosses the outlet stream from Helen Lake and meets the John Muir Trail, onto which our route turns right (south). From this junction to Helen Lake the ascent is steep. The first part of the climb is densely forested as it works its way up the east side of the outlet stream from Helen Lake, and midway up, the trail passes several alternative meadowed campsites on the right. Beyond these campsites the trail becomes rocky, exposed and eroded as it makes the last steep climb to Helen Lake. One has excellent views back down the U-shaped valley with which to fill the breather stops, and as the trail crests at the granite lip of the Helen Lake cirque, one can see whence the glacier emanated that carved the valley below. Anglers will want to fish Helen Lake — and Bobs Lake about ½ mile southeast. Both offer good-to-excellent angling for brook (to 9").

The trail then rock-hops the outlet of Helen Lake, passes two small alpine tarns, and branches right, leaving the John Muir Trail, which continues south to Silver Pass. Our route passes below rocky Papoose Lake, which offers good fishing for brook, as does Warrior Lake, a short distance over the granite to the east. At the outlet stream of Papoose Lake our route branches north, away from the Goodale Pass trail, and descends over a dusty traverse to the good, grassy-pocketed campsites at the southwest end of Lake of the Lone Indian (10200'). Firewood is ample, and fishing is good for brook and rainbow (8-14").

4th Hiking Day **(Lake of the Lone Indian** to **Lower Graveyard Lake,** 5.2 miles) : See 5th hiking day, trip 95.

5th Hiking Day **(Lower Graveyard Lake** to **Vermilion Campground,** 8.4 miles) : See 2nd hiking day, trip 90; and 1st hiking day, trip 89.

cony   £.w.

Mammoth Lakes to Lake Edison   100

TRIP   From Coldwater Campground (Mammoth Lakes) to Vermilion Campground (Lake Thomas A. Edison), via Cascade Valley, Tully Lake and Grinnell Lakes (shuttle trip). Topo maps (15') *Mt. Morrison, Mt. Abbot, Kaiser Peak*. Best late season; 35.9 miles.

Grade	Trail/layover days	Total recommended days
Leisurely	8/2	10
Moderate	5/2	7
Strenuous	4/2	6

HILITES   Employing a short but strenuous cross-country route over the Silver Divide, this unusual and remote trip should appeal to fisherman, hiker and naturalist — or any combination thereof. Travelers looking for a trip of lonely alpine grandeur will find it in the Silver Divide country.

DESCRIPTION (Leisurely trip)

1st Hiking Day **(Coldwater Campground** to **Purple Lake,** 8 miles) : See 1st hiking day, trip 98.

2nd Hiking Day **(Purple Lake** to **Cascade Valley/Fish Creek ford,** 3.5 miles) : See 2nd hiking day, trip 99.

3rd Hiking Day **(Cascade Valley/Fish Creek ford** to **Tully Hole,** 2.8 miles) : From the Fish Creek ford the trail ascends the sometimes-rocky valley floor on the south side of Fish Creek. This section offers splendid access to nice deep holes and gurgling riffles, but as the canyon narrows, the trail becomes steeper and the creek becomes faster, small waterfalls alternating with noisy cascades. Looking up at the sheer canyon walls, the hiker cannot help but be impressed with the glacial forces that polished their granite faces. Just below the junction with the John Muir Trail, the trail fords the outlet stream from Helen Lake. Our route turns left (north) onto the John Muir Trail and crosses to the north side of plunging Fish Creek via a steel bridge. The trail then climbs steeply by switchbacks, offering fine views back to the falls above the bridge. The climb is short, and the trail levels out somewhat as it rejoins Fish Creek. The reunion with the creek is startling, for its waters are now almost placid as they flow through deep green holes. The roar and thunder of the falls are but an echo, and beside the now-mellow Fish Creek the trail ascends to the lovely, open meadows of Tully Hole (9500'). Fish Creek is a pleasant, meandering background to the good campsites at the northwest edge of the meadow, and firewood is abundant. Here the angler should break out his rod for the good-to-excellent fishing for brook, rainbow, and some golden (to 12").

4th Hiking Day **(Tully Hole to Tully Lake,** 2.5 miles) : See 3rd hiking day, trip 95.

5th Hiking Day **(Tully Lake to Grinnell Lake,** 3.5 miles) : See 3rd hiking day, trip 97.

6th Hiking Day **(Grinnell Lake to Fish Camp,** 4.5 miles) : See 4th hiking day, trip 97.

7th Hiking Day **(Fish Camp to Quail Meadows,** 5 miles) : See 3rd hiking day, trip 96.

8th Hiking Day **(Quail Meadows to Vermilion Campground,** 6.1 miles) : See 4th hiking day, trip 96.

Trip Cross-reference Table

Trip No.	No. Hiking Days	Season			Pace			Trip Type			
		Early	Mid	Late	Leis.	Mod.	Stren.	Round	Shuttle	Loop	Semiloop
1	2	x	x		x			x			
2	3		x		x						x
3	6		x	x	x						x
4	2		x	x	x			x			
5	3		x	x	x			x			
6	2		x	x	x				x		
7	3		x	x		x			x		
8	6		x	x		x			x		
9	2		x	x	x			x			
10	5		x	x	x				x		
11	2		x	x	x			x			
12	2	x	x		x			x			
13	3		x		x				x		
14	2		x		x			x			
15	2		x		x				x		
16	2		x		x			x			
17	4	x	x		x			x			
18	4	x	x			x			x		
19	2		x		x			x			
20	2		x		x				x		
21	2	x	x		x			x			
22	4		x	x	x			x			
23	4		x	x	x			x			
24	5		x	x	x						x
25	7		x	x	x					x	
26	7		x	x	x				x		
27	2		x	x	x			x			
28	4		x	x	x			x			
29	2	x	x		x			x			
30	6		x	x	x			x			
31	5		x	x	x				x		
32	5		x	x	x				x		

Trip No.	No. Hiking Days	Season			Pace			Trip Type			
		Early	Mid	Late	Leis.	Mod.	Stren.	Round	Shuttle	Loop	Semiloop
33	7			x	x				x		
34	2		x	x	x			x			
35	3		x	x	x			x			
36	4		x	x		x					x
37	5		x	x		x					x
38	5	x	x			x			x		
39	2		x	x		x		x			
40	2	x	x	x		x		x			
41	4		x	x		x		x			
42	3		x	x		x			x		
43	3		x	x		x					x
44	2	x	x	x	x			x			
45	6		x	x			x		x		
46	6		x	x		x		x			
47	8		x	x		x					x
48	2	x	x	x	x			x			
49	4		x	x		x			x		
50	2		x	x	x				x		
51	2	x			x			x			
52	4	x			x			x			
53	4		x	x	x			x			
54	2		x	x	x			x			
55	2		x	x		x		x			
56	3		x	x		x			x		
57	5		x	x		x			x		
58	2	x	x	x	x					x	
59	2		x	x		x			.		x
60	2		x	x	x			x			
61	2		x	x	x			x			
62	4		x	x	x			x			
63	5		x	x	x				x		
64	3		x	x	x				x		
65	2		x	x	x			x			
66	2		x	x		x		x			

Trip No.	No. Hiking Days	Season			Pace			Trip Type			
		Early	Mid	Late	Leis.	Mod.	Stren.	Round	Shuttle	Loop	Semiloop
67	2	x	x	x	x			x			
68	5		x	x	x				x		
69	2		x	x	x			x			
70	2		x	x	x			x			
71	3		x	x	x				x		
72	2		x	x		x			x		
73	3		x·	x	x					x	
74	3		x	x	x					x	
75	3		x	x	x					x	
76	2		x	x	x			x			
77	3		x	x		x			x		
78	4		x	x	x				x		
79	3		x	x	x						x
80	5		x	x	x				x		
81	4	x			x			x			
82	4	x	x		x			x			
83	5	x	x		x				x		
84	5	x	x		x				x		
85	5	x	x		x						x
86	4	x			x			x			
87	10		x	x		x				x	
88	6		x	x		x			x		
89	2		x		x			x			
90	4		x	x	x			x			
91	2		x	x	x			x			
92	2		x	x	x			x			
93	2		x	x	x			x			
94	2		x	x	x			x			
95	7		x	x	x				x		
96	4			x	x				x		
97	6			x	x				x		
98	2			x		x		x			
99	5			x		x			x		
100	8			x	x				x		

Index